MIDI

THE COMPUTER MUSIC AND DIGITAL AUDIO SERIES
John Strawn, *Series Editor*

DIGITAL AUDIO SIGNAL PROCESSING
Edited by John Strawn

COMPOSERS AND THE COMPUTER
Edited by Curtis Roads

DIGITAL AUDIO ENGINEERING
Edited by John Strawn

COMPUTER APPLICATIONS IN MUSIC: A BIBLIOGRAPHY
Edited by Deta S. Davis

THE COMPACT DISC: A HANDBOOK OF THEORY AND USE
Ken C. Pohlmann

COMPUTERS AND MUSICAL STYLE
David Cope

MIDI: A COMPREHENSIVE INTRODUCTION
Joseph Rothstein
William Eldridge, *Volume Editor*

SYNTHESIZER PERFORMANCE AND REAL-TIME TECHNIQUES
Jeff Pressing
Chris Meyer, *Volume Editor*

VOLUME 7   THE COMPUTER MUSIC AND DIGITAL AUDIO SERIES

MIDI
A Comprehensive Introduction

Joseph Rothstein

A-R Editions, Inc.

Madison, Wisconsin

Library of Congress
Cataloging-in-Publication Data

Rothstein, Joseph
    MIDI: A comprehensive introduction / Joseph
Rothstein.
        p.   cm. — (The Computer music and digital
   audio series; v. 7)
    Includes index.
    ISBN 0-89579-258-3 : $39.95
    1. MIDI (Standard)   I. Title.   II. Series.
MT723.R68   1992
784.19′0285′46—dc20   91-39701
                                            CIP
                                           MN

A-R Editions, Inc.
801 Deming Way
Madison, Wisconsin 53717-1903
(608) 836-9000

Sections of *MIDI 1.0 Detailed Specification* reprinted by
permission of International MIDI Association

CONTENTS

PREFACE

· ·

When I first began making the transition to MIDI from music synthesis systems running on mainframe computers, I looked around for a book to supplement the *MIDI 1.0 Detailed Specification,* one that would enable me to make informed decisions about assembling and using a MIDI system. I read several of the MIDI books that were available and found that I learned little beyond what I already knew from the MIDI specification. More often, I found interviews with musicians, discussions of specific brands and models of MIDI equipment (most already obsolescent), and generalities regarding the fabulous possibilities of MIDI.

MIDI is a nexus of music, software, and computer technology. As a musician, I wanted to know precisely how MIDI could help me implement musical ideas. As a computer programmer of moderate skills, I wanted to know the specific requirements of MIDI programming, in greater detail and with more clarification than in the MIDI specification. Finally, as one who believes that all sufficiently advanced technology is indistinguishable from magic, I wanted to know which genies to summon to my cause and which to leave alone.

As I gathered information from books, magazine articles, conversations, and especially from often painful practical experience, the idea of writing a MIDI book began to form in my mind. I imagined it as the book I wish had been available when I was making the leap to MIDI.

I have tried to maintain mental images of several distinct readers. One is a piano or guitar player who has heard about MIDI, is intrigued, and wants to jump into the MIDI world—but wants to avoid the waste of time and resources that invariably stems from entering a new field without adequate preparation.

Another is the personal computer user, who may have heard for years about "computer music" but has used the computer's audio capabilities only for sound effects during game playing. MIDI music making is one of the most challenging and rewarding ways to use a personal computer. I believe that MIDI has attracted as many computer users to the delights of music as it has musicians to the enjoyment of computing, and I would like to acquaint as many computer users with MIDI as possible.

Finally, as one who has conducted MIDI seminars for beginning and advanced MIDI users, I wanted to develop a book that could serve as a comprehensive text for a MIDI class or seminar or for a music teacher who does not want to be left behind by technological developments.

My intention has been to concentrate on those topics of practical significance to such readers, omitting anything that does not contribute directly to the reader's understanding of MIDI or skill in using MIDI. I have similarly chosen not to focus on discussions of particular brands or models of MIDI equipment, computers, or software, concentrating instead on specific concepts appropriate to any hardware or software, irrespective of brand or model. It is also my intention and my hope that readers armed with the MIDI specification can use this book to bridge the gap between the specification and a functioning MIDI system.

MIDI is a means to music making, not an end in itself. There are only two kinds of music, "good" music and "bad"—and I like both. One of MIDI's greatest values is that it opens up the pleasures and possibilities of music making to a much wider range of practitioners. The only requirement of musicians is that we make music—so let's get to it!

ACKNOWLEDGMENTS

Many friends and associates have contributed ideas, suggestions, criticism, and materials for this book.

Portions of *MIDI: A Comprehensive Introduction* were written and rewritten at Pu'uhonua, the Molokai home of Dr. John Corboy, who generously permitted me to use his hideaway. It proved to be the perfect place for such an undertaking—quiet, relaxing, and free of distractions.

The Hawaii Musicians' Listening Group provided a forum for exchanging information, answering questions, and airing complaints and frustrations about MIDI. Those informal conversations helped clarify many MIDI concepts in my mind. In particular, Dr. Arthur Roberts offered valuable criticism and clarification of numerous technical points in several chapters, while Don Michael allowed me access to his equipment, expertise, and time.

Many equipment and software manufacturers have supported my work for *Computer Music Journal* over the years by providing press releases, photographs, evaluation units, and information. Some also contributed the photographs and computer screen images that are used here, along with others that could not be used due to space limitations and other factors. I thank all my friends among the MIDI manufacturers for their ongoing support and good humor.

Samuel Brylawski, reference librarian for the Recorded Sound Reference Center of the Library of Congress, found citations and sources that I was not sure existed except in my imagination. His friendship over the years has been even more important.

John Strawn, series editor for A-R Editions' Computer Music and Digital Audio Series, provided innumerable suggestions and criticisms that contributed significantly to the book's final form and focus.

I also want to express my gratitude to my parents for their unfailing encouragement—even when they had doubts about exactly what they were encouraging—and to Albert and Joan Rich, for all the things that good friends do.

Finally, it would be inadequate to thank Ann for her help during the making of this book. Thank you, Ann, for *everything,* and especially for saying yes.

Mahalo no kakou—a special thanks to all of you.

■

OVERVIEW

. . . .

MIDI is an acronym for "Musical Instrument Digital Interface." Despite its impact on the world of music, MIDI is not a musical language, nor does it directly describe musical sounds. Rather, it is a data communications protocol, an agreement among manufacturers of music equipment, computers, and software that describes a means for music systems and related equipment to exchange information and control signals.

The difference between audio information and MIDI data is similar to the difference between a tape recording of a pianist performing a piano sonata and the sheet music for that same sonata. The recording captures the musical information itself, storing the actual sounds that came from the piano.

Data, on the other hand, symbolically represent information for the purposes of storing or transmitting it in a more compact or more easily transmitted form. Thus, each notational symbol in printed piano music stores not the sound of the piano music but the instructions necessary for a human performer to re-create that music by converting the symbol back into the information it represents—that is, by striking the key indicated by the note symbol, using the indicated amount of pressure, and holding the key for the indicated length of time. Notational symbols in printed music are thus forms of data.

MIDI represents yet another level of abstraction from piano music. While printed piano music symbolically describes musical sounds, MIDI symbolically describes the electronic steps required to generate the sounds. That is, we can think of MIDI as specifying exactly which electronic circuits should be turned on and exactly how long they should remain on rather than describing a musical result that must be created by a human performer who interprets the instructions.

The MIDI protocol thus enables us to manage the complex information representing the performance of a musical work on electronic instruments. MIDI represents the information needed to re-create a performance as many individual pieces of data, whose meanings are specified by the MIDI protocol, and provides a means to store, manipulate, transmit, and re-create the information using symbolic data.

For anyone involved in music making using digital electronics—and increasingly for anyone involved in any art form using digital electronics—the significance of MIDI is that it permits a wide variety of equipment from many different manufacturers to work together in a single system. Each piece of MIDI equipment adheres to the same rules of information management specified by MIDI, so that they have a common system of communication.

MIDI APPLICATIONS

One of the simplest and most widely used applications of MIDI is to connect two or more synthesizers together so that playing one produces the same note on each. That way, a player at a single MIDI keyboard or other controller can produce sounds that have a rich, layered, complex timbre rather than a single, easily identifiable sound. MIDI devices other than just synthesizers can become part of that single system under the control of a single player. With the advent of MIDI-controlled reverberators, mixing consoles, lighting control panels, and other special effects boxes, a player at a master MIDI controller can run a complex multimedia setup of lights, sound, and effects, all by sending MIDI messages from the master controller to the correct device.

More powerful applications of MIDI technology involve a computer, making it an integral part of the MIDI system. The computer can be used to record MIDI messages, much as a tape recorder records audio signals. Because MIDI messages are digital data, the full power of digital computers can be brought to MIDI recordings. With appropriate software, the computer can simulate a multitrack tape recorder, not using just four, sixteen, or forty-eight tracks but hundreds of tracks, and in some cases unlimited numbers of tracks.

Rather than simple recording, playback, and cut-and-splice editing, a MIDI recorder includes powerful facilities that provide the user a tremendous range of creative controls. Certainly, MIDI recordings can be edited—toa precision of hundredths of a beat. But in addition the pitch, rhythm, tempo, or repetition of a single note, a longer passage, or an entire piece can be adjusted quickly and accurately. Each track can hold musical information intended for a particular synthesizer or control information for any MIDI device. The same recording that plays a synthesizer track can control a reverberator or a mixing console, setting reverb, equalization, or mix levels with a precision and accuracy that would be impossible otherwise.

Some MIDI programs are intended specifically for composing. These "intelligent instruments" let composers arrange musical ideas, concepts, and structures, with the computer making some (or many) of the specific decisions about notes, chords, and rhythms. The composer can hear the results as they occur and make changes as the music plays. As artificial intelligence concepts are applied to music composition programs, they are likely to gain an ever wider range of capacities.

Other computer programs translate MIDI data into printer control data so that the computer becomes a powerful composer's and arranger's assistant. The capabilities of MIDI scoring programs vary widely, but most such programs will let the composer enter music from a MIDI controller or the computer's typewriter-style keyboard along with tempo, meter, and expression markings, then print out the completed score on a graphics printer.

With so many synthesizers and so much complexity, it is only natural that the computer should be used to cut down on the volume of data that synthesizer operators must remember. One approach uses patch librarian software, which stores synthesizer settings with appropriate identifiers and comments, then transmits selected patch data to the correct synthesizer at the correct time. In this way, the synthesizer operator need not be concerned with setting parameters from scratch each time the patch is used but need only select the desired patch from the library.

And of course, the computer is an ideal tool for education; it is patient, precise, and always available. Music education programs are available for ear training, sight-reading, keyboard skills development, and music theory, designed for a wide range of skill levels.

With so much software under development, it is hard to imagine what the future will hold, but chapter 5, "MIDI Software," surveys current applications and speculates on future directions.

THE MIDI SPECIFICATION

The MIDI protocol specifies conditions in two areas, and manufacturers must meet these conditions in order to call their product a MIDI device. The areas are the hardware interface, the physical connection between two separate pieces of equipment, and the data format, the arrangement and order of data messages that are transmitted from one device to another. The hardware portion of the MIDI specification describes the two parts of the physical connection between different pieces of equipment. The two parts are, first, a MIDI port, which converts MIDI data from its digital form to the series of electrical voltages that represent the MIDI data numbers (or vice versa), and second, a MIDI cable, which transmits the voltage signals to the next device's MIDI port, where the voltages are converted back to digital data.

MIDI Ports

A port or interface is a place where two otherwise incompatible systems perform the necessary conversions that enable them to pass data from one to the other. Computers use groups of electrical voltages to represent large numbers, while the MIDI cable carries voltages representing only the numbers 0 and 1; conversion from one form to the other takes place at the MIDI port. Although "MIDI interface" is redundant, it is more commonly used than "MIDI port."

The MIDI specification describes three types of ports, each represented by a female jack designed to receive the five-pin MIDI cable connector, as shown in figure 1.1. At the MIDI Out jack, data is converted from digital to voltage format for transmission along a MIDI cable to another MIDI device. The receiving device must be equipped with a MIDI In jack so that the incoming voltages can be converted back to their digital format. When connecting MIDI devices, it is important to be sure which is sending signals and which is receiving them and connect the cables accordingly.

A simple example involves using a "master" keyboard synthesizer to control a "slave" keyboard or rack-mount synthesizer so that the two will sound in unison when the master keyboard is played. The MIDI cable should plug into the master's MIDI Out jack and the slave's MIDI In. As obvious as this may seem, incorrect cabling is one of the most common causes of MIDI system problems. Check for proper cabling first when such problems occur.

Most MIDI devices have both MIDI In and MIDI Out jacks, but there is a third port defined in the MIDI specification, called MIDI Thru. It makes a copy of any incoming signals the device receives through its MIDI In port and immediately retransmits them, unchanged, out the MIDI Thru jack (figure 1.2). In a sense, MIDI Thru is like a Y-connector, which breaks a signal in two. There are advantages and pitfalls associated with using MIDI Thru, and they will be discussed in chapter 7, "Getting It All to Work Together."

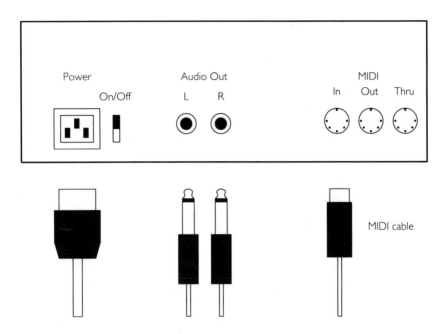

FIGURE 1.1   Rear-panel connections on a typical MIDI device, showing the location of MIDI In, Out, and Thru ports.

MIDI Cables

A MIDI cable consists of a length of wire with identical connectors at each end, as shown in figure 1.3. The cable transmits neither audio signals nor electrical power; rather, the changes in voltage transmitted through the MIDI cable represent binary data—the yes/no, on/off signals that, strung together, represent specific numbers whose purpose and meaning are defined in the MIDI protocol.

MIDI cables are generally no longer than 50 feet and usually much shorter than that. Voltages become weaker the farther they travel, so to avoid potential problems it is a good idea always to use the shortest possible MIDI cable.

Most MIDI cables use five-pin DIN connectors, one at each end of the cable. DIN connectors have long been used in European electronic equipment; they are inexpensive and readily available. The current MIDI specification uses only three of the five pins, and most manufacturers have left the remaining pins unused in case some future addition to the MIDI

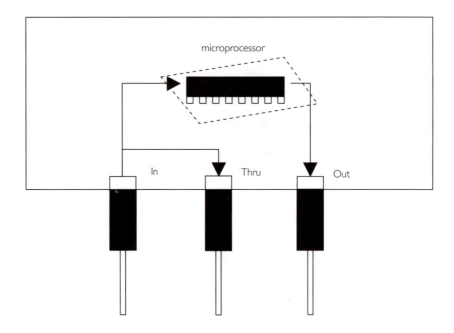

FIGURE 1.2   MIDI In, Out, and Thru ports, indicating the direction of data flow.

specification defines uses for them. But a few manufacturers have used the two pins for their own purposes. The documentation of any piece of MIDI equipment should indicate if more than three pins are used; if so, try to find an alternative that uses only the three pins specified by MIDI.

One problem with DIN connectors is that they are not particularly durable and may break after repeated disconnecting and reconnecting. A tougher but more expensive three-conductor XLR connector is used by many manufacturers of professional audio equipment; the MIDI specification permits manufacturers to use XLR connectors, provided that they also furnish adapters for connecting them to DIN connectors.

MIDI cables themselves can also be a source of problems if they should pick up stray electrical signals given off by electronic equipment. Better-quality MIDI cables wrap the wiring inside a thin aluminum sheath before the entire cable is wrapped in an outer covering of plastic or rubber. The aluminum shielding cuts down on the cable's receptivity to such unwanted signals, so an important rule for any MIDI setup is to use only shielded cables. This goes for audio cables as well as MIDI cables—too many expensive setups are sabotaged by cheap cables. It is impossible to tell by its

FIGURE 1.3   MIDI cable—note the identical connectors at each end (courtesy Pro Co Sound, Inc.).

outside appearance whether a cable is shielded or not, so if you make it a rule to buy only shielded cables, you will have one less thing to worry about later. Remember—if the price is cheap, the cable probably is, too! (Since the humble cable is the source of so many potential problems, there is a lot more on cabling in chapter 7.)

MIDI MESSAGES

Each of the different number sequences in the MIDI data format specification is called a MIDI message. Each message describes a particular event—the start of a musical note, the change in a switch setting, the motion of a foot pedal, or the selection of a sound "patch," for example.

Because MIDI specifies a digital (that is, numeric) data format, every MIDI device must contain at least one microprocessor, a "computer on a chip" that can interpret and act on MIDI messages. The microprocessors in MIDI synthesizers and other MIDI-controlled equipment make sense of the vast amounts of numbers that MIDI uses to describe what is required to create (or re-create) a piece of music.

Musicians generally think of music as a series of notes, each one having a particular pitch, amplitude, and timbre. For musicians, then, a note can be considered the most basic of musical messages. Likewise, the most basic MIDI message is the Note On message, though a Note On message differs from our usual understanding of a musical note. Both contain pitch and loudness data, but elements of expressiveness such as vibrato and pitch bend are treated as separate MIDI messages rather than as part and parcel of each note that they affect.

Many types of MIDI messages can be generated by a performer playing a MIDI instrument; such messages might include on/off switch settings or continuously varying controller information such as modulation, which changes the timbre or tone color of the note.

MIDI messages are often stored in prerecorded material called a sequence. Such messages most often describe notes, so that different MIDI devices know which notes they are supposed to play and how loud to play them. Other messages request that a particular MIDI synthesizer change from one instrumental sound to another. A device or computer program called a sequencer stores the messages, maintains the time relationships among the various messages, and transmits the stored messages at the appropriate times to MIDI devices connected to the sequencer, enabling those devices to re-create the performance specified by the stored messages.

Since the developers of the MIDI specification could not foresee all the ways that musical instruments might develop and change, they left a way for individual manufacturers to control specific aspects of their equipment that are not defined as part of the MIDI specification by using System Exclusive messages, which apply only to particular equipment from a particular manufacturer. The specifics of the System Exclusive messages are defined by each manufacturer and are ignored by equipment from other manufacturers.

Understanding MIDI messages is crucial to making full use of MIDI, and chapter 8, "Understanding MIDI Messages," describes each type in detail.

A BRIEF HISTORY OF MIDI

Producing music using electronic technology has been around as long as electronic technology itself. Though such electronic musical instruments appeared as early as the beginning of the twentieth century, the first popular electronic synthesizers were probably the Theremin and the Ondes Martenot, which were widely used during the 1920s and 1930s. Their unique sound qualities were especially appropriate in dramatic settings, and numerous movie scores of the period featured their synthesized sounds.

As vacuum-tube and then transistor technology evolved, musicians were quick to put the technology to use. The analog synthesizers that resulted represented sound as a constantly changing electrical voltage whose charge was analogous to the sound pressure the voltage represented. Such synthesizers of the 1940s, 1950s and early 1960s were generally large, expensive to build and maintain, and difficult to operate. Aside from an occasional movie score or public exhibition, analog electronic synthesizers were confined mostly to academic research institutions, music conservatories, and the studios of avant-garde composers.

The first widely popular analog electronic synthesizer was designed by Robert Moog in the 1960s. A 1968 recording of the music of Johann Sebastian Bach performed on a Moog synthesizer by Walter (now Wendy) Carlos set the recording industry and listening public on its ear. *Switched-On Bach* became one of the best-selling classical music albums of all time, and it continues to sell well, more than two decades later.

As millions of people became enchanted by the unique sounds used in *Switched-On Bach,* Moog became a household name, even if it was consistently mispronounced (it rhymes with "vogue"). Many of *Switched-On Bach*'s young listeners formed rock bands, and many of those bands used Moog synthesizers, along with a flood of analog synthesizers that followed from ARP, Sequential Circuits, and other manufacturers.

But the newer analog synthesizers were still beset by problems. Though smaller in size than their earlier counterparts, they were still difficult to set up and operate. "Programming" such synthesizers involved using patch cables to make temporary electrical connections among the synthesizer's various sound-generating oscillators, filters, and other components.

Most synthesizers of that era were monophonic—that is, they could play only one note at a time—so it was a common sight at concerts to see a keyboard player surrounded by a wall of synthesizers, each with its own tangle of patch cables and a bewildering array of buttons, switches, and sliders. To make matters worse, the tuning of analog synthesizers was prone to drift (particularly as their components heated up), so that every few minutes or so, the entire system had to be retuned, one synthesizer at a time. And of course, multiple synthesizers meant multiple keyboards, multiple oscillators, multiple patch-cord setups, and multiple headaches.

Computer music synthesizers—in which sounds are represented by numbers within a computer's memory—had also been around for almost two decades by the early 1970s, but the high price of computer components had kept them out of reach of most musicians.

When low-cost microprocessors and integrated circuits began to appear, music manufacturers eagerly adopted them. Digital circuits are inherently more stable, more reliable, and cheaper (when produced in large quantities) than their analog counterparts, so replacing analog oscillators and other voltage-based components with digital microchips resulted in more reliable, cheaper, and "smarter" synthesizers.

By the end of the 1970s many music manufacturers had begun to offer digital synthesizers, and the tangles of patch cords—the hallmark of analog synthesizers like the early Moog designs—began to disappear, replaced by control panels and software that allowed the user to change voices at the touch of a key. Furthermore, once they leave the factory, most digital synthesizers never need retuning.

But the problem of duplicate components (especially keyboards) remained. Keyboards are mechanical and therefore more expensive than similarly complex electrical devices. Since each manufacturer used a different design scheme, each synthesizer had its own keyboard and control panel. Using a wide range of synthesizer sounds still meant a wall of equipment and the prospect of dashing from one keyboard to the next. Musicians were still limited to playing only one or two synthesizers at a time or having multiple players for the multiple keyboards—neither one an appealing choice.

In 1981, three synthesizer company employees decided to do something about it. Dave Smith of Sequential Circuits, I. Kakehashi of Roland Corporation, and Tom Oberheim of Oberheim Electronics met during that June's show held by the National Association of Music Merchants (NAMM) and discussed ways that synthesizer manufacturers might standardize their control signals so that different companies' synthesizers might work together.

Since the new breed of synthesizers were really digital computers disguised as musical instruments, they considered the ways that computer manufacturers had addressed the same challenges of intermachine communication. One of the most successful approaches is the Local Area Network (LAN), a hardware and software system that permits computers from different manufacturers to share data and equipment such as printers. Local Area Networks had many of the characteristics the synthesizer group wanted: They can be relatively simple and inexpensive to set up and run, they can be nonhierarchical (that is, they can handle all the computers in the network on an equal basis), and they clearly define the hardware requirements for physically connecting the computers and the data format of the messages that pass among the computers.

Dave Smith wrote up the proposal, called the Universal Synthesizer Interface, and presented it at the November 1981 meeting of the Audio Engineering Society.

During the next NAMM show in January 1982, the original companies were joined by such major Japanese synthesizer manufacturers as Yamaha, Korg, and Kawai. The new, larger group refined and expanded the proposed standard, and by the June 1982 NAMM show, the basics were in place for what was to become MIDI—the Musical Instrument Digital Interface. Companies began developing synthesizers according to the early MIDI specifications, and those early efforts were used to test and further refine the MIDI specification based on "real-world" experience.

The full *MIDI 1.0 Detailed Specification* was first released to the general public in August 1983. The International MIDI Users Group (IMUG) was formed and given the responsibility for distributing the MIDI specification to musicians and music manufacturers. IMUG soon evolved into the present-day International MIDI Association (IMA), whose primary purpose is to be a clearing-house for information about MIDI. (For more about IMA, see chapter 11, "Getting Help.")

The manufacturers, concerned that they would lose control over MIDI, formed the MIDI Manufacturers Association (MMA) to safeguard the MIDI specification and implement changes in an orderly fashion. Together with the Japanese MIDI Standards Committee (JMSC), the MMA controls the MIDI specification. Before any changes can be adopted as part of the evolving MIDI specification, both the MMA and JMSC must review and agree on the proposals.

LIMITATIONS OF MIDI

MIDI is not without its shortcomings, however. One is that the MIDI specification does not describe what MIDI devices must do, only how to communicate something if the manufacturer decides to do it. Few MIDI devices will incorporate all the potential power of MIDI, so it is up to the person who buys and uses a MIDI device to find out what it can and cannot do. Capabilities range from simple one-voice Note On/Note Off generators to complicated systems with touch sensitivity, keyboard splits, and modulation control.

It should be no surprise that, within limits, the price of an instrument offers as good an initial guideline to its capabilities as any. Even though prices of MIDI equipment seem to drop as technological capabilities increase, there will probably always be disparities between expensive and inexpensive instruments, and even between similarly priced equipment. "Caveat emptor," as the Romans used to say: Buyer beware.

Nor does MIDI specify particular sounds that an instrument must make or the quality of the sounds that it does make. The range and quality of sounds from MIDI synthesizers vary from numerous and wonderful to few and awful, and MIDI itself will not help you determine which synthesizer has which.

Those are artistic limitations of MIDI, but there are technical limitations as well. One is that MIDI sends data serially—that is, one small piece of each message at a time—and the rate at which MIDI messages travel is relatively slow (compared to some other data transmission protocols). If many devices in a single MIDI setup are each generating many messages, all at the same time, the tremendous number of simultaneous MIDI messages can overwhelm MIDI's ability to handle them, a condition called MIDI clog.

In complicated setups, there can be an audible delay, called MIDI lag, between the time a message is initiated and the time you hear the result of the message. Our ears are sensitive instruments, and we can sense (even if not consciously hear) delays in the range of thousandths of a second.

Finally, MIDI provides for only sixteen channels of data. As more and more devices use MIDI for their control signals, the limit of sixteen channels has become inadequate for many complex setups. With one channel devoted to your mixer, another to your digital effects processor, and another to your equalizer, there are not nearly enough for that forty-voice orchestral spectacular you have been dreaming of—and that does not even count the channel you need to control the lighting panel!

Fortunately, the MIDI specification has room to grow and develop, though its development will be tightly controlled to prevent a tangle of incompatible "innovations." Already, multiport interfaces are available; with the right software, they can handle more than sixteen channels without defying the MIDI specification. (See chapter 4 for more on multiport interfaces.) Also underway are discussions that might lead to a solution of MIDI's transmission-speed limitations — perhaps they will become part of an updated MIDI specification.

Despite MIDI's limitations and shortcomings, it has changed the way many musicians work and indeed the way they think about music making. It is safe to say that no new technology has so changed the musical landscape since the introduction of the piano, and it is likely that MIDI's effects will be equally widespread and long-standing.

■

MUSICAL ACOUSTICS

. . . .

Although an understanding of acoustics, the science of sound, is not a requirement for music making, such an understanding can provide insights as well as save time and energy compared to a "hit or miss" approach to learning about music and sound synthesis. Those in a hurry to plug in their MIDI gear and start making sounds can skip this chapter, returning to it at a later date—or not at all. However, I am convinced that a basic understanding of why your music setup works will help you understand how it works, so I hope you will take the time to read this chapter.

The incredible complexity of "live" instrumental sounds makes them hard to synthesize—and even sounds that do not imitate acoustic ones must be similarly complex if they are to be interesting to the ear. Many synthesizer users are so intimidated by the acoustics involved in "designing" a sound that they do not even try to do it, relying instead on factory presets. That puts unnecessary restrictions on the music you create. It also explains why so much of today's popular music uses the same limited palette of sounds and often seems so much alike. With so few synthesizer sounds in circulation, compared to the much wider range of sounds it is possible to create, it is especially important and useful for synthesists to have an understanding of the acoustic principles involved in sound production and to experiment by changing your synthesizer's factory settings.

THE CAUSE OF SOUND

The term *sound* describes a complex interaction between a vibrating object, a transmission medium (usually the air around us), the ear, and the brain. The vibrations of the transmission medium are also referred to as "sounds."

In order for human beings to hear the sounds produced by a vibrating object, the object must oscillate—vibrate back and forth—in the range of roughly 20 to 20,000 times each second. As the object oscillates, it sets the air around it in motion. The moving air in turn moves the air near it, and so forth, and the vibration is carried away from the source of the sound in a pressure wave, or sound wave. The sound wave presses against the listener's ear, and the listener's brain interprets the changing pressure pattern as a particular sound. If there are no such changes in ambient air pressure, we hear silence, as shown in figure 2.1a.

A sound wave has pressures greater than the surrounding air at rest, called crests, and pressures less than the surrounding air at rest, called troughs. A waveform is a two-dimensional pictorial representation of the changes in pressure, with one dimension representing instantaneous pressure and the other representing elapsed time. Figure 2.1b shows a waveform with a recurring pattern of pressures higher and lower than ambient air pressure, such as are typical of the sound wave caused by striking a tuning fork.

As sound waves travel away from their source, they become weaker because they must cover a larger and larger area, moving successively larger masses of air as they propagate. At a sufficient distance from the sound source, the changes in pressure become too small to detect, and the sound dies away.

Even complex waveforms can be made up of repeating segments, as shown in figure 2.2. If the waveform's shape repeats itself at regular intervals, the length of time the wave travels before it repeats is called the period of the sound wave. The period depends on how fast the sound-emitting object is vibrating.

The vibrating object can be a string, as on a violin or guitar; a column of air set in motion by a reed or mouthpiece, as with an oboe, organ pipe, or trumpet; or a piece of wood or metal, as with a marimba or cymbal. Most often, the sound of a musical instrument is produced by the interaction of different materials. The vibrating strings of a violin cause vibrations within the wooden body of the violin and in turn within the air inside the violin body, all of which contribute to the characteristic sound of the violin.

Synthesizers do not produce sounds by their own vibration. Rather, they generate weak electrical signals, or waveforms, that are analogous in

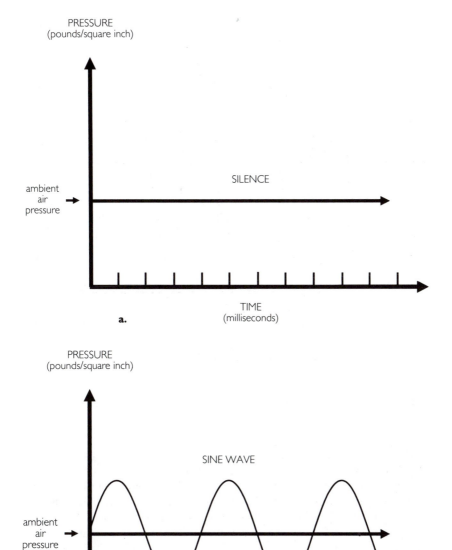

FIGURE 2.1 Simple pressure functions: a) With no change in ambient air pressure, we hear silence; b) Changes in air pressure caused by a vibrating tuning fork.

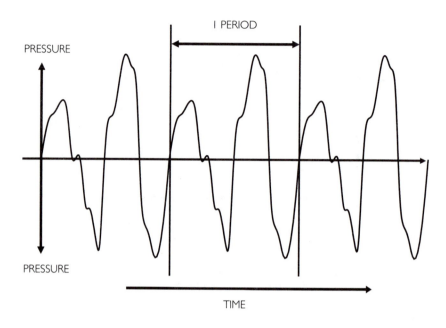

FIGURE 2.2   A typical periodic waveform.

shape to the sound waveform they produce. The electrical signals must be amplified enough to drive a speaker; as paper cones inside the speaker cabinets move back and forth in response to the changing electrical waveform, they produce changes in the surrounding air pressure, which changes are characteristic of the sound waveform—assuming, of course, that all the equipment operates perfectly, without any distortion or coloration of the signal. (For more on the process of converting sounds to electrical waveforms and back again, see chapter 3, "Computer Music Basics.")

One advantage that sounds produced by MIDI synthesizers (and other electronic sound sources) have over acoustic sounds is that the air pressure changes caused by the speaker cone's movement can be larger or smaller than the air pressure changes produced by most acoustic instruments producing similar sounds, resulting in a wider range of soft to loud sounds. (That advantage is negated, however, if the electronic sound source introduces its own sounds—noise—into the sounds it is creating, as is sometimes the case with MIDI equipment and other electronic devices.)

CHARACTERISTICS OF SOUNDS

Three terms are used in music to describe a particular sound: *pitch, timbre,* and *loudness.* Any given sound lasts for a specific length of time, and each of the three qualities may change during the duration of a sound. The way these three qualities combine and change during any given sound allows us to distinguish among different sound sources and different sounds.

Pitch

For a periodic sound source (one whose waveform repeats at regular intervals), the number of waveforms that the sound source produces each second is called the frequency of the sound. Within the limits of human hearing, we hear higher vibration rates as "higher" sounds and lower vibration rates as "lower" sounds; that sense of "higher" or "lower" is described by the musical term *pitch.*

In acoustics, frequency (which musicians call pitch) is usually measured in units called Hertz (abbreviated Hz), named after acoustics pioneer Heinrich Rudolf Hertz (1857–1894). A sound source vibrating at a rate of 100 vibrations per second is said to have a frequency of 100 Hertz.

The hearing range of an average young person is from about 20 Hz to about 20,000 Hz. Some animals can hear sounds outside the range of human hearing. Dog whistles, which produce frequencies above the range of human hearing and thus are silent to human ears, generate a pitch well within the hearing range of dogs.

As we get older, the upper limit of frequencies we can hear falls. Extended exposure to excessively loud sounds can also cause us to lose our ability to hear sounds at the upper end of the frequency range. A growing awareness of the fragile physiology of human hearing among performers and audio engineers has heightened their concern that loud monitoring or performance sound pressure levels can cost them the primary tool of their trade—their hearing. Studio monitor systems designed for accurate reproduction at lower sound pressure levels and headphone monitor systems for performers are becoming more accepted and widely used as the impact of sustained loud sounds on the ability to hear high frequencies becomes more widely recognized.

Two instruments playing at the same frequency will sound at the same pitch or, in musical terms, at the unison. Next to the unison, the two frequencies that sound most similar in pitch have a frequency ratio of 2:1, what musicians call an octave. Pitches at 200 Hz and 400 Hz will sound an octave apart; so will pitches at 800 Hz and 1,600 Hz. The octave, then, is defined not by a specific difference in Hz, but by the ratio of two frequencies. The higher one frequency is, the greater the frequency difference needed for the next higher octave to sound. Such relationships, based on constant ratios rather than constant absolute difference, are called logarithmic.

Frequency is a continuous spectrum, and we could distinguish many different frequencies or pitches within any octave. However, most musical cultures divide each octave into a smaller, fixed number of pitches—in most Western music, only twelve different pitches per octave are used. In the music of other cultures, there are sometimes fewer, sometimes more divisions of each octave. Regardless of its divisions, the octave appears to be a foundation of music in almost every culture.

Timbre

Timbre (from French, pronounced tam'ber) means "tone color." It is timbre that allows us to distinguish between two sustained sounds of the same pitch. We can determine, for example, that one sound source is an oboe and another a harmonica.

Rather than producing a single vibration pattern at a single frequency, most complex sound sources vibrate at several frequencies simultaneously. The combination, interaction, and relative strengths of these frequencies, or overtones, result in a single sound waveform that we interpret as timbre.

The lowest frequency in any sound produced by most musical instruments gives the sound its identifiable musical pitch (though there are exceptions, in which the frequency we identify as the musical pitch is not actually produced by the instrument). The lowest frequency we hear in any given instrumental sound, which is usually also the lowest frequency produced, is called the fundamental.

The overtones of most musical sounds are close to whole-number multiples of the fundamental, although the exact relationship between fundamental and overtones typically varies slightly during the duration of the sound. Overtones of this type are called harmonics; the fundamental is referred to as the first harmonic, and each successively higher overtone is referred to by number—the second harmonic has a frequency twice that of the fundamental, the third harmonic has a frequency three times that of the fundamental, and so on, theoretically continuing upwards to infinity. A fundamental and all of its harmonics is called the natural harmonic series. Most musical sounds involve many harmonics, but even among those harmonics in the audible range, not all are necessarily present, nor are all the harmonics present at equal intensities. The complex vibration characteristics of different sound sources produce sounds with different harmonic contents. Even the waveform of a single instrument may change depending on how the instrument is played.

Each of the strings on a violin, for example, has its own characteristic distribution of harmonics. The thicker strings are stiffer and cannot vibrate as freely at higher frequencies as the thinner ones. With the thicker strings, the higher harmonics tend to die away more quickly than the harmonics of the thinner ones, so even the same pitch played on two different strings of the same violin will have a slightly different timbre. One reason for that difference is that the harmonics are distributed differently on the two strings; another reason has to do with how the harmonic distribution of each string varies over the duration of each note played.

Furthermore, the timbre of a violin string is affected by where along its length it is plucked or bowed. Most often, the string is set to vibrating near one of its ends, producing sounds that are rich in harmonics. But if the string is plucked or bowed near its center, certain harmonics will be missing or of lower intensity. Similarly, the position of the pickup relative to the strings of an electric guitar influences the resulting timbre, so many guitars have pickups at different locations on the guitar body, giving the guitarist greater control over the instrument's timbre.

An understanding of timbre helps violinists decide where on the string to play and helps guitarists decide which pickup to use. Such an understanding helps synthesists choose synthesizer sounds and build sounds "from scratch," and it helps producers and engineers decide what kind and how much sound processing to use—subjects that will be covered in subsequent chapters.

Some sounds, particularly those made by the percussion family of musical instruments and those sounds we generally call "noise," produce overtones that fall outside the natural harmonic series. There can be so many of these inharmonic overtones, and they can be so strong, that they drown out the fundamental, making it impossible for us to hear any specific musical pitch among the unrelated overtones. With cymbals, for example, the inharmonic overtones give the sound its metallic "clanging" timbre, typical of sounds produced by vibrating metal plates or bars.

Resonance and Its Effect on Timbre

Two objects may naturally vibrate at the same frequency. If one is set into vibration with the other placed nearby, the first object may induce "sympathetic vibration" in the second, a phenomenon called resonance.

In addition to their primary function as radiators of sound energy, the bodies of most instruments resonate at various frequencies when they are played. The air mass inside the bodies of such instruments as violins, acoustic guitars, and drums resonates as well. All these resonances interact with each other and with the source of the original vibrations. As a result, some overtones produced by the vibrating sound source are strengthened while others are diminished. In some cases, overtones produced by the original source of the vibrations are completely canceled.

Even the room in which a sound occurs contributes its own resonances, which interact with the original sound and influence the timbre of that sound.

Amplitude, Loudness, and Intensity

Whereas frequency is a measure of the number of vibrations within a given time period, amplitude is the maximum sound pressure (measured in comparison to air pressure at rest) at a particular point in time. Instruments measure amplitude differences more consistently than the human ear can; the term *intensity* refers to such measurements of amplitude by machine.

The musical term *loudness* refers to perceived amplitude—a subtle distinction, but an important one. The loudness, or perceived amplitude of a sound depends upon its intensity, but also depends upon the frequency of the sound and the peculiarities of human hearing. The human ear "favors" frequencies in the 2,000 to 5,000 Hz range and is less sensitive to lower and higher frequencies. Thus, we may hear one pitch as louder than another, even though their amplitudes are the same. Tests have shown that varying intensities are required in order to make test tones at various frequencies sound as loud as a 1,000 Hz reference frequency of a given intensity. For example, at low intensity levels high frequency tones sound louder than low frequency tones of the same intensity.

It is easy to understand why so much confusion arises—the reality and perception of amplitude can be slightly different, and each has its own scale of measurement. Despite the differences between loudness and intensity, the two terms are often used interchangeably, and from a musician's point of view the differences are less important than the similarities.

A commonly used unit of sound-level measurement is the decibel (usually abbreviated dB), named after Alexander Graham Bell (1847–1922), sound research pioneer and inventor of the telephone. The decibel does not measure the amplitude of a single sound. It is a measure, on a logarithmic scale, of the magnitude of a particular quantity (such as sound pressure) with respect to a standard reference value for that quantity. The number of decibels difference between the two sounds does not describe the absolute amplitude of either; rather, it describes the relationship of the amplitudes of the two sounds to one another.

It is not important for musicians to understand all the mathematics and physics behind the decibel measurement scale, only to understand the practical usefulness of decibel ratios. For the average person, two sounds exhibiting the smallest audible difference in amplitude are described as being approximately 1 to 3 dB apart (though such factors as the frequency of the sounds might cause the listener's response to differ slightly). In other words, two otherwise identical sounds played in succession would have to be approximately 1 to 3 dB different in loudness before a listener would notice the difference.

The term *sound pressure level* (abbreviated SPL) is used to relate decibels to standard atmospheric pressure. The threshold of hearing level is used as a reference point and assigned the value 0 dB SPL. Other sounds can then be expressed in relation to this 0 dB SPL level, providing a measure of their absolute amplitude. Often a single reference stated in decibels implies dB SPL.

The difference, in decibels, between the softest sound a system can produce and the loudest is called the dynamic range of the system. The dynamic range of a live symphony orchestra can surpass 120 dB—that is, it can produce sounds at 0 dB SPL that are barely audible, and its loudest passages can exceed 120 dB SPL, approaching the threshold of pain, at which sound is felt rather than heard. (The actual dynamic range would vary for each listener, depending on the listener's seat location.)

Most inexpensive MIDI gear cannot match this dynamic range; indeed, only better-quality MIDI equipment has a dynamic range as high as 96 dB. Since MIDI equipment must be connected to amplifiers, speakers, and other electronic equipment, the lower limit at which MIDI systems can produce audible sound is determined by the overall noise level of the complete system, and the upper limit is determined by the level at which distortion occurs. The ratio of noise a sound reproduction system introduces relative to the signal it is reproducing is called the signal-to-noise ratio; the higher the signal-to-noise ratio, the larger the effective dynamic range. Chapter 4, "MIDI Hardware—How to Choose It, How to Use It," will have more information on reading MIDI equipment specifications and evaluating the price/performance trade-offs in light of your own particular needs.

As most sounds are produced, their amplitudes will vary during their production. This changing amplitude during the course of a single sound is called the envelope of the sound. The amplitude envelope is one of our most important clues to the identity of the sound.

The time required for the amplitude to rise to its maximum level is called its attack time. The time it takes for the sound to die away from the dissipation of its vibratory energy is called its decay time. If the sound is stopped before it has had a chance to die away completely, the time it takes before it stops sounding is called its release time.

For example, the characteristic amplitude envelope of a piano sound is a fast attack time, a slight decay followed by a slow, steadily fading sustain, and a fast release. Compared to a piano sound, an organ sound has a slightly slower (or longer) attack, very little decay, a sustain that lasts as long as the performer holds down the key, and a slightly longer release. A trumpet sound, by contrast, has a slower attack. The sound then decays slightly and sustains as long as the player continues to blow. The release (resulting from the interaction of the player's tongue, lips, and breath once the player begins to stop blowing) is slower than a piano's. Figures 2.3a, b, and c show typical amplitude envelopes for a piano, organ, and trumpet tone, respectively.

In addition to the overall amplitude envelope, the amplitude of each overtone of a sound relative to the other overtones present in the sound also affects its timbre. The high overtones of a cymbal crash, for example, are of greater relative amplitude than the lower overtones. Because the overtones are inharmonic, and the fundamental is undefined, we hear a cymbal crash as unpitched. Many metal percussion instruments have a similar emphasis on the inharmonic, higher overtones and a similarly weak fundamental, making it difficult for the ear to assign them a pitch.

NOISE

Unlike the common usage of the term, the acoustic term *noise* has a more specific meaning than "unpleasant sounds." Rather, noise describes a sound in which none of the harmonics are of significantly greater amplitude than the others, resulting in a sound that lacks a discernible pitch. Two categories of noise are important to an understanding of acoustics: *white noise* and *pink noise.*

Like white light, which combines equal amounts of all colors, white noise combines equal amounts of all audio frequencies. Because of the logarithmic nature of frequency, each octave of white noise contains twice as many frequencies as the octave immediately below it. Each frequency of white noise has the same energy, so the octaves with more frequencies (the upper octaves) have more total energy. Using decibel ratios, each octave is 3 dB higher than the octave below it. Since there are more high frequencies than low frequencies, the higher frequencies are more noticeable, giving white noise its characteristic hissing sound.

Pink noise, on the other hand, has the same amount of sound energy in each octave — there are still more frequencies in the upper octaves, but each higher frequency has less energy. Since all octaves have equal energy, we do not hear any particular frequency range as predominant, giving pink noise its characteristic sound similar to that of surf or a waterfall.

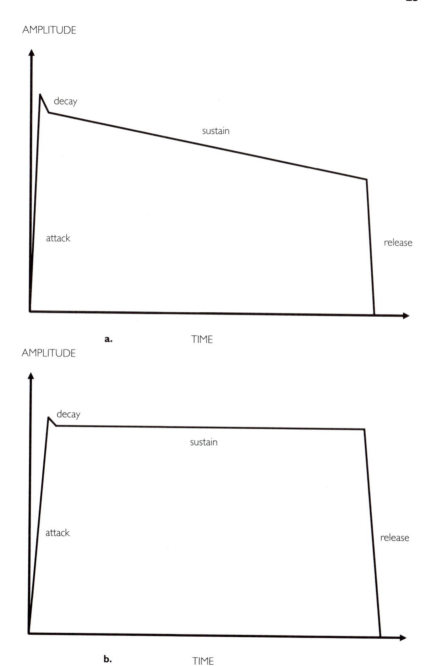

FIGURE 2.3 Typical amplitude envelopes for various instruments: a) a typical piano tone; b) a typical organ tone; c) a typical trumpet tone.

AMPLITUDE

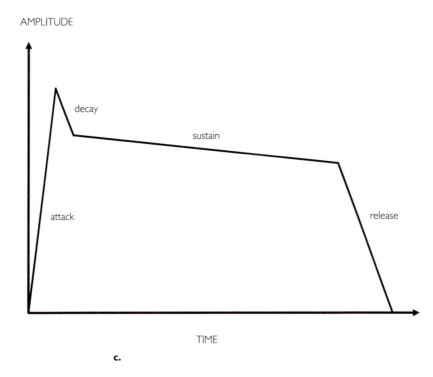

TIME

c.

FIGURE 2.3   continued.

PITCH RELATIONSHIPS IN MUSIC

The difference in pitch between two pitched sounds is called an interval. The interval described by two pitches with the same fundamental is called the unison, and in the interval known as the octave, the fundamental of the upper pitch is exactly twice that of the lower pitch; in other words, the second harmonic of the lower pitch is the same as the fundamental of the upper pitch.

In the music of most Western cultures, the octave is usually divided into twelve equal parts. Musicians use letter names (called notes) to indicate pitches within an octave rather than specifying frequencies. For example, the pitch to which orchestras tune prior to performing has a frequency of 440 Hz and is called A. Figure 2.4 shows two-and-a-half octaves of a piano keyboard, centered on the notes commonly called middle C and A-440, along with the MIDI note numbers and frequencies of each note. In

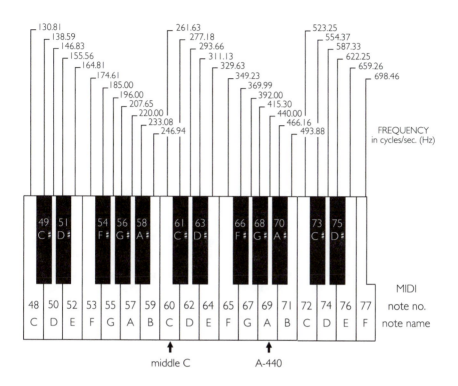

FIGURE 2.4 Piano keys, note names, MIDI note numbers, and their associated frequencies.

ascending order, the pitches, or notes, within an octave are named A, A-sharp, B, C, C-sharp, D, D-sharp, E, F, F-sharp, G, and G-sharp. (Each of the sharps can be named enharmonically as the flat of the note above it—thus, C-sharp can be enharmonically named D-flat, D-sharp can be enharmonically named E-flat, and so forth.) The note above G-sharp is the A that begins the next octave. An octave may be counted starting on any note; simply progress through the notes until you have reached the same note name on which you began. This note begins the next higher octave.

Prior to the eighteenth century, the music of European cultures used tuning systems based on the theories of the ancient Greek philosopher Pythagoras. Pythagoras divided the octave into intervals whose frequencies form a series of small whole-number ratios. In the Pythagorean system, as in all tuning systems, the unison has a frequency ratio of 1:1, while the octave has a frequency relationship of 2:1. Those intervals whose frequency ratios can be expressed in the smallest integers such as 1:1, 2:1, 3:2, and 4:3 sounded most pleasant to sixteenth- and seventeenth-century musicians, who used a tuning system based upon the Pythagorean model; that system is now known as mean-tone temperament. Frequency ratios involving larger integers such as 9:8 or 15:8 sounded more dissonant. Composers of the time felt constrained to "resolve" dissonant intervals by following them with nearby intervals that listeners considered consonant. In such tuning systems, a melody consisting of a series of intervals starting from a specific note does not sound like the same series of intervals if a different note is used as the starting point.

Around the time of Bach, there arose a system called equal temperament, in which each octave is divided into twelve equal parts. In equal temperament, the frequency ratio between any two adjacent notes (semitones or half steps) is almost exactly equal to the twelfth root of 2—approximately 1.05946—regardless of which octave is considered, as a few minutes with a calculator and figure 2.4 should confirm. This allows for transposition, when a melody sounds as if it uses the same intervals regardless of which note it begins on. No other tuning system permits such transposition to any starting note without altering the sound of the interval relationships.

The trade-off in using equal temperament rather than the Pythagorean system is that the intervals of equal temperament deviate slightly from simple integer ratios, so that the intervals are less consonant than their Pythagorean counterparts.

The switch from tuning systems based on the Pythagorean model to one based on equal temperament was largely an accommodation to the limitations of the fixed-tuned instruments of the era—harpsichords and flutes, for example. The technology of computer synthesizers is more flexible, making it possible once again to enjoy the more acoustically pure intervals of the Pythagorean system or the convenience of equal temperament, as we wish. Indeed, synthesizers have sparked a renewed interest in all manner of tuning systems including historical systems that once enjoyed a measure of popularity, more recent tunings designed by avant-garde composers, tunings used among non-Western cultures, and unique tunings devised by individual experimenters. Chapter 4 describes how to evaluate a synthesizer for its potential to use new tunings and how to experiment with alternate tuning systems.

C H A P T E R   T H R E E

COMPUTER MUSIC BASICS

· ·

It is quite possible to use MIDI musically and effectively without understanding how MIDI devices store or manipulate their information. Many users of MIDI—particularly those who are just starting out—are unconcerned with the theory behind how digital systems work, and such users can skip this section entirely, returning to it if they wish when their understanding of the operating principles of MIDI is stronger.

However, MIDI users who want to work with their equipment at the most fundamental level—by changing the equipment's operating characteristics, configuring complex multidevice setups, or writing programs to manipulate MIDI data, for example—will likely deal with specific data messages at the symbolic level. Since individual MIDI messages are represented by numeric data, a basic understanding of how computers represent musical information and the number systems used by computers is indispensible.

ANALOG AND DIGITAL REPRESENTATIONS OF SOUND

Sound pressure is a continuously changing phenomenon. Many electric sound sources represent the sound pressure wave by a continuously changing electrical signal, whose strength at any instant is analogous to the strength of the sound's pressure at that instant. Systems

27

that represent one continuously changing phenomenon by an analogous continuously changing phenomenon are called analog systems. Most home stereos are analog systems, as were early synthesizers.

Computers and MIDI synthesizers, on the other hand, deal with discrete numbers rather than continuous changes. Such digital equipment represents the sound wave as a series of "snapshots" of the wave, each snapshot taken at successive small increments of time, as shown in figure 3.1. The amplitude of the wave at each time increment is assigned a single number that represents the amplitude at that instant. If the snapshots are taken frequently enough, and if the numbers assigned are adequately precise, the digital equipment can develop a close approximation of the wave itself. An analog (electrical) signal may be converted into a numerical value (called sampling), or the computer may itself generate the numbers that describe the analog signal (called synthesis).

BINARY NUMBER SYSTEMS

The presence or absence of voltage in a single circuit within a computer—a two-state phenomenon—is represented by the number symbol characters (digits) 0 or 1, called binary (two-state) digits or bits. With only one bit, the computer can represent only the two values 0 and 1. But if two bits are considered together as a group, four different values can be represented—00, 01, 10, and 11. With each additional bit that is added to the grouping, the range of numbers that can be represented doubles.

We use the placement of each digit within a number as well as the digits themselves when we interpret both decimal and binary numbers. For example, the decimal number 139 represents 1 times 10 to the power of 2, plus 3 times 10 to the power of 1, plus 9 times 10 to the power of 0, or $(1 \times 10^2) + (3 \times 10^1) + (9 \times 10^0)$. The same value might be represented in binary as the eight-bit value $10001011 - (1 \times 2^7) + (0 \times 2^6) + (0 \times 2^5) + (0 \times 2^4) + (1 \times 2^3) + (0 \times 2^2) + (1 \times 2^1) + (1 \times 2^0)$, which in decimal notation equals $128 + 0 + 0 + 0 + 8 + 0 + 2 + 1$, or 139. Most often, computer data is structured in groups of eight bits. Each eight-bit group is known as one byte. Within a byte or other multibit grouping, the bit with the largest power of 2 is called the most significant bit, while the bit representing 2 to the 0 power is called the least significant bit (figure 3.2).

Because MIDI messages are all non-negative integers, MIDI uses this simple binary number representation system, called pure binary. Other binary number representation systems are also able to represent negative numbers and fractions.

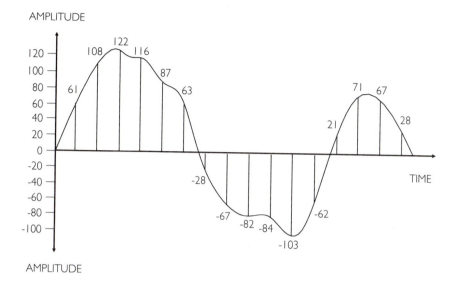

FIGURE 3.1 An analog waveform with digital values assigned to periodic instantaneous voltages of the waveform.

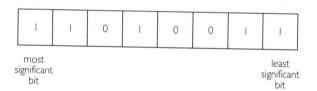

FIGURE 3.2 Binary byte, showing the most significant bit (MSB) and the least significant bit (LSB).

Representing large binary numbers requires a great many 0s and 1s, so a shorthand representation system called hexadecimal notation is often used instead. Each of the sixteen possible bit patterns in a 4-bit group is assigned a particular hexadecimal digit—0 through 9 as with decimal numbers, along with A to represent 10 decimal, B to represent 11 decimal, and so on, through F, which represents 15 decimal, as shown in figure 3.3.

Using hexadecimal notation, the binary value 11011001 is broken up into two 4-bit groups—1101 1001. Each group of four bits is represented by a single hexadecimal digit, resulting in the hexadecimal value D9. Larger binary numbers can be similarly represented more compactly using

BINARY	DECIMAL	HEXADECIMAL
0000	0	0
0001	1	1
0010	2	2
0011	3	3
0100	4	4
0101	5	5
0110	6	6
0111	7	7
1000	8	8
1001	9	9
1010	10	A
1011	11	B
1100	12	C
1101	13	D
1110	14	E
1111	15	F

FIGURE 3.3   Binary, decimal, and hexadecimal notation.

hexadecimal notation: 1010111001011111 is broken up into 1010 1110 0101 1111, expressed in hexadecimal as AE5F.

To convert hexadecimal notation back to binary, reverse the encoding process, substituting the appropriate 4-bit pattern for each hexadecimal digit. Thus, B40A hexadecimal equals 1011010000001010 binary.

RESOLUTION IN SAMPLING AND SYNTHESIS

The number of bits used by a digital system to represent each value is called the resolution of the system. With higher resolution, the system can more accurately represent the different amplitudes within a waveform. An 8-bit binary code (or byte) can represent 256 different amplitude values; a 16-bit binary code (or word) can represent 65,536 different values.

The difference between the system's capability to represent a waveform and the errors introduced into the waveform by the system itself is called the system's signal-to-noise ratio. The ratio is the relationship, in decibels, between the largest signal amplitude the system can handle without distortion and the noise created by the system itself.

As a general guideline, we can calculate the theoretical maximum signal-to-noise ratio for a digital audio system by multiplying its number of bits by 6. Signal-to-noise ratio is expressed in decibels; for example, a 12-bit digital audio system typically has a theoretical maximum signal-to-noise ratio of $12 \times 6 = 72$dB.

No digital audio system can achieve more than its theoretical maximum signal-to-noise ratio, and most perform far below the theoretical maximum in actual use. Specifications are at best only a guideline to actual performance and at worst serve to mislead rather than inform. Your ears are a better guide to audio performance than simple specifications—a point that will be repeated in chapter 4, "MIDI Hardware—How to Choose It, How to Use It."

The difference, in decibels, between the softest sound a system can produce and the loudest is called the dynamic range of the system. The signal-to-noise ratio of an audio system influences how much of the system's dynamic range can be produced without significant added distortion, and in electronic sound systems the two terms are often used interchangeably. Since the dynamic range of a live symphony orchestra can be more than 120 dB, a 12-bit system with a 72 dB signal-to-noise ratio is unable to represent the full dynamic range of orchestral sounds, or indeed to represent an individual waveform whose harmonic components differ in amplitude by more than 72 dB.

The professional recording industry has settled on a minimum of 16-bit resolution, yielding a dynamic range approaching 96 dB. When professional-quality digital recorders are used, most listeners are unaware of noise generated by the recording medium itself. More often, any audible noise present in the recording is due to microphone input circuitry or the limitations of other equipment used in the recording.

When noise is present in digital recordings, it can be particularly annoying. Quantization noise, which can occur during the process of converting sounds into numbers for use by computers, is focused on particular frequencies and results in a sound many listeners describe as "granular." The random noise of analog recordings, in contrast, may more easily fade into the background of the listener's perception.

Systems with 16-bit resolution and a 96 dB dynamic range do not usually suffer from quantization noise. To solve the quantization noise problem in digital recording systems with less than 16-bit resolution, a slight amount of random noise called dither may be added to the signal input to randomize the effects of quantization. While dithering decreases the dynamic range of a digital recording, the resulting sound may prove more pleasing to the listener.

SAMPLING RATES AND NYQUIST'S THEOREM

Just as the number of bits per sample is important in determining the signal-to-noise ratio, the sampling rate is important in determining the bandwidth, or range of frequencies, the system can represent. The smaller the time interval between each sample, the closer the system can get to an accurate representation of the waveform. In figure 3.4a, the sampling rate is so low that the number representing each sample inaccurately quantifies the waveform for most of the time that elapses until the next sample is taken. Figure 3.4b shows that a higher sampling rate more accurately quantifies the waveform; with a high enough sampling rate, the differences between the sample value quantity and the actual waveform pressure quantity at any given time become negligible.

Nyquist's theorem states that the maximum frequency a digital system can represent is approximately one-half the sampling rate. Since the range of human hearing can extend upward to 20,000 Hz or higher, the sampling rate must be in excess of 40,000 samples per second (or 40 kilohertz, written kHz) in order to be able to reproduce the full bandwidth of human hearing. Compact discs, for example, store sounds in digital format using a 44.1 kHz sampling rate so that the highest frequency they can reproduce (called their Nyquist frequency) is approximately 20 kHz. Many professional digital recorders use a 48 kHz sampling rate, yielding an even higher Nyquist frequency.

THE DIGITAL RECORDING PROCESS

The heart of the digital recording process is the conversion of signals from the electrical (analog) domain into the digital domain of numbers, called A/D conversion (pronounced "A-to-D conversion"). The incoming analog signal is fed to a sample-and-hold circuit, which is updated at the system's sampling rate. During the interval between samples, an A/D converter (or ADC) determines the amplitude of the input signal's level and assigns it a numeric value, or quantizes it. The time it takes for the A/D converter to do this is called its settling time.

If input frequencies above the Nyquist frequency are allowed to enter the sampling process, these signals, upon playback, will be transferred down an equal amount below the Nyquist frequency, or aliased into the audible range. For example, if the Nyquist frequency is at 15 kHz and a 20 kHz signal is sampled, the signal will be aliased down to 10 kHz. Most sampling systems use a low-pass filter—set at or slightly below the Nyquist frequency—before analog-to-digital conversion takes place, in order to eliminate from the input signal any frequencies above the low-pass setting, thus preventing aliasing from occurring.

One advantage of digital recording over the analog recording process is that, for each bit of each digital word, only one of two states must be determined—0 or 1. As long as the digital recorder can distinguish

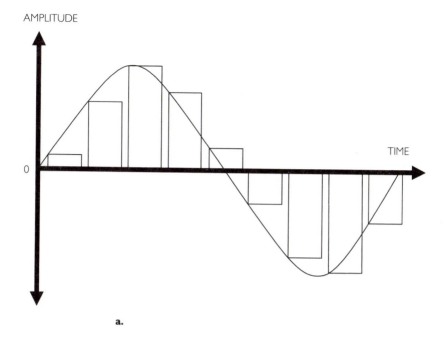

AMPLITUDE

TIME

0

a.

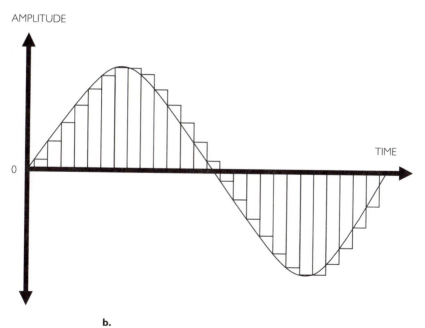

AMPLITUDE

TIME

0

b.

FIGURE 3.4 Two sampling rates: a) low and b) high.

between the two digits, tape noise and distortion are irrelevant. Furthermore, there is no noise buildup when digital recordings are copied in the digital domain. If the identity of digital data can be determined at all, it can be copied accurately and completely. A first-generation digital copy should be no noisier than the original, and successive generations should be identical to the first.

In addition, the computing power in digital recording systems can be used to generate a verification code that can determine when errors have occurred and often can regenerate a damaged portion of the digital code. Any noise or signal recording error in an analog recording, by contrast, becomes a permanent part of the recording and is difficult to remove. And because the recorded analog signal must match the complexity of the original electrical waveform, it is difficult to copy precisely, and each successive generation of copies will be further and further from the original signal.

Since a digital signal contains only digital words composed of 0s and 1s, a digital recording can be stored almost indefinitely, manipulated within a computer, transmitted to another digital device, or converted back into its original analog form—all without the introduction of signal errors.

To re-create the original signal, each word is successively converted from the digital domain into an analog electrical signal, called D/A conversion. Once processed by the D/A converter (or DAC, pronounced "dack"), the resulting analog signals pass through a smoothing filter to remove the discrete steps created during the quantization process, and the resulting signal can be so close to the original signal that it appears identical to the listener's ears. A block diagram of a complete digital audio recording and playback system is shown in figure 3.5.

TRANSMITTING DIGITAL DATA

MIDI is *not* a digital audio recording system as described above, though MIDI borrows many of digital audio recording's basic principles. In particular, since MIDI is concerned primarily with the storage and transmission of large volumes of digital data, it draws on similar principles and techniques developed for storing and transmitting digital audio data.

Digital data can be transmitted from one device to another in one of two ways. In parallel transmission, multiple bits (typically one byte) are sent along multiple transmission lines all at once as shown in figure 3.6a. In serial transmission, bits are sent along a single wire, one bit at a time, according to some predetermined formula, as shown in figure 3.6b. The

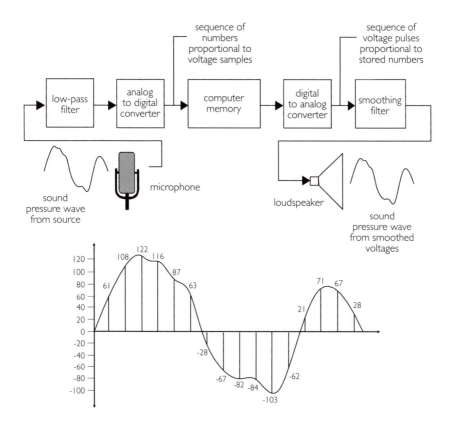

FIGURE 3.5 A digital recording and playback system.

bits are then reassembled at the receiving end, according to the same formula that was used to transmit the bits.

The advantage of parallel data transmission is that it can be much faster, but serial data transmission has a cost advantage—it requires fewer wires in the connecting cable, since each bit travels along the same wire rather than its own dedicated wire. An added advantage of serial transmission is that its cables can be longer than parallel cables, since serial cables are not as susceptible to radio frequency interference (RFI)—signals from other electronic equipment that may scramble the data signal.

Since MIDI was intended from the start to be a low-cost data transmission protocol, its designers settled on serial data transmission. Each MIDI transmitting device sends its information out along the cable as a series of voltages representing the 1s and 0s in each 8-bit byte, along with an extra

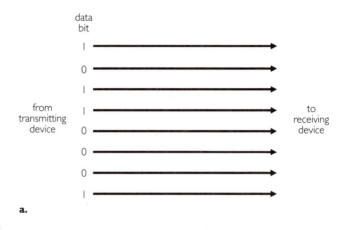

a.

from transmitting device

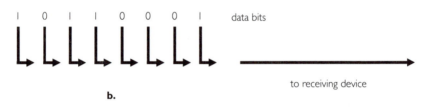

b.

FIGURE 3.6   Two types of data transmission: a) parallel; b) serial.

0 bit before and 1 bit after each byte, called the start and stop bits. These start and stop bits are stripped off by the receiving device as it reassembles the data. In order for MIDI devices to communicate with one another, they must all send and receive information at the same speed—31,250 bits per second. Each byte is preceded by its start bit, then its least significant bit, followed by each more significant bit successively until all eight bits have been sent, followed by the stop bit.

MIDI messages fall into several categories based on the type of instruction the message represents. The MIDI specification clearly spells out the particulars of each message, including how many bytes are required for the message and the value of each byte.

MIDI MESSAGES

The data communicated between MIDI devices do not describe sound waves but rather are numerical codes that specify particular events such as the press of a key or the turn of a controller wheel. The MIDI specification assigns a message number to each type of event MIDI is capable of describing.

This aspect of MIDI is one that is most commonly misunderstood, so let me repeat—MIDI does not describe specific sounds but rather sends instructions, in the form of voltages that represent the 0s and 1s of binary numbers, to a device such as a synthesizer that can interpret the numbers as a call for a particular type of event, causing the synthesizer to produce the sounds. Because MIDI cables do not carry audio signals, plugging a MIDI cable from a MIDI port into a connector on a piece of audio equipment can damage both pieces of equipment, since the voltages transmitted might be outside the range of voltages the audio equipment was designed to handle.

Even if cables are correctly connected to two MIDI devices, that alone does not guarantee that they will work together as desired. Two different synthesizers might produce entirely different sounds in response to the same MIDI message from a keyboard controller. Similarly, a MIDI message sent to a different kind of device—a mixing console or lighting control panel, for example—might not produce a sound at all. The interpretation of the MIDI message is a function of the device that receives the message, and it is up to the user to make sure that the device can respond appropriately.

One common type of MIDI message, Note On, specifies a particular note. Generally, if the message is sent to a synthesizer, it will produce the specified note. But if the message is sent to a drum machine it might produce a percussive noise, or, if it is sent to a lighting control panel, it might turn on a particular colored light.

Another type of MIDI message called a program change message is often used to select a particular sound from among the many that a synthesizer might be able to produce. Because MIDI does not specify the exact nature of the sound that is associated with any particular program change message number, selecting program change number 41, for example, might produce a flute sound on one synthesizer and a trombone sound on another synthesizer. General MIDI, an addendum to the *MIDI 1.0 Detailed Specification,* attempts to address this problem. But as described in chapter 4, General MIDI is neither a certain solution nor a complete one.

It is the responsibility of the MIDI user to know how each piece of equipment in a particular MIDI setup responds to the messages it is sent. Chapter 8 will describe each message type in detail, discuss potential problems that can arise from misinterpretations of MIDI messages, and offer suggestions for ways to avoid them.

■

MIDI HARDWARE— HOW TO CHOOSE IT, HOW TO USE IT

. . . .

This chapter is intended to acquaint you with the most widely used categories of MIDI hardware—the "things" that compose a MIDI system—and the most important capabilities and features of each. It will cover the following categories of MIDI hardware: MIDI keyboard controllers and keyboard synthesizers; rack-mount synthesizers and drum machines; samplers and sample players; MIDI workstations; alternative (nonkeyboard) MIDI controllers; hardware sequencers; and MIDI-controlled studio equipment. The final section of the chapter provides an overview of MIDI interfaces for personal computers and for retrofitting non-MIDI electronic equipment; offers guidelines for choosing, using, and fabricating MIDI cables; and introduces personal computers as a part of MIDI systems.

The market for MIDI products is highly competitive, with a great many product categories, brands, and price ranges. Because of intense competition, prices generally are a reflection of underlying value, though, as always, there are bargains to be found if you know what to look for. Before selecting any MIDI equipment, decide what capabilities you need and how much you can afford to spend. Then compare the specifications, features, and quality of several models in your price range before making your choice. A MIDI setup can represent a considerable investment, so be prepared to invest your time learning about the equipment by getting a hands-on demonstration or (better yet) working with a friend's system so that you will have an understanding of what you are buying before making your commitment.

KEYBOARD CONTROLLERS

Controllers generate MIDI signals for other devices to interpret and act upon, while synthesizers produce the sounds specified by the incoming MIDI messages. There are an increasing number of types of controller. Although MIDI guitars, MIDI saxophones, and MIDI trumpets are becoming commonplace, the first (and still most widely used) MIDI controllers were keyboards (figure 4.1)—and there are now dozens of brands and styles.

If a keyboard is to be your primary means of interacting with MIDI, the choice of which keyboard may be your most important hardware decision. Mechanical technology is relatively more expensive than solid-state, and keyboards are very much mechanical devices. Therefore, the range of keyboard prices and capabilities is relatively wider than for many other MIDI devices.

One way to limit mechanical costs is to limit the number of keys. Few MIDI keyboard controllers feature a full eighty-eight key piano-style keyboard, and those that do are generally the most feature-rich and expensive. Other common keyboard sizes include seventy-six keys, sixty-one keys, and fifty-two keys, though even smaller keyboards are also manufactured. Most synthesizers can transpose in real time, as you play, and MIDI sequencers let you transpose music once it has been recorded. The number of keys you will need, then, depends on your playing style and circumstances. For composing, a smaller keyboard may be sufficient, but for live performance using a full range of notes, more keys is probably better.

Regardless of the number of keys, the simplest (and cheapest) keyboards send only two types of information: when and which keys are pressed, and when those keys are released. These correspond to MIDI's Note On and Note Off messages. Any MIDI keyboard can generate these messages, but some keyboards are incapable of anything more.

Some MIDI keyboards, like pianos, can detect how fast each key was pressed. A velocity component is part of each MIDI Note On and Note Off message, and velocity sensing is most often used to signal loudness. Keyboards without velocity sensing send all Note On and Note Off messages at a uniform velocity.

Some high-end keyboards sense and send messages in response to how hard you press a key as you hold it down, called aftertouch. If the keyboard

FIGURE 4.1   A-80 keyboard controller (courtesy RolandCorp US).

controller can send Aftertouch messages (and the synthesizer can react to them), increasing aftertouch pressure can cause the sound of a trumpet, for example, to swell in volume or waver in pitch as it sustains a note.

Monophonic aftertouch assigns the aftertouch value of the hardest-pressed key to all keys currently held down. Polyphonic aftertouch (usually found only in the most expensive keyboards) permits each key to have its own aftertouch value. With polyphonic aftertouch, pressing one key in a held chord harder than the other keys might cause that note's sound to grow louder within the chord; with monophonic aftertouch, all the notes in the chord would grow louder.

Keyboard splits can be especially useful in live performance situations. They allow the user to assign one sound (often called a patch or program) to the notes below a particular split point and a different program to all the notes above the split point. A single keyboard player, for example, could play acoustic bass sounds with the left hand and pipe organ sounds with the right. Some keyboards have user-assignable split points, while others have multiple splits, with each section assignable to a different program (figure 4.2).

Other features found on keyboard controllers include jacks for foot pedals, transposition (over the entire keyboard or within individual splits), and the capability to transmit MIDI Program Change messages.

If you are likely to need complex keyboard setups, look for a keyboard that can store setup data in its own battery-backed memory. Then once you have created a keyboard setup involving, for example, multiple splits with a transposition and MIDI program assigned to each, you can store and recall it rather than having to enter it from the keyboard's control panel each time you want to reuse that setup.

A word of caution that applies to all MIDI equipment applies particularly to keyboard controllers: MIDI does not specify what features are required of any MIDI device, it only specifies how the equipment communicates what it does do. If your keyboard controller sends out polyphonic

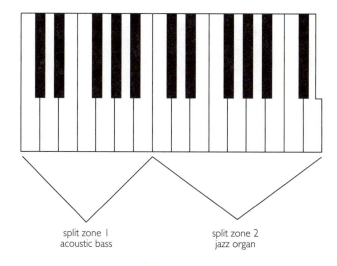

split zone 1
acoustic bass

split zone 2
jazz organ

FIGURE 4.2   Keyboard splits.

aftertouch but your synthesizer does not implement aftertouch, you will not hear the results of aftertouch. Chapter 7 describes how to make sure that all your MIDI gear has the features you plan to use.

NUMBERED CONTROLLERS

The term *controller* is used both to indicate a MIDI performance device like the keyboard controllers described above and a performance control with an identifying number implemented in that device. MIDI recognizes three types of numbered controllers (figure 4.3). Continuous controllers are usually implemented as one or more sliders or wheels, which can stop at any position along their path of travel. They are used to control aspects of the sound (parameters), which may be set anywhere along a spectrum of values, usually 0 to 127, according to the user's choice. Modulation wheels are often used to set vibrato depth, for example. The farther the wheel is turned from its minimum setting, the more vibrato is added to the sound.

Bidirectional controllers usually take the form of wheels that return to a center position (most often representing a value of 64) when they are released. They can be used to control such parameters as pitch bend. When the wheel is not used, the pitch is centered at its usual frequency.

FIGURE 4.3   MIDI numbered switch, continuous, and bidirectional continuous controllers (photo by Don Michael).

Moving the wheel up or to the right (depending on its orientation) increases the parameter value toward its maximum (usually 127) and raises the pitch, while moving it down or to the left decreases the parameter value toward its minimum (usually 0) and lowers the pitch. The farther the wheel moves from its centered position, the more noticeable the pitch change. When the wheel is released it returns to the center, the parameter value returns to its original setting, and the pitch returns to its original frequency.

Switches usually appear as buttons or foot pedals that are either on or off. Rather than controlling a parameter value over a range, switches have only two possible values, usually 0 or 127. Switches are used to control parameters that are either on or off, such as a sustain pedal attached to a keyboard. When the sustain pedal is pressed, the sound currently being produced continues even if the player releases the keys. When the pedal is released, the sound stops.

Each controller generates an identifying controller number as well as its parameter data. Many controllers have standard functions and are assigned unique controller numbers in the MIDI specification. The modulation wheel usually used to control vibrato, for example, is assigned to controller 1, while Pan—the movement of a signal in the left-to-right stereo field—is assigned to controller 10. Other commonly used preassigned controller numbers include Volume (7), Sustain Pedal (64), Sostenuto Pedal (66), and Soft Pedal (67).

Since controllers are assigned numbers, manufacturers are free to use any form of controller device, provided that it generates the correct controller number. A synthesizer may use a multiposition foot pedal to control vibrato if the foot pedal identifies itself as controller 1. Similarly, any on/off switch may be implemented as controller 67 and used as a soft pedal.

Not all MIDI equipment implements all controllers, so it is important to find out if the equipment you are considering can use your preferred type of controllers to affect the parameters you want. Some keyboard controllers, for example, provide extra flexibility by allowing the user to assign any of its controllers to any controller number. That way, you could assign a wheel to controller 1 and use it to control vibrato, then reassign it to controller 67 and use it as a soft pedal, moving it to one extreme for on and the other for off. The MIDI specification also left many controller numbers unassigned, and each manufacturer may implement them as it wishes.

One clever approach to numbered controllers is the "universal" MIDI controller, usually implemented as a separate device with several faders, buttons or switches (figure 4.4). Each can be assigned any controller number, MIDI channel, and other appropriate operating characteristics. In that fashion, the single device can be used to control one or more MIDI devices with great precision and flexibility, since the user can reconfigure it as necessary and use it to control any MIDI device that responds to any numbered MIDI controller.

Using alternative controllers with your MIDI gear can help you add expressiveness to your sounds and make controlling the quality of the sounds much easier.

KEYBOARD SYNTHESIZERS

Many keyboard controllers have synthesizers integrated into their single housing or cabinet. Strictly speaking, devices that integrate a keyboard controller and a synthesizer should be called keyboard synthesizers, but they are often referred to simply as synthesizers, MIDI keyboards, or synths.

For some MIDI users, a keyboard synthesizer may be all they will ever need. While most synthesizers have audio output connectors that must be cabled to the audio input of a stereo system or other amplifier, some keyboard synthesizers even have a small amplifier and speakers or a

FIGURE 4.4   FaderMaster universal MIDI controller (courtesy J. L. Cooper Electronics).

headphone outlet built in. Power up one of those, and you are ready to start making music.

A keyboard synthesizer is often a good first choice even for those who plan to add additional synthesizers from the same or other manufacturers to their MIDI setup. A keyboard can be the most convenient way to generate MIDI data for performance or sequencing, even if it is not your primary instrument, so it may be worth having along with your MIDI guitar or wind controller.

That first keyboard can serve as the controller for your whole MIDI system, so make sure that it suits you. Use the same guidelines described above for a keyboard controller without the integrated synthesizer. In addition, a switch or other control (called Local Control Off) that will let you disable the synthesizer portion of the keyboard synthesizer is a useful feature, so you can use the keyboard to generate messages intended for another synthesizer without it causing the built-in synthesizer to play. An alternative that achieves the same effect is simply to turn the controlling synthesizer's volume all the way down.

On the other hand, it may be to your advantage to purchase a keyboard controller rather than a keyboard synthesizer. If you intend to use rack-mount equipment primarily, you might not want to pay for a keyboard that contains a synthesizer you don't need. Furthermore, you might not be satisfied with a keyboard synthesizer's size, feel, and control options; you may prefer to buy a high-end controller with a full eighty-eight key keyboard and a weighted, piano-like action, features rarely found in keyboard synthesizers.

RACK-MOUNT SYNTHESIZERS

Buying a keyboard synthesizer or MIDI workstation (discussed below) is much like buying a stereo system-in-a-box from a single manufacturer: Choosing it takes less research than choosing individual components, the pieces are more likely to work together, and the controls for each section are likely to have a similar design.

As mentioned above, the all-in-one approach has problems, too. Every person has unique needs, but keyboard synthesizers and MIDI workstations are designed to achieve a balance between the parts rather than matching the particular approach of an individual user. Your needs will probably change over time, but with a keyboard synthesizer or MIDI workstation, you would have to buy a whole new unit to get a better keyboard controller. Furthermore, most MIDI users want more than one synthesizer, though one keyboard is usually plenty.

All these problems can be solved with a keyboard controller or a single keyboard synthesizer, plus one or more suitable rack-mount synthesizers (figure 4.5). Lacking keys, rack-mounts are usually compact and streamlined in appearance and generally cost hundreds of dollars less than

FIGURE 4.5   MIR rack-mount synthesizer (courtesy Korg USA, Inc.).

keyboard versions of the same synthesizers. They get their name from the fact that many such boxes are designed for mounting in equipment racks using bolts through holes in flanges at each side of the front panel, though many "rack-mount" models (sometimes called tone modules) cannot actually be mounted in that manner.

GENERAL MIDI

Each synthesizer sound, or patch, is identified by a unique program number. The MIDI specification does not establish a correspondence between particular program numbers and specific patches, so the same program number might produce completely different sounds from different synthesizers. General MIDI, an addendum to the *MIDI 1.0 Detailed Specification,* establishes a standard list of 128 program numbers and corresponding instrumental sounds. It also sets certain minimum hardware capabilities and required operating characteristics.

General MIDI is optional, so synthesizer manufacturers are free to implement or ignore it as they wish. Even synthesizers that implement General MIDI may have the capability to toggle between programmable and General MIDI modes, using a Universal System Exclusive message designed by the MIDI Manufacturers Association for just that purpose.

The most important aspect of General MIDI is its Instrument Patch Map, a list of 128 sounds and corresponding MIDI program numbers. The sounds are loosely grouped into sixteen families, each with eight variations. The families include such familiar sounds as pianos, guitars, brass, reed, and percussion instruments, as well as widely recognized synthesizer sounds, sound effects, and ethnic instruments. Sounds other than the 128 specified by General MIDI are not considered and may be assigned program numbers that are peculiar to each synthesizer.

General MIDI also includes a Percussion Key Map, based on assignments of MIDI note numbers to drum sounds implemented on several of the first popular MIDI drum machines. Although the MIDI specification itself does not require that any particular sound be assigned a specific MIDI channel, General MIDI restricts drum sounds to MIDI channel 10.

A synthesizer that complies with the General MIDI standard must respond to all sixteen MIDI channels, with dynamic voice allocation and a minimum of twenty-four voice polyphony (both discussed below). Other requirements of a General MIDI synthesizer include velocity response and implementation of modulation wheel, pitch bend, aftertouch, sustain, expression, volume, and pan controllers (see "Numbered Controllers" above), as well as All Notes Off and Reset All Controllers messages (see chapter 8).

The default General MIDI pitch bend range is plus or minus two semi-tones. Middle C must correspond to MIDI note number 60, and master tuning must be adjustable.

General MIDI does not specify anything regarding synthesis methods or minimum acceptable sound quality. Rather, it enables users to play a sequence over any General MIDI synthesizer and hear a predictable set of sounds. Although General MIDI was originally conceived of as a "consumer version" of the MIDI specification, it is likely to be implemented in a wide range of MIDI synthesizers, which may be identified by a label or logo indicating that they meet the General MIDI standard.

DIGITAL WORD LENGTH AND SAMPLE RATE

Many manufacturers do not provide specifications—designs, measurements and test results of the device's internal architecture—so it is difficult to use specifications as a basis for comparison. When available, however, specifications can guide you in evaluating synthesizers, though even specifications do not tell the whole story. The two most useful specifications that are likely to be available are word length and sample rate.

Generally speaking, synthesizers that use a larger digital word length produce a better sound. Most use words of 12 bits or more. Digital words using fewer than 12 bits usually means poor sound quality; a 14- or 16-bit word length is often an indication (though not a guarantee) of a better-sounding synthesizer.

Another specification worth knowing is sample rate—generally, the higher the better. Many popular synthesizers use a 30 kHz sample rate, while the best professional-quality models use sample rates of 44.1 kHz or 48 kHz. Like all specifications, word length and sample rate are subject to interpretation, so let your ears be the final judge.

SYNTHESIS METHODS

Synthesizers, unlike samplers, do not work like tape recorders, playing back sounds they have recorded. Rather, they generate (synthesize) the sounds from scratch. One way to categorize a synthesizer is by the synthesis method it uses. Direct synthesis involves storing in the synthesizer's memory the series of numbers that represent the amplitude values of a waveform at each sample interval and recalling the stored values to produce sounds. In frequency modulation (FM), simple wave-forms change the frequencies of other simple waveforms at least twenty times a second to produce a harmonically rich new waveform. Additive synthesizers (also called Fourier synthesizers) add together a number of harmonics at different frequencies and amplitudes to produce a single harmonically rich waveform. Subtractive synthesis, on the other hand, starts with a waveform that is already rich in harmonics, then filters out unwanted harmonics to produce the desired sound. In phase distortion, a simple waveform is altered (distorted) to produce a more complex one.

A variety of other synthesis methods exists as well. One reason for the variety is that each can more easily and accurately produce some sounds than others. Rather than relying on one "best" synthesis method or syn-thesizer, MIDI lets you combine different kinds of synthesizers into a single music-making system and use each synthesizer for the best sounds it produces.

The conventional wisdom, which sometimes holds that "FM is best for bells and brass sounds," or "additive synthesis is best for percussion sounds," is wrong as often as it is correct and should not be considered more than a guideline. Instead, judge each synthesizer by listening to as many of its built-in sounds as possible at a variety of pitches, amplitudes, and articu-lations, and give each sound an extended listening test. Your ears can judge what an individual synthesizer can and cannot do well—use your ears, and trust them.

POLYPHONY AND MULTITIMBRAL CAPABILITY

Regardless of the synthesis method you choose, you will probably want a synthesizer that can make more than one sound at a time. Unlike many monophonic analog synthesizers from the 1960s which lim-ited players to one note at a time, most MIDI synthesizers can play polyphonically—many notes at once.

The maximum number of notes a polyphonic synthesizer can play at once is fixed for a given synthesizer but varies from one synthesizer to another. Maximum polyphony is usually related to the synthesizer's price—six or eight notes at a time is common on low-cost synthesizers, while more expensive models may have the capability to play twenty-four notes or more at once.

Multitimbral synthesizers are able to play different instrumental sounds, or voices, at the same time. Only polyphonic synthesizers can play multi-timbrally, but the maximum number of notes may be different from the maximum number of voices. For instance, a multitimbral synthesizer with dual voice capability and eight-note polyphony could play all eight notes with the same instrumental voicing or two voices of four notes each. The maximum number of notes can be allocated equally or unequally among voices, so that a four-voice synthesizer with ten-note polyphony might have three notes assigned to the first voice, three notes to the second voice, two notes to the third voice, and two notes to the fourth voice.

Some synthesizers, particularly older ones, assign voices statically, so that each voice has a predetermined number of notes it can play at once, with the total not to exceed the maximum polyphony. Most recent synthesizers instead use dynamic voice allocation, in which the number of notes any voice can play is a function of how many voices are playing. Synthesizers that use dynamic allocation assign notes to voices "on the fly"—if a musical passage played on a multitimbral synthesizer with sixteen-note polyphony used only one voice, it could play sixteen notes at once, while a later passage using more voices could use any combination of notes per voice, provided that the total at any one time did not exceed sixteen notes.

ALTERNATE TUNINGS

The option to adjust the frequency of each note provides alternatives to the usual equal-temperament tuning system. Some synthesizers let the user select from among preset choices of alternate tunings; these choices might include historical, non-Western, or experimental tunings. Others permit the user to define the exact frequency of each MIDI note. Even when an alternate tuning is in use, the synthesizer responds to the usual MIDI Note On messages. But instead of an equal-tempered note, a synthesizer using an alternate tuning will produce a note whose frequency differs slightly or considerably from its equal-tempered value.

DRUM MACHINES

A drum machine (figure 4.6) is a synthesizer that is designed to produce only drum sounds and contains special hardware that lets the user program and produce drum sounds comfortably. The drum machine may use any of the synthesis methods to produce its internal sounds, and, as with any synthesizer, the quality of those sounds is determined not only by the synthesis method but by such factors as the data

FIGURE 4.6   Hr-16:B drum machine (courtesy Alesis Studio Electronics).

word length and sample rate the drum machine uses. As with any synthesizer, the best way to judge the quality of a drum machine's sounds is to spend as much time listening to as many of them as you can.

Like other synthesizers, drum machines usually have a display window that describes its status and prompts the user to act. The display window should be large enough to read easily, and the messages should be clear and easy to understand—just as any synthesizer's should be.

Instead of the piano-style keys found on a keyboard synthesizer, drum machines are played by tapping fingertip-sized buttons, one for each drum sound that is currently available. Most drum machines have at least eight different drum sounds available at once, while some have as many as sixteen. The more sounds that are available at once, the better.

Each button/sound sends and receives a specific MIDI note number. Most drum machines allow you to customize this MIDI note map, assigning, for example, the snare drum sound to MIDI note number 60 (middle C).

Better-quality drum machines have velocity-sensing buttons. Like velocity-sensing keys, these are usually programmed to produce louder sounds when they are struck with greater force. Drum machines generally produce a smaller number of velocity values than velocity-sensing keyboards do, though, so it is important to find out by testing or reading the manual what an individual drum machine's velocity increments are.

Some drum machines that do not respond to velocity when the buttons are pressed are able to respond to incoming velocity data from another MIDI device. That way, you can use a keyboard, sequencer or other device that generates velocity data to control the drum machine, with the controlling device determining the drum machine's velocity settings. In the same fashion, some drum machines can respond to a wider range of velocities than their buttons are capable of generating.

Most drum machines have built-in sequencers that store and replay rhythmic patterns. Even if you use another sequencer, the one inside the drum machine can be helpful. It is usually designed to store short patterns, which are then looped and combined with other patterns in a particular order to produce a complete drum track. The more complex the rhythmic tracks you plan to create, the more patterns your drum machine must accommodate. Each individual pattern has a maximum number of notes or beats, so you must determine if the drum machine's sequencer matches your requirements.

Although drum machine sequencers are more pattern-oriented than most hardware or software sequencers, the drum machine's sequencer must be capable of many of the same functions as any sequencer. These should include programmable metronome and tempo, quantization, event editing, and step programming. Other sequencer considerations, such as resolution, also apply to drum machine sequencers. For more on sequencers, see chapter 6, "Choosing and Using Sequencer Software."

Like other synthesizers, drum machines vary in their number of audio outputs. Some offer only a single output, others provide stereo outputs, while some have individual outputs for each drum sound so that each can have its own signal processing.

Like other synthesizers, a drum machine's usefulness and flexibility are determined in part by its expandability. A good-quality drum machine should be able to use more than just a single set of drum sounds, either by selecting a different "bank" of sounds from its internal programs or by loading in alternate sounds from an external source. External data storage on floppy disks or data cartridges also provides more options for expanding the library of available sounds, though the number of sounds available at any one time is always the same.

While drum machines generally benefit less than general-purpose synthesizers do from software running on personal computers, such basic programs as patch librarians can be helpful if the drum machine can load any of numerous banks of sounds. If you are considering a high-priced full-featured drum machine, check to see if any personal computer software supports it and whether those programs will run on your brand of computer.

SAMPLERS

One of the most versatile MIDI instruments is the sampler (figure 4.7), which acts as if it were an intelligent tape recorder. It records sounds that are played into it, but unlike a tape recorder it converts the sounds into digital format and stores them in the sampler's memory. The contents of the sampler's memory can be controlled by the sampler's built-in computer, so you can not only record sounds but change them as well.

Sampling involves recording live or prerecorded sounds into the sampler, either directly through a microphone or from a conventional tape recorder, compact disc, or digital tape recorder. As with a conventional tape recorder, you must first set record levels, then begin recording. The sampled sound can then be played back by playing a designated note of the MIDI system's controller. Playing other notes on the controller causes the sampled sound to be replayed at a different pitch from the original, with transposition typically over as much as a two-octave range.

As the sampled sound is played back at higher pitches, the samples are played back faster than the original, causing the result to sound sped up; playing it at a lower pitch causes the result to sound slowed down. For this reason, sampled sounds have an increasingly different character from their original sources as they are transposed more than a few semitones from the original recorded sounds.

A sampler that permits stereo recording will render recorded sounds more accurately than a similar monaural sampler, but sampling in stereo requires twice as much memory, twice as much signal path circuitry, and so forth. As a result, stereo samplers are priced correspondingly higher than comparable monaural units.

Most samplers permit multisampling, recording several versions of the original sound at different pitches and assigning them across the keyboard so that playback sounds more natural over a wider range. Since multisampling takes up more memory than a single sample, the same amount of memory can hold a single longer sample or several shorter multisamples.

In the same fashion, the sample rate determines both the bandwidth of the recorded samples and the maximum duration of each sample. A higher sample rate means that a wider range of frequencies can be recorded, but it also requires more memory to store the recorded sound than at a lower

FIGURE 4.7   EPS-M performance sampler (courtesy Ensoniq).

sampling rate. If you are considering a sampler with a fixed sampling rate, make sure it is high enough to handle the full range of frequencies you want to record. Since Nyquist's theorem states that the sampling rate must be approximately double the highest frequency recorded, many professional samplers have sample rates of 44.1 kHz or higher. Less expensive samplers may save on memory costs by having a maximum sample rate of 30 kHz or less, which can result in less faithful reproduction of complex, harmonically rich sounds.

At any sample rate, the amount of memory determines the maximum duration of a recorded sample. Make sure that the maximum duration is long enough to store the sounds you want to sample at the sampling rate you plan to use. Some samplers offer the option of adding additional memory if you require it.

Ideally, a sampler should offer variable sampling rates. A low rate can be used to record longer samples of low-fidelity source material, while a higher rate can be used for shorter samples when the widest possible bandwidth is important.

Other options found on many samplers include capabilities for on-board sound processing. Such options can make sample recording and playback much easier. Truncation enables the user to edit out small or large increments of the recorded sound, to remove noise, or change the character of the recorded sound.

Looping lets you set start and end times within the recorded sound and repeat the selected segment indefinitely. With this option, you can sustain any sound for as long as you like, without the need for additional memory.

Cross-fading uses two samples, making a smooth transition from one to the other. A sound that begins with one timbre can gradually or abruptly fade into another sound with a similar or unrelated timbre. The technique can yield much more complex sounds than a single sample and can result in sounds that are truly unique.

Instead of interpolating between two samples, layering mixes the two samples together over their entire duration while retaining the identity of each. It allows a single controller to call up both sounds at once, resulting in a "thicker" sound.

The capability to transfer samples from the sampler's memory to a storage device like a cartridge or floppy disk lets you build up a large library of samples, then transfer the ones you want to use for a particular session back into the sampler's memory for playback. Different storage devices have different capacities and transfer speeds. Floppy disks are much slower and hold much less than hard disks, for example, but they cost correspondingly less.

If you cannot afford a high-speed mass-storage device at the time you first buy your sampler, check to see if such a device can be added later. Some samplers are "closed boxes" that can never be enhanced, while others can be upgraded with additional memory, hard disks, and multiple audio outputs. A sampler equipped with a Small Computer System Interface (SCSI) port, for example, can be upgraded with a high-performance hard disk that can give it a new lease on life.

You can also use sample editing software to transfer samples to a personal computer for storage on the computer's hard disk (see chapter 5, "MIDI Software—How to Choose It, How to Use It"). Some samplers with SCSI ports can transfer samples directly to a computer. Transferring samples via MIDI is much slower but gets the job done.

SAMPLE PLAYERS

Recording samples takes some practice and skill. Sample players (figure 4.8) are playback-only units that sidestep the need for sample recording by providing access to the growing library of commercially and informally available samples. Since the recording circuitry is omitted, sample players generally cost considerably less than comparably equipped samplers.

Aside from recording capability, samplers and sample players share the same range of features, options, and specifications. Sample players must rely on samples from an external source, so storage capacity and compatibility are particularly important. Ideally, a sample player should have its own mass-storage device and be able to use a range of storage media such as small and large floppy disks, data cartridges, or plug-in memory cards. It should be able to play back samples recorded on (or intended for) sampler models or brands other than its own.

FIGURE 4.8 Proteus sample player (courtesy E-Mu Systems).

THE MIDI SAMPLE DUMP STANDARD

To make it easier to exchange samples among samplers and sample players from different manufacturers, the MIDI specification includes a special group of System Exclusive messages known as the Sample Dump Standard (SDS). It describes a standard format for sample data and the associated messages used to request, send, and acknowledge receipt of sample data so that the data can be transferred from one sampler to another.

Any sampler that implements the Sample Dump Standard should be able to receive samples stored in SDS format or transmit samples in SDS format for playback on another unit. The Sample Dump Standard has brought us closer to universal exchangeability of samples; unless you plan to create all your samples yourself, never exchanging them with anyone else, consider samplers that implement the MIDI Sample Dump Standard.

MIDI WORKSTATIONS

Some manufacturers have taken the multifunction keyboard synthesizer yet another step further. In addition to the keyboard controller and synthesizer hardware, a typical MIDI workstation includes a drum machine, a sampler or sample player, and a sequencer as well.

The idea behind a MIDI workstation is to have a complete MIDI production studio in a single unit. All the strengths and weaknesses of the keyboard synthesizer approach are magnified when the concept is expanded into a MIDI workstation. That is, the workstation can provide an integrated production environment, conveniently grouping all the hardware and software the MIDI user needs into a package that is more compact, less expensive, and requires less setup than a similar component system. By the same token, MIDI workstations limit their users' ability to expand their MIDI setups incrementally by adding components and capabilities as their needs, knowledge base, and budgets dictate. With a fast-changing technology like MIDI, it is hard to imagine that users will not want to upgrade some part of their systems from time to time; with a workstation, that would involve redundant equipment and expense or scrapping the workstation and beginning again. Until general-purpose computers become powerful enough to act as true stand-alone MIDI workstations, upgradable simply by the addition or substitution of new software, users must decide if the convenience of the current MIDI workstation approach outweighs its disadvantages.

DISPLAYS

Although the control and display panels of keyboard controllers, synthesizers, and other MIDI equipment perform different functions, the same set of design criteria applies to all. Controls such as buttons and sliders let you tell the equipment what you want; displays let the equipment tell you what it is doing. On most MIDI equipment, the display takes the form of a small "window" where messages appear. As a general rule, the bigger the window, the better. More characters per line and more message lines usually mean more comprehensive messages that are easier to read and understand.

Since the control and display panels provide the means by which you interact with the equipment, they should be appropriately designed. Each control device should be clearly labeled, comfortable to manipulate, and logically grouped and arranged. Look for plain English messages rather than codes. A message like "Select Parameter Number" makes more sense to most people than one that reads "SEL PARM #."

Some equipment can display graphic messages as well as text. This can be especially useful for such things as showing envelope shapes. The graphic representation of an envelope is much easier to grasp than a set of numbers describing it.

As an alternative to the small display window, some manufacturers offer the option of connecting their equipment to an external video monitor. That way you can see full-length messages instead of scrolling within the smaller display window. Both graphics and text can be larger, crisper, and easier to read.

Finally, software programs running on external personal computers offer many advantages, including a way to bypass the limits of the display window altogether. Synthesizer editors, for example, let you set all the values on your synthesizer directly from your computer, without having to use the synthesizer's controls or look at the synthesizer's display window. Librarian programs let you store complete synthesizer setups, organize them into groups of sounds or patches, and recall the complete set of patches—all from the computer keyboard. (For more on MIDI software, see chapter 5, "MIDI Software—How to Choose It, How to Use It.")

Even if you do not currently use a computer with your MIDI setup, you may decide (like many MIDI users) that the extra power and convenience of external computer control is worth the investment of time and resources. Before buying MIDI gear, check to see if there are editor or librarian programs available to support it. Equipment that has no software support has fewer opportunities than well-supported hardware for expanded power and simplified operation.

Fortunately, "universal" editor and librarian programs are beginning to appear on the market. These include editing templates for most current synthesizers, and most also permit the user to construct custom templates for synthesizers that were overlooked or that will appear on the market in the future.

ALTERNATIVE MIDI CONTROLLERS

In its early days, MIDI was limited to musicians with keyboard skills. Guitarists, saxophonists, and drummers had no way to work with MIDI equipment because the only controllers available were piano-style keyboards. All that has changed. Now, practically any instrumentalist can join the MIDI world, since a variety of alternative controllers is available.

Like keyboard controllers, most guitar controllers (figure 4.9) have no built-in synthesizer and must be connected to an external synthesizer in order to produce sounds. If you are considering a guitar controller, check to see if it is limited to transmitting on a single MIDI channel or whether it can be programmed to transmit on any channel. Make sure that it handles chords correctly as well as melody lines.

Some guitar controllers allow the player to assign each string to a different MIDI channel, which provides much more flexibility. The low string on the guitar can be assigned to a bass sound, for example, while the upper strings can be assigned the sound of a melody instrument.

Since it is a guitar, it should have the feel and playability of a comparable quality standard electric guitar. Many MIDI guitar controllers incorporate standard guitar controls such as wham bars and volume knobs. Some permit pitch bend using the standard technique of bending fretted notes, while others require the player to use a pitch bend wheel like the

FIGURE 4.9   MIDI guitar controller (courtesy Zeta Music Systems, Inc.).

ones on keyboards. A particularly useful option is the capability to transmit MIDI program change data directly from the guitar controller so that you can change instrument voices on the fly.

Wind instrument players likewise have a range of choices. Some wind controllers (figure 4.10) are blown and fingered like a flute or saxophone, while others have valves like trumpets. In either case, the keys or valves should be comfortably spaced and responsive.

FIGURE 4.10   WX7 MIDI wind controller (courtesy Yamaha Corporation of America).

Most wind controllers feature velocity sensing, in which breath pressure at the start of a note establishes a velocity value that determines the loudness of the note. A more sophisticated option uses aftertouch data or MIDI controller 7 (MIDI Volume) messages to enable the player to change the loudness of a note as it sustains.

Other wind controller options include transposition; transmitting on any MIDI channel; sending program change data directly from the controller; automatically adding a second melody line in parallel with the one played or sustaining one note while playing others; and selecting the overall key of the instrument—typically C, B-flat, or E-flat.

Pitch followers, also called pitch-to-MIDI converters, provide an alternative for wind players who do not like the available choices in wind controllers or who will not give up their familiar instrument. In fact, pitch followers can be used together with any melody instrument—including the human singing voice. Pitch followers are not instruments themselves; rather, they "hear" the notes of a melody instrument or vocalist and translate those notes into their equivalent MIDI Note On messages.

Some pitch followers are built into a standard microphone, while others are free-standing boxes to which a microphone is connected. In either case, the performer sings or plays into the microphone, and the output of the pitch follower drives a MIDI synthesizer.

Most of the options and features found on wind controllers can be found on pitch followers, including velocity sensing, volume control, transposition, and sustain. Some pitch followers have other features as well. One feature found on many pitch followers is pitch auto-correct. If a singer or player is out of tune, auto-correct generates MIDI Note On messages for the pitches that are closest to the out-of-tune ones.

A related feature found on some pitch followers is a tuning display, which shows the relationship between each note the performer plays and the correct pitch for that note. In one such implementation, each correct pitch appears as a line or bar in the center of the display screen or window. The actual note the performer plays is on the bar or line if it is in tune and away from the correct-pitch line if it is out of tune. The farther apart the two are, the more out of tune. Such a feature can be a great help to singers or instrumentalists who want to learn to play better in tune — just adjust the intonation of each note you play or sing so that the two lines or bars on the display overlap.

Another option found on some more expensive pitch followers is intelligent harmonization. Unlike the parallel melody feature found on some wind controllers, intelligent harmonization produces major or minor chords that harmonize each note played or sung into the microphone. Some pitch followers can even be programmed with a specific chord sequence, which is then used to harmonize each successive note in the melody.

Pitch followers perform a difficult task — selecting the correct MIDI note from a complex sound that might include rapid fluctuations in pitch and timbre and may contain noise from the environment or the performer. As a result, pitch followers are generally slow to respond to rapid changes and may pick a different note than the one the user expects. Pitch followers show great promise as MIDI controllers, but so far they are not as technically successful or as widely used as some of the other alternate MIDI controllers.

While drum machines can be played easily by almost anyone, skilled drummers are likely to achieve their best results by using MIDI drum controllers. A drum controller is not a synthesizer like a drum machine but a modified drum pad or kit that makes little or no sound when struck with drumsticks. Instead, each hit generates a MIDI Note On message that is routed to a drum machine or other synthesizer. Some drum controllers produce different pitches depending on where on the strike surfaces they are hit or produce different sounds depending on how hard they are hit.

Drum controllers should have as much expressive capacity and flexibility as other controllers. Features to consider include velocity sensing, sustain pedals, pitch bend controllers, and MIDI program change signal buttons. Each pad or piece in the drum kit should be assignable to its own MIDI channel so that each can be assigned its own synthesizer and its own patch — even a patch we might never expect from a drum. With a rich enough array of features, drum controllers provide drummers as much control over MIDI systems as keyboard and wind players have.

Imaginative designers are also inventing controllers whose appearance is unlike that of conventional instruments. Examples include motion-sensing gloves, which let the performer control a synthesizer by hand movements; hand-held sticks, which sense changes in position and transmit MIDI data in response to the changes; and sensors attached to a dancer's body, which turn the dancer into a living MIDI controller. As these designs are refined and improved we are likely to see new generations of MIDI controllers with more flexibility, subtlety, and expressiveness than any that are currently in use.

HARDWARE SEQUENCERS

A sequencer stores MIDI messages for subsequent playback, editing, and manipulation, acting like a "smart tape recorder"—not for sounds, but for MIDI message data. Sequencers can be implemented within a synthesizer or sampler, as a separate piece of equipment, or as a program run on a personal computer.

Generally, sequencers implemented within other MIDI hardware are limited in the number of notes they can store, the breadth and ease of editing controls, and their ability to synchronize to other equipment. They are most often useful as "note pads" for storing simple musical ideas, improvisations, and sketches quickly and with a minimum of interruption to the creative process.

Stand-alone hardware sequencer units generally provide more capability and flexibility than sequencers implemented within other equipment and cost much less than a computer and sequencing software—often comparable in price to sequencer software alone. Since hardware sequencers are typically smaller, lighter, sturdier, and simpler to operate than personal computers (some can even fit in the palm of a hand), they are usually easier for traveling musicians to take on the road.

Sequencer programs run on personal computers harness the computational power and memory storage of the host computer, so they are often more capable, more flexible, and easier to use than hardware sequencers or sequencers built into other MIDI instruments. A variety of sequencer programs is available, so computer users can choose the one best suited for their needs, while hardware sequencer users needing more features usually have no alternative but to buy another hardware sequencer. The same computer that can run sequencer software can run other software as well, further increasing its value and flexibility.

Regardless of where the sequencer is implemented, its features and operating characteristics are much the same. Sequencers are such an important tool that they are covered separately in chapter 6, "Choosing and Using Sequencer Software."

MIDI-CONTROLLED STUDIO EQUIPMENT

MIDI has become so widely accepted that a variety of equipment manufacturers have implemented it—even manufacturers of devices that are not, strictly speaking, musical instruments. These MIDI-capable devices can include recording studio equipment such as mixing consoles (figure 4.11), tape recorders, reverberators, and delay units. MIDI is even finding its way into nonmusical equipment such as lighting control panels.

Such equipment usually implements MIDI control in one of two ways: snapshot state capture or dynamic MIDI control. Snapshot state capture is easier to implement and is more likely to be found on less-expensive equipment, while dynamic MIDI control is more often found only on better-quality, more expensive gear.

In snapshot state capture, the current settings of some or all of the equipment's controls are stored as a "snapshot" of the equipment's status at the instant of the snapshot. The stored snapshot is assigned a MIDI program change number. By assigning the piece of equipment its own MIDI channel over which it receives data, a controller or sequencer can send it a program change request for the desired snapshot over the specified MIDI channel. Upon receipt of the Program Change message, the equipment recalls the stored snapshot and sets its controls to the positions at the time the snapshot was originally taken. A MIDI-controlled equalizer, for example, could store different equalization settings as snapshots. You could then insert MIDI Program Change messages into a recorded sequence at the points where the equalization changes are needed. On playback, the equalizer settings will change at the appropriate spots in the sequence.

Equipment that can be dynamically controlled usually has snapshot capability but also stores or responds to moving fader data or other changing controller settings as well as fixed equipment states. Since MIDI Control Change messages act on a specific controller number rather than a specific controller device, the manufacturer of a MIDI-controlled mixing console, for example, might program its equipment to use incoming MIDI controller 7 Control Change messages for volume fader control. Unlike Program Change messages, which are on/off data appropriate for selecting fixed machine states, Control Change messages can be transmitted or received over a range of values and used to modify settings in real time.

The advantage of dynamic control is that gradual changes in the equipment's settings can be recorded into a sequencer track and replayed. Rather than simply recording the appropriate Program Change message in your sequencer you might record MIDI controller 7 Control Change

FIGURE 4.11   DMP7 MIDI-controlled mixing console (courtesy Yamaha Corporation of America).

messages, and, on playback, the volume fader (for example) would move in real time. In other words, playing back recorded sequencer tracks that control a synthesizer while recording changes to volume faders on the MIDI-controlled mixer would store the fader settings as part of the sequence. When the entire sequence is replayed, the fader positions change as they did when they were moved during live recording.

THE MIDI INTERFACE

The MIDI interface, which allows a MIDI device to be connected to other MIDI devices, is what differentiates a MIDI device from other electronic equipment—MIDI synthesizers, samplers, keyboard controllers, and other MIDI instruments have MIDI interfaces built into them. It is easy to tell if a device has a MIDI interface—just look for MIDI In, Out, and Thru jacks on the device (though not all MIDI devices have a MIDI Thru connector). If the jacks are present (see figure 1.1), so is the interface.

MIDI interfaces are responsible for taking data from a MIDI device, one byte at a time, and performing the necessary buffering so that the data (along with the required start and stop bits) can be sent out along the MIDI cable at the appropriate speed, one bit at a time. At the receiving end, the MIDI interface collects data coming in along the MIDI cable one bit at a time and reassembles the data into one-byte units before passing it along to the MIDI device to which the interface is connected.

MIDI interfaces most often need to be added to three classes of devices—acoustic instruments such as pianos, which were not designed with MIDI in mind; older synthesizers, which predate the widespread acceptance of the MIDI specification; and computers, few of which are MIDI-ready when they are shipped from the factory.

MIDI retrofit kits for acoustic instruments are generally costly and often hard to come by. They are limited primarily to pianos and organs, though retrofits for accordions and even for saxophones have appeared on the market. Kit manufacturers seem to come and go, so the best way to find out what is currently available is to call instrument dealers, talk to other instrumentalists (see chapter 11, "Getting Help," for information on computer bulletin board systems for musicians), and read instrument-specific magazines. Retrofit kits usually need to be installed by a professional technician, and repair service may also be costly or hard to come by, so consider carefully before deciding to retrofit your harp or bagpipes for MIDI.

Many early analog synthesizers manufactured by Moog, Oberheim, Sequential Circuits, and others remain popular and in widespread use because people like their sounds and have learned the techniques for programming them. These synthesizers use a system of control voltages (CV) for external control of system parameters, much as MIDI messages are used to control MIDI devices. CV-to-MIDI converters can be used to connect such synthesizers to MIDI equipment and combine the repeatability and editability of MIDI sequencing with the desired sounds and programming techniques of the non-MIDI gear. Retrofit kits for pre-MIDI synthesizers are more common than such kits for acoustic instruments, but my suggestions are the same for both: Check around, research carefully, and do not make the decision to retrofit lightly.

While the MIDI retrofit market for musical instruments is small and unsettled, MIDI is among the most popular add-ons to personal computers, so there are several large, well-established manufacturers of MIDI interfaces for computers. Although many computer manufacturers have come and gone and the market is far from stable, several personal computer brands are popular among musicians and likely to remain so for some time. Because of design differences among computers and the lack of a single MIDI interface specification, most MIDI software is designed for a specific computer and interface.

The least expensive computer for musicians is probably the Commodore 64 and 128 family. For the most part, any MIDI interface designed for a Commodore 64 or 128 will work fine. The Amiga line of mid-priced computers followed the original Commodore specification in its early models, and those models can use MIDI interfaces designed for the Commodore family. Design changes to the serial port in more recent Amiga computers may require a special MIDI interface, so be sure to tell the vendor the model number and serial port type of your Amiga computer before purchasing a MIDI interface—and make sure you can return it if they sell you the wrong one.

Atari designed its low-cost ST family of computers with the musician in mind—Atari ST systems have a built-in MIDI interface as standard equipment. Other Atari models may need a MIDI interface, and any add-on MIDI interface designed for Ataris should do the job.

At the high end, many MIDI computer users prefer either Apple's Macintosh or IBM's PC family (including IBM-PC compatible computers). Each has a MIDI interface that is so widely adopted it is considered "standard," and each has alternatives to consider.

Most IBM-PCs and compatibles use a MIDI interface that is similar in design to Roland's MPU-401, which consists of an external connector box and a card to plug into one of the PC's vacant slots. (One notable exception is Yamaha's C1 Music computer, a portable IBM-PC compatible computer. Its built-in multiport MIDI interface is not compatible with the MPU-401.) The MPU was one of the earliest MIDI interfaces for PCs and became so widely used that most PC MIDI software is written with the MPU in mind. Several manufacturers make interfaces that are functionally equivalent to Roland's, so it is common to see software specify that an "MPU-401 or compatible MIDI interface is required." Figure 4.12 shows an MPU-401 compatible interface for IBM-PC or compatible computers.

More recently, IBM introduced its own plug-in card called the Music Feature, which incorporates an eight-voice synthesizer onto the card as well as the MIDI interface. The Music Feature is incompatible with software designed for the MPU-401, so it is not supported by as many software developers, but because of IBM's backing it may earn a place in the IBM MIDI marketplace.

Although IBM's newer PS/2 line of personal computers is not hardware-compatible with the original IBM-PC family, PS/2s can run software designed for the earlier line of IBM-PCs. As a result, most MIDI interfaces for PS/2 series computers are software-compatible with the MPU-401, though their MIDI interface hardware is different.

Differences among Macintosh MIDI interfaces involve clock speeds and ports rather than competing plug-in card designs. Since the computer communicates data to the interface at a fixed speed, the hardware and software developers must agree on a clock speed—the rate at which such data exchanges take place. Early Macintosh music software developers used one of three different clock speeds, and many early Macintosh MIDI

FIGURE 4.12   V-4000 "MPU-401 compatible" MIDI interface for IBM-PC or compatible computers (courtesy Voyetra Technologies).

interfaces could be set to operate at the speed that would match the particular software in use. Eventually, a clock speed of one megahertz (written 1 MHz—one million clock cycles per second) became the unofficial standard, though many software developers continue to provide an option by which the user can set the program's clock speed to match an older interface.

Be aware, though, that many software developers now simply assume a 1 MHz clock speed. New MIDI interfaces for the Macintosh should not have any problems, since all the recent MIDI interfaces for the Macintosh use the 1 MHz clock; but if you are using an older interface that works at one of the nonstandard clock speeds only—500 kHz or 2 MHz—you must either find software that supports your interface speed or buy a newer interface.

MIDI interfaces for the Macintosh can connect to either of the computer's standard serial ports—printer or modem. Some programs can take advantage of both, letting you double the number of MIDI channels you can use at one time from sixteen to thirty-two. Channels, MIDI's data communication pathways, are like lanes in a highway — the more lanes, the more traffic can move along the highway at one time. The developers of the initial MIDI specification thought that sixteen data channels would be enough, but many users of complex MIDI setups find they need more. Since the MIDI specification does not define a standard for implementing more than sixteen channels, make sure the MIDI software you choose will support both of the Macintosh's serial ports if you plan to use them.

Multiport interfaces are becoming more common among users of other computers as well. They serve a valuable function because they overcome MIDI's limit of sixteen channels. Instead of a single MIDI Out with channels 1 through 16, a multiport interface has two (or more) MIDI Outs—each one of which can be "addressed" by the MIDI software running on the computer (typically as port A and port B). By specifying the port as well as the channel, a two-port interface doubles the number of available channels. Since each MIDI device may require from one to several channels devoted to it, increasing the number of channels allows you to use your computer to control more MIDI devices.

Unfortunately, there is no MIDI specification for multiport interfaces—yet—so they are more likely to have compatibility problems. If you decide to use a multiport interface, choose one that emulates, or acts identically to, the existing standard for your computer. In particular, make sure that any software you want to use with the multiport interface supports the particular brand of interface you have. Better yet, talk to other users of the same interface and find out what kinds of problems they have encountered and what solutions they may have found.

Aside from the compatibility issue, there are options to consider when choosing a MIDI interface, whether single or multiport. Some provide a metronome, which counts off the tempo for performers to play along with, built into the interface hardware. Others generate metronome sounds that are played over the host computer's built-in speaker. Still other interfaces require that you devote a channel of your synthesizer to generating metronome tones. Using a synthesizer-generated metronome lets you choose the pitch and tone of your metronome sound, but it ties up one channel of your synthesizer. Relying on a metronome from the interface frees up that MIDI channel but limits you to whatever metronome sound the interface or host computer can produce.

A more significant choice involves tape synchronization capability. Briefly, tape synchronization involves recording a special synchronization tone, which stores timing information onto the tape, before anything else is recorded onto it. Subsequent recording can then be synced up with the prerecorded sync tone.

The synchronization tone recorded on tape can be generated by the MIDI interface or by an external sync box. The advantage of tape sync built into the MIDI interface is that it is economical and easy—there are fewer boxes to be concerned with, and the cost is usually lower than the combined costs of a MIDI interface without tape sync plus a sync box.

The disadvantage of built-in tape sync is that it is limited and inflexible. Many sync boxes offer capabilities that are not available on MIDI interfaces with built-in sync, including such features as chase lock and MIDI Song Position Pointer. Furthermore, many MIDI interfaces that generate sync tones work only for one type of tone, frequency shift key or FSK. While this is a widely used sync tone arrangement, other synchronization methods, such as SMPTE, are proving more powerful and convenient to use. Despite spending extra money now for a MIDI interface with built-in sync generator, you may still end up buying an external sync box later.

FSK, SMPTE, Chase Lock and the like will all be covered in chapter 9, "Synchronization." For now, if you just want to be able to get started with synchronization, a MIDI interface with built-in sync generator is an economical way to do it. If, however, you know that your synchronization needs are likely to be (or become) complicated, or if synchronization is a regular part of your musical routine, buy the simplest MIDI interface that does its basic job, and worry about tape sync separately.

MIDI CABLES

Choosing MIDI cables is easy, if you keep in mind three simple rules. To minimize cable headaches:

1. buy lots of them, in assorted sizes;
2. make sure they are all shielded and properly wired;
3. use the shortest possible cable for each connection.

Always keeping a supply of spare cables on hand is the best way to avoid the most common problems that plague MIDI systems and to isolate those problems that occur. Cables wear out through repeated disconnection and reconnection. People trip over them, and they can get folded around a corner or back on themselves with a weight atop them. Any of these and other common conditions can cause cable failure. Without a ready replacement, a lost cable could mean a useless module or, worse, a useless system.

Shielding protects cables from mistakenly picking up electrical signals in the surrounding environment. Even one unshielded cable can pick up noise—spurious electrical signals from the operating environment—which can cause the digital data represented by the current levels within the MIDI cable to become scrambled. The solution is simple—buy only shielded cables from the very beginning.

Just as you cannot tell shielded cable from unshielded by looking at it, you cannot tell by looking if a cable is wired up correctly. The MIDI specification uses only three of the five pins on a MIDI connector. The other two should be left unconnected, but some manufacturers use those pins for their own purposes. Using such a cable can cause problems, so use only cables that meet the MIDI specification. If a particular piece of hardware requires a nonstandard cable, tag the cable with an identifying label so that you will not accidentally use it on another piece of equipment.

The best approach is to check with other MIDI users. They can usually suggest a brand of cable that has worked well for them (and probably warn you about some that have not). If there are knowledgeable salespeople at your MIDI music store, ask them to recommend a good shielded cable that conforms to the MIDI specification. Once you find a cable manufacturer you trust, try to stick with them.

Quality cables do not come cheap, though. First-time cable buyers are often surprised that MIDI cables are as much as five times the price of audio cables of the same length. The investment is worth it.

If price is no object, you might want to consider buying cables in a rainbow of colors rather than just basic black. Color-coding cables can help you remember which cable is used where and help make sense of the inevitable tangle of MIDI cables that accompanies a complex setup.

Whether your cables are color-coded or not, it is a good idea to tag each cable with a legend that tells where it is coming from or going. Keep a supply of plain white peel-off mailing labels on hand, and as you plug in a cable write its source or destination on a label, peel the label off its backing, and wrap it around the cable, near the connector, sticking the two ends of the label together. The labels are easy to tear off when the setup changes, you can tell at a glance how the system is wired, and it is easy to follow cables from connections at one end to the other.

The longer the cable, the more it acts like an antenna, picking up stray electrical signals. Use the shortest cable that will reach between the two devices you want to connect. This is true regardless of how simple or how complex a MIDI setup you have.

Rather than purchasing ready-made MIDI cables, some MIDI users prefer to fabricate their own. Homemade MIDI cables offer several advantages over the store-bought variety: They are less expensive, they can be made to the precise length required, and, most important, you can be sure that they are properly shielded and wired up.

All that is necessary are two five-pin male DIN plugs, the proper length shielded twisted-pair cable (figure 4.13), and soldering supplies—all readily available at most electronics supply stores.

Each pin of a DIN connector is numbered (figure 4.14). Solder the end of one of the two wires twisted together inside the cable to pin 4 of the DIN connector. Solder the other end of the same wire to pin 4 of the other DIN connector. Each wire of the pair has a uniquely colored or patterned

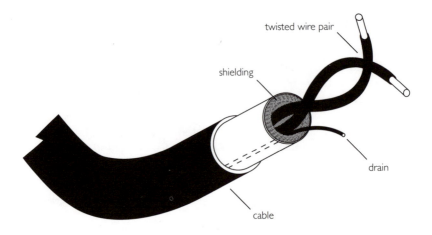

FIGURE 4.13   MIDI cable, cut away to show shielding.

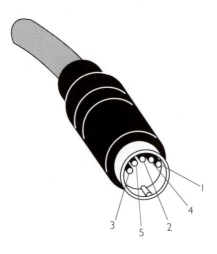

FIGURE 4.14   Male five-pin DIN connector, showing pin numbers.

plastic sheath, so you should have no difficulty telling them apart. In the same fashion, solder one end of the other wire to pin 5 of one DIN connector, and the other end of the same wire to pin 5 of the other DIN connector.

Many MIDI cable manufacturers fail to connect the shielding to pin 2 of the DIN connectors as required by the MIDI specification, a condition called "floating ground." While you may be able to get away with not

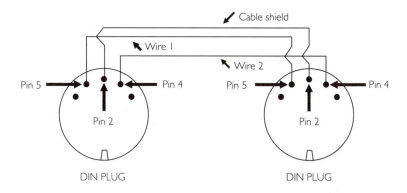

FIGURE 4.15 Cable connections between two five-pin male DIN plugs.

connecting the shielding, it is risky, and it is a better idea to connect the shielding in accordance with the specification.

There are two types of shielding—foil and wire mesh. A low-capacitance continuous-coverage foil shield is generally preferable, both because it is easier to work with and because it offers the best performance. Foil shielding looks like tinfoil; to make soldering connections easier, a "drain wire" is attached to the shielding. If your cable uses foil shielding, solder the shield's drain wire to pin 2 of the DIN connectors at each end. Wire mesh shielding, on the other hand, must be gathered up, partially trimmed away, or both, until there is a bundle of wire mesh shielding tight enough that it can be soldered to pin 2 of the DIN connector at each end. Figure 4.15 shows the proper cable connections between two male five-pin DIN plugs.

Wrap each end of the cable with insulating tape or heat-shrink insulation where the wires meet the connector, both to protect the wiring from electrical short-circuits and to strengthen the cable at its weakest point.

MIDI AND PERSONAL COMPUTERS

Almost any capability of MIDI equipment can be duplicated by an appropriate program run on a personal computer. Since most personal computers have more computational power, more memory storage, better display capabilities, and more precise input capabilities than their MIDI hardware counterparts, the personal computer can be considered the ultimate MIDI instrument. Even such sophisticated functions as synthesis and sampling can be performed directly from within a personal computer, and as computer designs grow increasingly powerful and sophisticated it is likely that personal computers will become genuine all-purpose MIDI workstations, capable of any current MIDI function and upgradable to include those that develop in the future.

Until such MIDI workstations become widely available, we can harness the power of the personal computer to extend the capabilities of an existing MIDI setup. For example, why be limited to a four-line display on a synthesizer when, with the right software, we can take advantage of a computer monitor's larger screen and graphics capability?

The range and power of MIDI software has become so comprehensive that personal computers can enhance almost any MIDI setup. We turn to this subject in the next chapter.

MIDI SOFTWARE— HOW TO CHOOSE IT, HOW TO USE IT

When the proper software is used to control a MIDI system's hardware, a personal computer can become the focal point of a comprehensive musician's workstation. Instructional software, for example, enables the student to practice the mechanical skills of music making, at a pace and skill level appropriate to the individual. Instructional software topics include ear training, instrumental performance technique, and the rules of Western classical music or other systems of music theory.

Other software can be used to simplify the complex exchanges of data involved in a multidevice MIDI setup, making the entire system easier to use. Almost any MIDI setup involving more than one or two instruments can benefit from such system-management software.

A third category of programs performs musical tasks directly— recording performances played on MIDI instruments, transcribing such performances into traditional music notation, or extracting parts from a score.

SOFTWARE PRICES

Software developers take many different approaches to pricing software. Some try to charge as much as they think the market will bear, while others try to price their programs as low as possible, hoping for larger sales volume. Others charge whatever they think their competitors are charging.

This confusion means that software prices, unlike hardware prices, offer little insight into the underlying production costs, capabilities, or value of the product. It is usually true, for example, that more expensive synthesizers provide more features and capabilities than less expensive ones, but the same is not as often true of software. In every software category there are great values to be found, but it requires an investment in research to ferret them out.

One indicator that is more reliable than just the price tag is the software author's or distributor's "track record." Some software authors and publishers sell only powerful, high-priced software, while others sell only low-cost programs suitable for beginners. Still others develop a reputation for good programs at reasonable prices, and some become known for offering great values. If you are looking for a patch librarian, for example, it pays to find out if the same source offers a sequencer or editor and what reputation those products have earned.

With new products from unknown authors or distributors, you are more likely to have to rely on reviews, advertising, and especially on word of mouth. Develop a network of contacts in the MIDI world and exchange information. Particularly in a field as young as MIDI, a little cooperation and mutual assistance goes a long way. Seek opinions from others, and share the knowledge that you have gained.

EVALUATING MIDI SOFTWARE

The best way to become acquainted with any computer program—perhaps the only way—is to use it, and this is especially true of MIDI music software. If your musical instrument store stocks software, ask for a demo and an opportunity to spend some time using the program yourself. Try to "test drive" the software using the same MIDI equipment and the same computer you expect to use, or as similar a setup as you can find.

If you are unable to find a store that stocks music programs for the type of computer you plan to use, try to find a friend or associate who is already using the type of program you are interested in—even if it is not the same computer or software brand as yours, if necessary. Get a demo and try out the software yourself.

Whether in the store or elsewhere, spend enough time, working on projects similar in scope if not in size to your own to get a feel for what the software can and cannot do. Even if the computer is a different type than your own, experience using any similar program on any computer will help you in your subsequent evaluations and judgments.

Many software manufacturers offer demo disks at a nominal price. Typically, these demo disks offer all the capabilities of the "real thing," except that they are usually limited in the number of MIDI events they will store in computer memory at once, and they generally will not let you save your work. For the purposes of familiarizing yourself with the product, demo disks are a bargain—you should not pass them up. As an added incentive, most manufacturers will credit you the cost of the demo disk if you decide to buy their product.

If you cannot get a demo version, your only other choice is to watch the magazines and journals for a review of the program you are interested in and hope that the reviewer is interested in the same sorts of features and capabilities that you are (for a list of magazines and other information sources, see chapter 11, "Getting Help"). Someone else's review is no substitute for first-hand experience, but it is better than nothing at all.

Make sure that any program you buy—whether a demo or a complete version—is designed to work with your computer system and MIDI interface. Otherwise, it will be useless. Even if it does match your computer and interface, there are other hardware factors to consider.

Hard Disk Support

Hard disk drives (or "hard disks") are faster than floppy disks and store more programs and data than a stack of floppies. They also cost several times more than floppy drives—typically $400 and up, versus around $100 for a floppy drive. For many computer users, musicians included, the cost is well worth it. When programs and data are stored on a hard disk, they are always close at hand, ready to run. No more searching for disks, swapping floppy disks in and out, or checking each disk to see which one you used to store the sequence you worked on last weekend. With periodic backups, hard disks are actually more reliable than floppies, since you do not handle them, risk bending them, or lose them.

Almost all computers with hard disks also have a floppy drive, both for making backups and so that you can transport data to another computer when you want to. Some systems, though, have no hard disk; such systems usually have two floppy drives instead. While many programs will run successfully on systems without a hard disk, some require so much storage for the programs themselves or the data they work with that they can only be run on hard disk systems.

Copy Protection

Copy protection is designed to protect software manufacturers' profits by preventing illegal copying and distribution of software, but skillful software "pirates" have found ways to sidestep copy protection schemes and make illegal copies anyway. Copy protection more often serves to frustrate honest users because it prevents such users from making backup copies for their own safety.

Some copy-protected programs require that the "key disk" always be in place in the computer's floppy disk drive, even if the program is running from a hard disk drive. Others require only that the key disk be used to start up the program, whether it is run subsequently from a hard disk or floppy disk.

Another copy protection scheme permits hard disk installation and operation but keeps track of how many times the hard disk installation has occurred. Such programs typically permit only two or three hard disk installations. Such programs cannot be backed up as other programs can and must be "deinstalled" before fully backing up or reorganizing the hard disk to improve its performance speed. Deinstalling the program decrements the installation counter to its former value, permitting multiple install/deinstall cycles.

In any case, copy protection burdens honest users with extra confusion, more steps to go through to run the program, and less protection against disk failure or accidental loss than programs that are not copy-protected. For those reasons and others I will not permit copy-protected programs in my studio unless there is no alternative or they are so much better than competing programs that I have no choice but to grit my teeth and put up with them.

I recognize the need for software authors to protect their livelihoods, and I understand that software authors must be paid for their work or they will stop producing it. I do not copy other folks' programs and I do not let anyone copy the ones I have bought. I urge everyone to respect the rights of software authors if they want to continue to see innovative software developed. However, I do not think the burden should be placed on the honest users who are the source of software authors' livelihood. Others have a different opinion and support copy protection wholeheartedly; the choice is up to you, but know what you are buying before you buy.

Pointing Devices

Many program operations require the user to point to commands or locations on the screen. Since pointing must be performed so frequently, the implementation of pointing commands is an important consideration.

Some computer operating systems, such as the Apple Macintosh's, use "graphical user interfaces," which rely primarily on pointing. All programs running on such computers operate in a similar fashion, so users need only learn one set of skills for entering commands. Other operating systems, like IBM's PC-DOS, use character-based interfaces, which typically require users to type in commands that may vary from one program to another.

Even many character-based programs require pointing, often by pressing special keys on the computer keyboards' called cursor control keys, usually marked with up, down, left, and right arrow symbols. (A cursor is a small symbol on screen that shows where the next character will appear.) Not all computer keyboards have cursor control keys, so some character-based programs provide the option of using special-purpose keys (sometimes the "Ctrl" or "Alt" key) in combination with letter keys for cursor control. Many touch typists prefer combination keys to arrow keys for cursor control, since the typist's hands can remain in the "home" position on the keyboard during cursoring. Other computer users do not like to have to memorize the key combinations, preferring cursor arrow keys instead.

In either case, pressing the cursor-control keys as many times as necessary moves a cursor or pointing symbol on the screen to the correct location. Once the on-screen pointer is correctly placed, the user presses another key to initiate the desired operation.

Cursoring is time consuming, so some programs support alternative pointing devices. The most common of these are mice and trackballs. A mouse (figure 5.1a) is a device about the size of a deck of cards connected by a thin cable to the back of the computer. As the user rolls the mouse on a desktop or special mouse pad, the computer interprets the movements of the mouse and moves the pointing cursor on the screen accordingly. Once the pointing cursor is positioned, the user can press a button on the mouse instead of the specified key on the computer keyboard.

A trackball (figure 5.1b), on the other hand, is a partially exposed ball mounted in a box that sits stationary on the desktop alongside the computer keyboard. Like the mouse, the trackball box is connected to the computer by a cable. Using the fingertips or the palm of the hand, the user rolls the ball in any direction, and the computer translates the ball's movements, moving the on-screen pointer accordingly. Like a mouse, a trackball has one or more buttons the user can press once the pointer is in position.

Each has its advocates, and studies indicate that both devices are faster than pointing using the cursor keys. Those same studies generally give a small edge to trackballs over mice for speed, accuracy, and ease of use.

Not all pointing devices work with all computers, though. Be sure that the device you plan to buy is designed to work with the computer you plan to use. Even then, not all programs designed for character-based systems can take advantage of the pointing device; such programs must have mouse or trackball support if you plan to use a pointing device with them.

a.

b.

FIGURE 5.1   Pointing devices: a) a mouse (courtesy Logitech, Inc.); b) a trackball (courtesy Kensington Microware Ltd.).

Command Entry

The two most common ways that users tell a program what to do are by typing in the required commands, called a "command-driven" system, or by choosing from a list of commands presented to the user by the program, called a "menu-driven" system. The advantage of a menu-driven system is that you see the available command choices before picking the correct one, while a command-driven system lets you enter commands as quickly as you can type them, without having to wait for the program to print the list of choices.

As a rule, menu-driven systems are easier for the inexperienced user to learn, while command-driven systems do not slow down experienced users who already know the necessary choices. Most new users cannot remember commands like "T/B4/BN4/C5:E5:C5/D5:B4/C5;". Experienced users do not want to wait while the program prints a menu of choices they are already familiar with. While most programs use only one approach or the other, the best ones provide menus for new users and let experienced users avoid the menus once they have learned the necessary commands.

Even among menu-driven systems, there can be important differences. Some programs require that you first move a highlight bar onto your chosen command in the list, either by pressing the cursor control keys or moving the mouse. Only when the correct command is highlighted will such programs let you press a key (typically the Enter or Return key) or push a button on the mouse to initiate the command.

Other programs will let you press just the first letter of the command you want, regardless of which choice is highlighted and without having to press anything else. That approach to menu-driven systems saves keystrokes, and in the long run it can increase the user's speed in command entry considerably.

One way to speed up command entry is by storing commonly used commands in macros—abbreviated keystroke sequences that cause longer text strings to be substituted in their place. By assigning a lengthy command string to a macro, you can then type the shorter macro each time you want to use the longer command string. Few music programs have macro capabilities, though, but memory-resident utility programs that add macro capability to any program are available. They are worth considering if the programs you want to use lack a built-in macro feature.

With so many different options and combinations it is hard to evaluate a program's command entry style during a quick demo, so try to spend enough time with the software to get a sense of how easy it will be to learn and how quickly you will be able to enter complex commands once you have learned them.

Documentation

Documentation includes not only the printed materials that come packaged with the program diskette but also on-screen prompts, messages, and help that can be called up on-screen at the user's request.

Start with the program screen itself. It should be clearly laid out, logically organized, and easy to understand. The very best programs are those that anyone can use right away, regardless of their computer background or skill level.

Many programs include explanations that the user can call onto the screen by pressing a special key (often a function key such as F1). One type of callable help presents an index or table of contents from which the user must select a topic; help on the selected topic then appears. An easier approach provides context-sensitive help, that is, help appropriate to what was happening on screen when the user pressed the help key. If you were selecting a value for a parameter, the context-sensitive help might explain the parameter and indicate the possible range of values. If you were choosing from a menu, the context-sensitive help might explain each menu choice.

The more on-screen help available, the less likely that thick manuals of printed documentation will be needed. In fact, a stack of thick manuals accompanying a MIDI program sometimes indicates a program that is unnecessarily complex, poorly designed, or inadequately documented on screen.

Some of the best MIDI programs include a reference manual (with a comprehensive index!) for advanced users, a separate tutorial for those getting started, and a quick reference card or template to fit over the keyboard, listing the most commonly used commands. Some programs are so well designed that printed documentation is almost unnecessary; you can learn everything you need to know by reading the screen and getting help when you need it.

The best way to evaluate documentation is to use the program. Check to see if the screens are easy to understand, if on-screen help is available, and if the printed documentation is readable and comprehensive. A brief test may not reveal if a program is well designed, but it is usually easy to spot one that is poorly designed. If it looks confusing, difficult to use, or unnecessarily complex, it probably is.

Upgrade Policy

Like textbooks, computer programs are likely to undergo revision over time, either to fix bugs—aspects of the program that do not work as the author intended—or to add features that make the program more powerful or easier to use. Often, an upgrade package will include new documentation as well as new program diskettes. Some companies offer upgrades to registered users free or for a nominal charge, while others charge a discount from full price, and some offer no discount at all. Upgrade prices can represent a significant portion of the total cost of a program during its useful life, so it is worth finding out about upgrade policies in advance.

Extensibility

Instead of relying on the software's authors to improve their product, some programs provide "hooks" that let users themselves add improvements. A user with programming skills might write a subroutine in C or a LISP function to provide a capability the program did not originally have. Very few programs provide such hooks, so if you want to be able to extend the functionality of a program, make sure it is capable of such extensions. Check to see if the extensibility is restricted to a particular programming language or dialect and how such extensions are added to the program.

One reason so few programs are extensible is that adding code to the program provides a way to add bugs to the program as well, causing problems ranging from trivial to critical. Before you add to an extensible program, test your code thoroughly, and back up the program before adding your routine. Better yet, back up everything on the disk that holds the program you plan to add to.

Extensibility is best left to programmers with considerable skill (or considerable confidence)—but there are ways to learn about MIDI programming without altering commercial programs. You can write programs yourself, from scratch. For suggestions on getting started in MIDI programming, see chapter 10, "Programming in MIDI."

MIDI SOFTWARE FOR EAR TRAINING

Ear-training software (figure 5.2) can help students develop aural acuity by repeatedly playing intervals, chords, or scales and prompting the student to identify them correctly. The student should be able to adjust the difficulty of any exercise to the appropriate level as well as set the tempo, range, and loudness of the exercises to provide a variety of challenges.

More advanced ear-training programs include melodic error detection and correction; recognition of intervals, scales, modes, and chords; and melodic and rhythmic dictation. The best ear-training programs retain a history of student achievement and provide a cumulative evaluation, showing the student's improvement over time in numbers or graphic representations. The program should also be able to flag those exercises on which the student most needs to practice as well as those the student has already mastered.

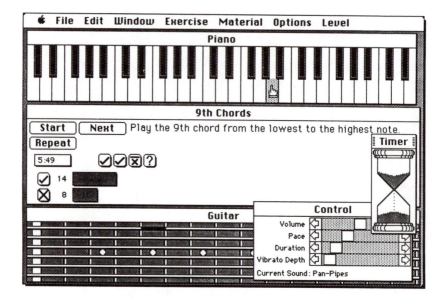

FIGURE 5.2   Listen ear-training software (courtesy Resonate).

INSTRUMENTAL PRACTICE SOFTWARE

Instrumental practice programs monitor the MIDI data stream generated by playing a MIDI keyboard or other controller and compare aspects of the data stream to a benchmark of the correct performance stored within the program. For example, the program might compare the student's performance of a keyboard exercise to the correct version and show the student any incorrect notes. The program should keep cumulative scores of correct and incorrect aspects of the performance, showing how the student's performance improves with practice and highlighting those aspects of the performance that the student should concentrate on.

The more aspects of performance the program can monitor, the better. Ideally, it should report on correct and incorrect notes, rhythmic irregularities (both incorrect rhythms and overall rhythmic precision), consistency of attack, and correctness of note durations.

The practice passages should be appropriate to the student's skill level, and they should progress in difficulty as the student's skills progress. For beginners, the program might simply display a note on a staff shown on the computer's video monitor and measure how often the student plays the indicated note correctly. The program might also measure response time so that it can present notes more quickly as the student's skills improve.

More complex performance practice programs might include major and minor scales; arpeggio performance and fingerings; major and minor triads in different voicings, played by each hand separately or both at once; major, minor, diminished and augmented chords; and complete passages from the instrument's literature.

You should be able to set the tempo for each performance of the exercise or musical passage, increasing the tempo as you gain mastery of the exercise. Some programs set the tempo based on an initial performance, automatically increasing the tempo as the student's performance improves.

SOFTWARE FOR SIGHT-READING PRACTICE

Like instrumental practice programs, sight-reading programs compare a student's performance with one stored in memory. The difference is that rather than exercises such as scales, sight-reading programs usually contain musical passages or excerpts that increase in difficulty as the student's sight-reading skills improve. Rather than playing the same exercises repeatedly and receiving reports on improvement, the student plays the passages in a sight-reading program once and receives a report showing errors and suggestions for improvement. Once the student reaches a certain level of competence, the program presents harder examples for sight-reading.

As with performance programs, the student should be able to set the tempo or let the program select a tempo based on the student's prior skill level. The program should also be able to generate reports on the student's skill level and improvement over time and make suggestions for further skill development.

SYNTHESIZER SOUND LIBRARIES

Rather than creating new synthesizer sounds from scratch by programming new patches, you can use preprogrammed sounds from libraries designed for your synthesizer brand or model. Such collections of patches may be grouped by instrument categories such as strings, keyboards, or brass instrument sounds. Some libraries include sound effects or a range of sounds from many types of instruments.

Sound libraries come in a variety of formats including floppy disks, data cassettes, and plug-in memory cartridges. The library you choose must be designed specifically for your synthesizer and must be stored on a device compatible with your synthesizer. Some libraries are published in book form and require the user to enter the synthesizer patch data they contain "by hand." Even then, the patch data in the book must be designed for the synthesizer you use.

The only way to evaluate the quality of synthesizer sound libraries is to hear them. Some manufacturers of sound libraries offer demo cassettes with examples at little or no cost; otherwise, you will have to rely on word of mouth or magazine reviews.

PATCH LIBRARIANS

Synthesizers can draw from only a limited number of instrument voices at one time from among the voices the synthesizer is capable of producing—an unlimited number in the case of programmable synthesizers. The active group of voices is usually referred to as a bank. Many synthesizers recall the bank in use when the power was turned off and automatically restore that bank when the power comes on again. Still, to use a different set of voices you must assign those voices to the current bank by pressing buttons or entering data from the synthesizer's control panel. Such data entry is usually tedious and time consuming. In live performance situations, the delays required for synthesizer bank reprogramming can be intolerable; in recording studios, time is money and delays are expensive. Even in the home studio, bank programming is unnecessarily cumbersome.

The solution is a voice (or patch) librarian program (figure 5.3) run on a personal computer linked to the synthesizer through MIDI. Librarians let you view many banks on the computer monitor and choose the one you want. All the required patch and programming data is transferred to the synthesizer, which is then ready to play the voices in the bank you have selected.

"Dedicated" librarians are designed for one particular synthesizer or synthesizer family, while "universal" librarians are designed to work with many different synthesizer brands and models. Typically, dedicated librarians better handle the one synthesizer they were designed for than universal librarians do, though as universal librarians become more powerful and customizable they compare favorably to dedicated librarians.

A good universal librarian should come preprogrammed with parameter settings for the synthesizers you use, including such data as the number of voices per bank and the system exclusive codes that identify the

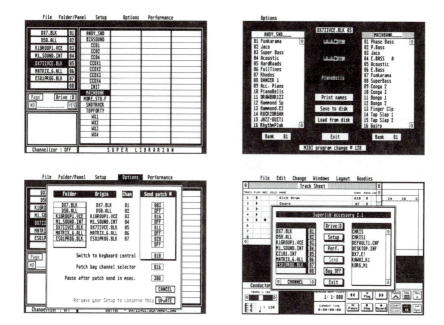

FIGURE 5.3   Super Librarian software (courtesy Pixel Publishing).

synthesizers, especially if those synthesizers are among the more popular models. You should also be able to program in the necessary data for synthesizers that the librarian is not already set up for. (For more on System Exclusive messages, see chapter 8, "Understanding MIDI Messages.")

The librarian should be able to list all the synthesizer's voices on the computer screen and let you organize the voices into banks however you like. Some librarians let you name each bank, then simply select the bank you want from the list of names, or see a list that displays both the name and the contents of each bank and select the bank from that.

The capability to compare banks and highlight their differences is useful in finding and eliminating duplicate or near-duplicate banks. Another option lets you store lists of banks to be transmitted in a specified order at your command—a particularly useful capability in live performance situations. Other features of a good librarian include the ability to copy, rename, or delete patches and banks; sort names alphabetically, by instrument, or by date; or build a menu of the instruments in your setup, then choose from the menu and see, change, or select only from the patches or banks for the selected instrument.

PATCH EDITORS

Editing programs, or patch editors (figure 5.4), allow you to change the actual parameters whose data values determine the sound quality of a particular patch. Because the way each instrument implements its patches is unique, patch editors usually work only with a single instrument or "family" of instruments from one manufacturer. If your setup includes several MIDI instruments, you may need a patch editor program for each, although universal editors have begun to appear recently; these universal editors may serve your needs just as well.

One style of editor duplicates as closely as possible the instrument's control panel on the computer screen. Another approach uses icons—small pictures that represent a concept, like a small loudspeaker representing "produce sound"—and groups parameters under appropriate icons. The control-panel approach builds on familiarity the user has developed with the equipment, while the icon-based approach may take better advantage of the computer screen's graphics capabilities to communicate more quickly. A third approach combines the two, organizing data into menus that may be organized like the instrument's control panel but showing all the possible choices on screen at once. Each approach has advantages and disadvantages, so try to work with several editors to learn which is most comfortable for you.

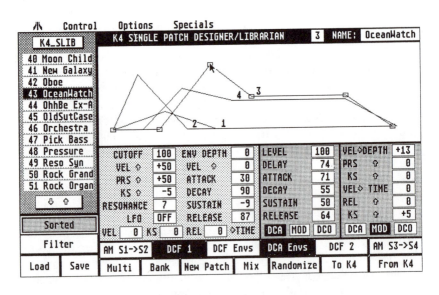

FIGURE 5.4 K4 Voice Development System software (courtesy Musicode).

To change a parameter value, the user moves the cursor to the area of the screen holding the parameter to be changed. Once the correct parameter is selected, the user enters the new data value. Some editors require the user to type in the value, while others offer the option of using a special key (often the " + " key) to increase the value and another key (often " − ") to decrease it.

Many editors require that you save the changes before you can hear the result, but some let you hear the changes in real time while you change the data values. Real-time auditioning lets you develop patches more quickly and with greater precision and is a feature most users feel is worth paying extra for.

Another option that many users find indispensable is a random parameter value generator. Instead of selecting a value for a particular parameter, the user can call on the generator to supply one. Some editors generate random values for one parameter at a time, while other editors feature complete random patch generation. Either approach helps the user discover new sounds and can also help the user learn how to specify patch parameters for particular sounds by observing how the random value affects the resulting sound.

AUDIO RECORDINGS FOR SAMPLING

Many sampler users lack the opportunity or microphone technique required to record original samples of sounds they would like to use. Commercial recordings became a popular source of samples—so much so that some recording artists claimed copyright infringement and sued other artists who sampled their original recorded sounds for use in subsequent commercial releases. Fortunately, there are alternative sample sources that are comprehensive, designed for sampling, and legal.

Audio recordings of sound libraries for sampling have appeared on long-playing record, tape, and compact disc formats. Such recordings usually feature sounds of instruments, nature sounds, or sound effects. Rather than being part of a performance, the sounds intended for sampling are recorded in an isolated context, usually for only a few seconds' duration each and generally without such postproduction effects as reverberation or equalization. To use the sounds in a recorded library, simply connect a cable from the audio equipment's output to the sampler's input and record the sounds directly into the sampler.

Compact discs are probably the most useful and convenient format for sample sound libraries, and numerous volumes of CD sampling libraries are available. CDs can hold more than an hour of recorded sounds; their sound remains consistent even after repeated playing; and better-quality CD players provide almost instant access to any sound on the disc.

For instrumental sounds, look for a recording that features many short examples of each instrument. For example, a sampling library of cello sounds might include a series of notes from the bottom to the top of the cello's range, each performed soft, loud, and in between, and each played bowed, plucked, and with various attacks. It is not necessary to include every note in an instrument's range, since samples can be transposed over a limited span without too noticeable a change in timbre.

SAMPLE LIBRARIES FOR PLAYBACK

Some samplers offer playback only but no way to record new sounds, and even some sampler users who can record their own samples prefer not to. Even so, sampler users can still expand their library of samples, provided that their sampler or sample player has a storage device such as a floppy disk or plug-in memory cartridge. Sampler manufacturers and third-party vendors offer collections of samples for playback. Rather than containing audio recordings that must then be sampled, such diskettes or cartridges contain sampled sounds that are already in digital sample format, ready for playback. All the sampler user needs to do is plug in the diskette or cartridge and load the samples into the sampler's memory.

In order to take advantage of such libraries, the samples must be in a compatible media format and a compatible sample format. Compatible media format goes beyond the correct diskette or cartridge size; samplers may store digital data on diskette or cartridge using one or more encoding arrangements or formats, so the sampler library diskette or cartridge must store its data in the same format that the sampler or sample player uses.

Even if the media and data format are correct, there are different ways to store or encode sample data. Most diskettes for sampler playback state clearly the sampler they are intended for, and the samples are stored according to the sampler manufacturer's specifications. Other sample library diskettes store the samples according to the MIDI Sample Dump Standard and can be used by any sampler that can read MIDI Sample Dump format data, provided that the media format is the correct one. Before buying a sample library diskette or cartridge, either make sure it is designed specifically for your sampler or sample player, or make sure that the media and sample format are compatible with your own.

Even if the samples play back correctly, there is no assurance that they will sound good. As with audio libraries for sample recording, the only way to be sure is to listen to the results. Get a demo from a store or a friend, read reviews, and check with other sampler users before you buy.

SAMPLE LIBRARIANS AND EDITORS

Librarians and editors for samplers, like their counterparts for synthesizer patches, let you organize and keep track of large numbers of samples and make changes to the samples in the computer's memory or once they are stored in the sampler itself. Look for sample librarian features similar to the ones described above in the section on synthesizer patch librarians, including the capability to organize, name, and compare banks of samples; copy, rename, or delete samples or banks; and use System Exclusive messages to specify a particular sampler from among several that you might use in a complex MIDI setup.

Sample editors include features beyond those of patch librarians. In addition to evaluating a sample editor's user interface for clarity and ease of use, check to see that it includes all the features of your sampler, such as cross-fading and setting loop points.

A graphic waveform sample editor (figure 5.5) shows a picture of the sample's waveform. Zooming in or out can help to determine more accurately the start and end points for looping and locations of noise to be edited out. The editor may also permit waveforms to be drawn from scratch using cursor keys or a mouse. The most powerful editors let you hear changes as you make them, while others require that you save the sound before you can hear the results of your edits.

Some sample editors provide editing capabilities that are not even present in the samplers they support, including such advanced functions as equalization, cross-fading one sample into another, or mixing two or more samples together.

Many sample editors are designed for a particular sampler model or several models. Others are generic and designed to work with any sampler that meets the MIDI Sample Dump Standard. Generally, generic editors trade off depth for breadth—they are likely to work with a wider range of samplers but may not take advantage of all the features of each. Sample editors designed for a specific model may more fully implement the features of that model, but you may have to buy a second editor if you add another sampler to your setup.

MUSIC PRINTING PROGRAMS

Sequencers (see below) let you record and play back MIDI data, enabling you to store and edit the MIDI data generated while performing music. Some sequencers are capable of transcribing MIDI data

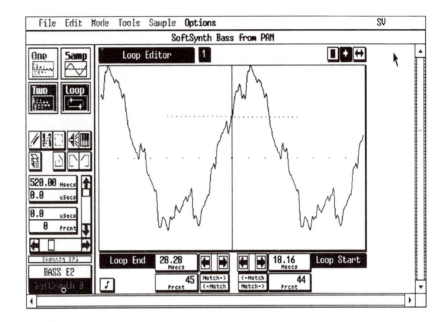

FIGURE 5.5   SampleVision sample editor software (courtesy Turtle Beach Softworks).

into conventional music notation. Other sequencers that lack transcription capabilities can transfer their sequencer files into a program designed specifically for notation.

Well-integrated software that combines MIDI recorders and notation programs should be able to convert data in either direction—that is, take a performance recorded from a MIDI controller and generate a printed score or take notation symbols and MIDI control data entered at the computer keyboard and synthesize the performance from the score.

Notation programs (figure 5.6) do not themselves have comprehensive playback facilities. Notation programs may be able to accept MIDI data directly from a MIDI controller; most use notation symbols entered via the computer keyboard or a mouse. They may read sequence files directly, or a utility program may be required to convert the sequence data into a format the notation program can use.

The printed notation that results can be as simple as a lead sheet for a song or as complex as a full orchestral score. Capabilities vary widely among notation programs. Some can generate only piano or piano/vocal scores, but most have user-definable page layouts with multiple staffs,

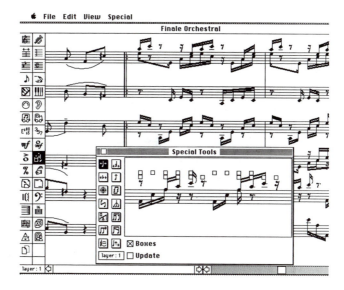

FIGURE 5.6   Finale music notation software (courtesy Coda Music Software).

clefs, beaming, key signatures, and meters. Programs with complex user-definable parameters should also let the user assign defaults—specific choices the program will always make unless the user selects something different.

Some notation programs also include MIDI output capability, which converts the music symbols on the screen into their equivalent MIDI messages, which can then be sent to any MIDI synthesizer for playback. Despite that capability, few music printing programs can yet equal the speed, flexibility, and powerful editing capabilities of full-function sequencing software.

Other features of music printing programs include capabilities to move and copy passages, insert lyrics, generate chord symbols, or automatically create piano reductions. A good-quality notation program should be able to handle arbitrary tuplets (irregular groupings of rhythmic values such as triplets, quintuplets, septuplets, and so on), performance instructions, measure numbers, and dynamic markings. The best notation programs let the user define new notational symbols and determine the size and shape of each staff.

Any printing program you plan to use must support your printer. Laser printer output, for example, can be comparable to typeset quality, but the sequencer's music printout or notation program must support the laser printer's features in order to take advantage of them.

COMPUTER-AIDED COMPOSITION

A basic function of computers is the capability for decision making, either according to guidelines established by a program or user, or on a random basis. This decision-making capability can be applied to composition as well. As musicians and programmers better understand the process of composing music, computer-aided composition programs (figure 5.7) grow in sophistication.

Generally, such programs take an interactive approach to the composition process, letting the user set guidelines within which the computer will make specific decisions. The guidelines might include a set of pitches a melody may include, while the actual choice of each individual pitch is left to the program.

The computer "improvises" within the framework established by the user; better-quality interactive composition programs provide the option of storing the improvisation as a MIDI sequence in the format of a particular sequencer program or in the standard MIDI files format. Once stored, the sequence can be edited and played back just as if it had been created in the usual manner.

One approach to interactive composition lets the user improvise or play a performance on a MIDI controller. The program then incorporates the user's playing style into its own variations on the user's performance.

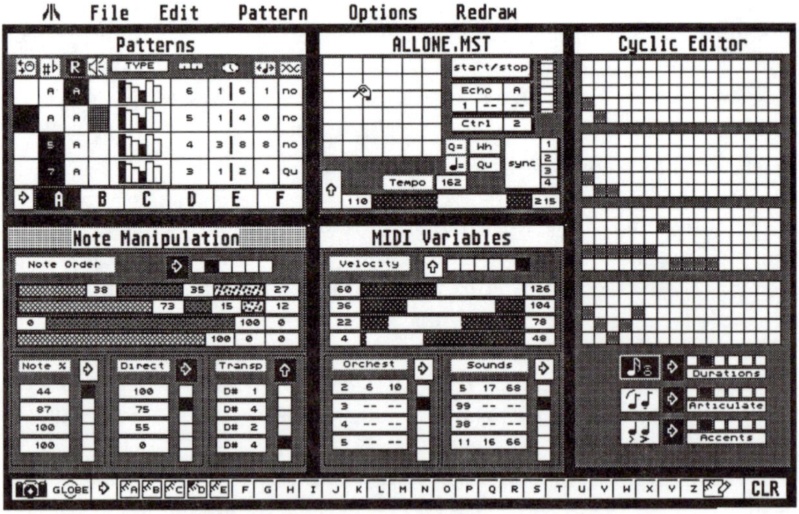

FIGURE 5.7 M™ algorithmic composition software (courtesy Intelligent Music).

Other computer-aided composition programs let the user change the computer's performance as it occurs, adjusting such variables as the tempo, key, time signature, or accents in real time.

Such programs can help composers expand their musical language, explore new possibilities for composition, or experiment with different approaches to the same musical idea.

SEQUENCERS

All MIDI sequencers perform the same functions, whether the sequencer is implemented in hardware, as a separate MIDI device or as part of a MIDI workstation, or in software, as a program running on a personal computer. In each case, sequencers record MIDI data and provide a way to store, edit, and replay the data. Of all the MIDI musician's tools, sequencers are probably the most widely used, and they are so important that they are the subject of the next chapter.

CHOOSING AND USING SEQUENCER SOFTWARE

. . . .

Of all the computer software available to the MIDI musician, none is so widely used as MIDI recorder/sequencer programs. They go by a variety of names—event recorders, MIDI sequencers, pattern editors, and the like—but they all have two things in common. They store MIDI messages for subsequent playback, editing, and manipulation, and they are all intended to automate the composer's tasks by combining the creative spontaneity of "live" performance with the precision and editing capabilities of "traditional" notation.

All such programs store the MIDI messages themselves, and also the timing and sequence in which the messages occurred, so I will refer to them all as "sequencers." They fall into two main categories, based on the composing approach they most resemble. The first category treats the computer as a smart tape recorder, often mimicking a tape recorder's controls on the computer screen (figure 6.1). Instead of recording sounds, though, the programs store a continuous stream of incoming MIDI messages. Once stored in the computer, the MIDI messages can be played back, edited, manipulated, and polished, without the problems of tape splicing and generation loss that plague analog tape recorder users.

The other approach treats a piece of music as a series of individual building blocks or patterns. Rather than storing all the MIDI messages that make up a piece of music in a continuous stream, pattern recorders let the composer store a chunk at a time. Each chunk can be edited individually

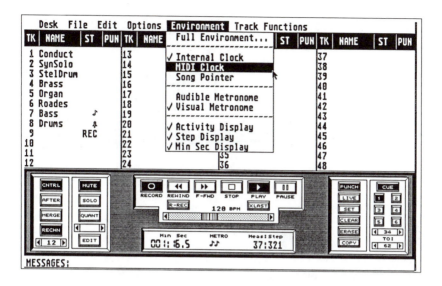

FIGURE 6.1 KCS tape recorder-style sequencer (courtesy Dr. T's Music Software, Inc.).

and manipulated in the same ways as in tape recorder-style sequencers. However, a pattern editor lets the composer assemble a piece by arranging these chunks in any order, repeating, transposing, and combining them at will (figure 6.2).

Your choice of a recorder-style or pattern-style sequencer depends on your approach to music making. If you primarily compose songs with repeating bass lines, a chorus/verse structure, and so forth, a pattern editor can help speed the construction of your music. If you work with larger-scale, more complex, through-composed musical ideas, you may find that a recorder-style editor lets your ideas flow more comfortably from one to the next, without the interruption of assembling patterns into a whole.

Regardless of which style you choose, there are a wide variety of features to look for. Like any other product, more features usually mean a higher price tag, so if your budget is limited, find the sequencer with the features you need, and skip those you think are unimportant.

STARTING YOUR EVALUATION

More than any other music software, a sequencer is the one program most MIDI musicians live with on a daily basis, so it is

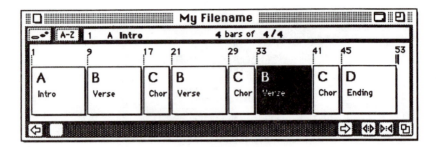

FIGURE 6.2 EZ Vision sequencer (courtesy Opcode Systems, Inc.).

especially important to invest the time and effort to get to know the package you choose before you commit to it. The general considerations in evaluating any software that were mentioned in chapter 5 apply equally— perhaps especially—to sequencers. You may want to review the appropriate sections of chapter 5 before proceeding, and certainly you should keep the criteria covered there foremost in mind when evaluating sequencers. This chapter will build on the material in chapter 5 by covering those issues of particular significance to sequencer users. The following is not a complete list of features that sequencers may have; rather, I have tried to include the ones most MIDI musicians consider important and those most likely to vary from one sequencer to another.

TRACKS AND CHANNELS

Borrowing from tape recording terminology, sequencers use "tracks" to describe separate areas in the sequencer's memory where MIDI messages may be stored. As with audio tape recorders, extra sequencer tracks provide more flexibility and control, so the rule of thumb is "the more tracks, the better." Many sequencers provide thirty-two, sixty-four, or more tracks. At the very least, look for a minimum of sixteen tracks so that each channel of MIDI information can be stored and manipulated individually. Additional tracks might be used to store special-purpose messages, such as program change or controller data, or for especially tricky passages that might have to be step recorded or entered through the event editor (see below) rather than recorded in real time.

Even if the number of tracks available is limited, some sequencers offset that shortcoming by letting you overdub newly recorded material onto an existing track. That way, you can record part of what you want played back over a particular MIDI channel onto a particular sequencer track, then play back what you have recorded while simultaneously recording new MIDI messages onto the same track for playback over the same MIDI channel as the original recorded messages. Some sequencers will even let you over-dub MIDI messages intended for playback over a different MIDI channel onto the same recorder track.

The current MIDI specification defines sixteen channels, and any sequencer worth using should let you record or play back over as few or as many of the sixteen channels as you choose.

MULTIPORT SUPPORT

While the MIDI specification defines sixteen channels for MIDI data, some MIDI musicians find that sixteen channels are not enough. An "orchestral" composition with forty different parts, for example, could not be accomplished in a single MIDI sequence but could be achieved only by using synchronized multitrack recording.

Manufacturers have begun to address this shortcoming with special MIDI interfaces. One approach uses a multiport MIDI interface, with two, four, or as many as eight separate MIDI ports on a single interface, designated Out A, Out B, Out C (or Out 1, 2, and 3), and so on. Another approach is to connect a second MIDI interface to the computer's printer port to complement the interface connected to the modem port. Some manufacturers make a double MIDI interface that can be connected to both of the computer's serial ports.

If you use a second or double MIDI interface on your printer port, or a multiport MIDI interface, make sure that the software can specify a particular MIDI port as well as a specified MIDI channel, for example, MIDI B, channel 8 or printer port, channel 3.

Perhaps the MIDI specification will be amended to extend the number of channels beyond sixteen, but meanwhile the marketplace will always try to address users' needs as it perceives them. Deviating from the MIDI standard has risks for both the manufacturers and MIDI users who choose that course, so it should be taken only if there is a compelling need with no alternative that is within the MIDI specification.

RESOLUTION

Dividing a musical beat into a large number of very small units of time lets the composer position rhythmic values with greater precision. The MIDI specification does not define a standard resolution, but most sequencers use from ninety-six to 600 "ticks," or parts, per quarter note. A higher resolution lets the composer more subtly position notes slightly before or after the beat, called "pushing" or "lagging" the beat in musical terms. It also permits more accurate representation of complex tuplets, such as eleven thirty-second notes in the time of eight. If you write march music, low resolution might be adequate, but if your pieces are rhythmically more complex, or you are trying to capture the "feel" of a live performance, a higher resolution would better serve your purposes.

RECORDER FEATURES

Programmable Metronome

You should be able to set the sequencer to generate an audible metronome click only while recording, only during playback, during both, or neither. For many musicians, listening to the metronome during playback is an annoying distraction from the music, though it may be a necessity during recording. Turning the metronome on and off each time you switch from playback to record and vice versa is bothersome, so look for flexibility in how the sequencer handles the metronome following a change of mode.

Some sequencers' metronomes can play only a predetermined sound using the computer's speaker. Others play a predetermined sound but require that the metronome output from the MIDI interface be passed through a channel of the mixing console to an external amplifier. Still others let you direct the metronome to any MIDI channel you specify so you can synthesize a metronome sound you like, perhaps even controlling the pitch. Again, this will probably require that you devote a channel of your mixer exclusively to the metronome.

As always, a variety of options is most desirable. If you have plenty of mixing console channels available, or plan to upgrade your system to include them, look for a sequencer that will let you direct the metronome output to the computer speaker or to the preferred device and channel. If synthesizer or console channels are at a premium, choose a sequencer that can use the computer's speaker for metronome output.

No matter how you set up the metronome, you may want to hear some counts of the metronome to establish your rhythm before starting to record. Some sequencers will "count off" only by playing a single measure in the tempo you have set before recording actually begins, while others can be programmed to play any number of beats in any tempo you specify before switching into record mode, at which time the metronome may switch to a different meter or tempo. Your need for countoff control depends on the rhythmic complexity of your music. One bar of four beats in the actual meter is usually sufficient for rock and roll, while jazz, ethnic, or contemporary classical music may have more complex countoff requirements.

Quantizing

Some sequencers can move the start, end, or both start and end of each note to the nearest exact rhythmic unit of a value you specify (figure 6.3). Depending on the sequencer, the quantizing may be performed while recording or later during editing. In either case, recording a string of eighth notes, for example, and quantizing the Note On and Note Off messages to the nearest eighth-note value, assures that each note will be aligned precisely with the beat.

The larger the unit used for quantizing, the more noticeable the change is likely to be. One approach is to start by quantizing to the smallest rhythmic unit available—often, a sixty-fourth note. Listen to what results, and if you are still not satisfied with the accuracy of the placement of each note, quantize to the next larger unit. Repeat the process until the desired accuracy results.

Some sequencers allow for partial quantization, in which notes are quantized by a specified percentage. Fifty percent quantization would move notes halfway toward the quantize value, increasing metrical accuracy while retaining some of the original feel of the performance.

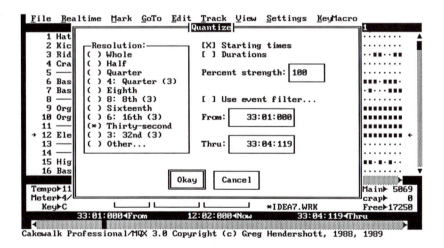

FIGURE 6.3 Cakewalk sequencer's quantization options (courtesy Twelve Tone Systems, Inc.).

If you quantize a track that has already been recorded rather than quantizing during the recording process, make a copy of the original track before you quantize it. Quantizing is a mechanical process, not a creative one. The sequencer simply moves each Note On or Note Off message to the nearest specified rhythmic unit whether or not it makes the most musical sense. The results can be different from what you expect or want, so copying the original track to another gives you a backup if you want to erase the quantized track and start over.

Even done correctly, quantizing should usually be used sparingly. Too much quantizing gives music a mechanical feel, particularly if you quantize both the start and end of notes so that each note is the same duration as all others of the same rhythmic value.

Message Filtering

A sequencer should be able to record, edit, and play back any sort of MIDI message including continuous controller data, program changes, aftertouch, and the like. However, MIDI systems can generate enormous quantities of data, some of which may not be worth recording. If your sequencer lets you set filters, you can tell it to ignore incoming messages of types you specify—System Exclusive or Aftertouch messages, for example—conserving your computer's memory and permitting you to record longer sequences than otherwise as well as eliminating the clutter of unwanted messages in your recording. If your sequencer has overdubbing capability, you can set note filtering on, for example, while letting pitch bend information pass through for recording, to add pitch bend effects to an existing track that was originally recorded without pitch bend.

Patch Thru

The ability of a sequencer to receive incoming messages and immediately retransmit them over the same or a different MIDI channel is known as Patch Thru. This is useful when, for example, you want to use a voiceless MIDI controller to send messages to both the sequencer and the synthesizer for which the track you are recording is intended.

Sequencers implement Patch Thru in either or both of two different modes. Direct echo sends incoming MIDI data out over the same channel on which it was received. Auto-channelize sends the data out over the channel to which the track you are recording is assigned.

If you are using a synthesizer as a controller and it is set to send and receive messages over the same MIDI channel, during recording your sequencer may send messages from the synthesizer back to it, setting up a feedback loop and a variety of unwanted consequences. If you hear "double notes" like a quick, one-time echo as you play, chances are good that Patch Thru is the cause of the problem. Being able either to set Patch Thru to a channel other than the one over which incoming MIDI messages were transmitted or to disable Patch Thru altogether prevents this sort of MIDI feedback. An alternative is to set the sending synthesizer to receive on a different channel.

Real-Time and Step Recording

Normally, your sequencer acts as a smart tape recorder, storing messages and their timing relationships as you generate them in real time. For passages that are difficult to play "up-tempo," but easier to play at a slower speed, you can slow the sequencer's metronome during recording, then reset the metronome to a faster tempo during playback.

Some passages, though, might be too complex to play in real time regardless of the tempo. A sequencer with Step Recording lets you make a recording outside real time so that you are not constrained by the need for physical dexterity.

Typically, you would assign duration and step advance values as default units—for example, a quarter note for each. Then, with your sequencer set in Step Recording mode, each time you play a note it will automatically be assigned a duration of a quarter note, no matter how long or short a time you hold down the key. The next note you play will be assigned to the next quarter note—no matter how much real time has elapsed between notes. By changing the defaults as necessary, you can enter complex or hard-to-play rhythmic passages at your leisure and play them back in perfect rhythm.

If the step recorder lets you specify the default duration and default step advance in clock ticks, not just rhythmic values, you can achieve precise control over the note placement and rhythmic effect. If, for example, your default duration is less than the advance value, the result will be a staccato or tenuto passage, depending on the amount of the difference, with a break between each note. If the default duration is slightly more than the advance value, the passage will be played back legato, with a slight overlap between successive notes.

An "extender" key—typically a special function key or cursor arrow key—is sometimes used as an alternative to changing the default rhythm frequently. If you want a duration longer than the default, you would first press the key for the note you want and, as you hold it down, press the extender key, which adds a specified duration to the note's default rhythm. Until you release the original note key, the extender key will continue to add the specified duration to the original note each time you press the extender key. If your default rhythm is a quarter note and your extender key is assigned an eighth-note duration, pressing a key on your keyboard and holding it down while you press the extender key three times yields a single note whose duration is quarter + eighth + eighth + eighth—a half note tied to an eighth note.

Some sequencers operate only monophonically in step mode—that is, you can enter only one "melody line" at a time, but not chords. Most will let you enter chords, with two different approaches to chord entry in step mode. One approach requires that you press all the keys in the chord at once. All are assigned the default rhythm, regardless of how long you hold down the keys in the chord. An easier approach lets you press the first key of the chord, then as you continue to hold down that key, press the remaining keys of the chord. When you release the first key pressed, the sequencer considers that the end of the chord, and all notes in the chord are assigned the default rhythmic value.

Punch-In/Punch-Out

You may play most of a passage perfectly as you record it in your sequencer, except for one section with lots of errors. Rather than having to record the entire passage again, some sequencers let you specify the section with the errors, then "punch" in and out of record mode automatically so that you can simultaneously erase and rerecord only the section with problems.

The sequencer will begin playback before the specified section to help you get your place, then automatically go into record mode at the correct spot while you replay the problem section. Once you have reached the end of that predetermined section, the sequencer will automatically stop recording, leaving you with the best of both "takes."

EDITOR FEATURES

Track Editing

After you have recorded one or more tracks, you may want to change an entire track or specific group of tracks (figure 6.4). Useful track-wide editing transformations include:

Transpose—Shift the pitch of each note in the track up or down a specified interval.

Invert—Change the direction of a melody, while keeping the interval distances the same. For example, a middle C followed by the E above it, then the G above that (a major third up followed by a minor third up) becomes a middle C followed by the A-flat

```
======================= Main =======================
Song TAKE 1                                         ┌──────┐
                                                    │ STOP │  Mem 221248
Tk   3 Electric Piano        BPM 114   CK: INTERNAL └──────┘
                                                      26:0
────────────────────────────────────────────────────────────────────
Trk Name                Chn Grp Prg  Trans Quant Loop Mute  Offset  │      Bars
  1 Drums                 8  A  49   ───── ───   ───  ───── ─────── │  1   109
  2 Bass                  6  A  26   ───── ───   ───  ───── ─────── │  2   112
  3 Electric Piano        1  A  11   ───── ───   ───  ───── ─────── │  3   112
  4 Brass                 3  A   2   ───── ───   ───  ───── ─────── │  4    51
  5 Alto Sax              5  A  22   ───── ───   ───  ───── ─────── │  5   101
  6 Tenor Sax             4  A  62   ───── ───   ───  ───── ─────── │  6   107
  7 Trumpet               2  A  12   ───── ───   ───  ───── ─────── │  7   101
  8 Guitar Solo           7  A  54   ───── ───   ───  ───── ─────── │  8   109
  9 Background Brass      3  A   2   ───── ───   ───  ───── ─────── │  9   102
 10 Melody (tenor sax)    4  A  62   ───── ───   ───  ───── ─────── │ 10   102
 11 ───────────────────  1  A  11   ───── ───   ───  ───── ─────── │ 11     0
 12 ───────────────────  1  A  11   ───── ───   ───  ───── ─────── │ 12     0
 13 ───────────────────  1  A  11   ───── ───   ───  ───── ─────── │ 13     0
 14 ───────────────────  1  A  11   ───── ───   ───  ───── ─────── │ 14     0
 15 ───────────────────  1  A  11   ───── ───   ───  ───── ─────── │ 15     0
 16 ───────────────────  1  A  11   ───── ───   ───  ───── ─────── │ 16     0
===================== Main Menu =====================
Record  Delete  Mute  Loop  Name  Solo  Tempo  Chase  GROUP  EDIT  FILES
VIEW  XLIBRARIAN  OPTIONS  PUNCH-IN  H_MULTI  Quit
```

FIGURE 6.4 Sequencer Plus track editing options (courtesy Voyetra Technologies).

below it, then the F below that (a major third down followed by a minor third down), and so on throughout the track.

Retrograde—Rearrange the order of the notes in the track so that they are stored and played back from last to first rather than first to last.

Quantize—Lets you "clean up" rhythmic inaccuracies by moving each note to the nearest specified rhythmic unit.

Velocity change—Some sequencers let you adjust the overall MIDI velocity parameter (loudness) of specified tracks, either by adding a fixed amount to each note's velocity or multiplying each note's velocity by some fixed percentage. The most powerful velocity change editors let you specify the starting and ending velocity. The computer then adjusts the velocity of each note in the track, progressing from the starting to the ending velocity you set. The result is a track-long crescendo or diminuendo. The sequencer may even let you choose either a linear curve—a steady increase in note velocity from beginning to end—or an exponential curve—larger increases at the beginning with successively smaller increases toward the end.

Event Editing

Once a string of MIDI messages is recorded in the sequencer, an event editor lets the composer make precise changes and adjustments, on an event-by-event basis if needed. Generally, the MIDI messages are shown on the screen one by one or on a "message list" from which you can specify the message you want to edit.

Some sequencers offer only minimal event editing, limited to inserting or deleting specified MIDI messages. Others let you change only the pitch or duration of a note. If you want do more precise editing, choose a sequencer whose editor lets you examine and change any aspect of any MIDI message.

Beyond simple inserting and deleting, desirable note control parameters for editing include pitch, duration, start and end time, velocity (volume), and MIDI channel assignment. You should be able to insert, delete, and edit non-note MIDI messages as well—the synthesizer patch number in Program Change messages or the range of Continuous Controller message values, for example. The best event editors also give you control over the structure of the piece itself, allowing you to insert, delete, or edit meter and tempo changes within a single sequence.

An important distinction among event editors is that some permit editing only one track or channel at a time, while others permit editing of any user-specified tracks or channels. The message list of a single track or channel at a time may be easier to follow than one cluttered with messages from many tracks or channels on a single list. If on the other hand, for example, you need to transpose a specified segment of track 2, track 9, and tracks 12 through 15, track-by-track editing can be cumbersome and slow. Ideally, you should have quick and easy control over the domain of editing commands, choosing the appropriate region (see "Region Editing" below) and tracks or channels on which editing commands act.

Measure Editing

While event editors let the composer work at the most detailed level, measure editors (figure 6.5) show the "big picture." Typically, measure editors display as many tracks as will fit vertically on screen at once and display each track's measures horizontally across the screen. Measures that contain no MIDI events are often represented by dots or dashes, while measures containing events appear as solid boxes.

During playback, the measure view makes it easier to correlate what has been recorded with what is being played back. The composer can use the measure view to locate the general area where editing is required, then use the event editor to locate the precise MIDI event to edit.

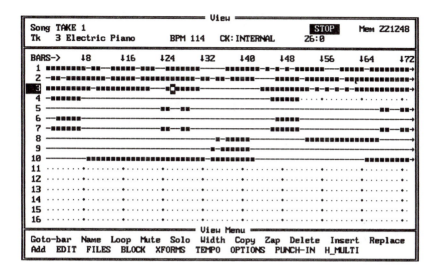

FIGURE 6.5 Sequencer Plus measure editor (courtesy Voyetra Technologies).

Many of the most commonly used editing commands can also generally be used in the measure editor. By marking certain measures within one track or across several tracks, you should be able to perform such functions as transposition, quantization, velocity scaling, and so forth. The change should affect only the selected measures of the selected tracks.

Graphic Editing

Graphic editors display MIDI messages in a visual format rather than as text. Two popular approaches to graphic editing are the score approach, in which notes are shown on screen as they would appear on manuscript paper, and the "piano-roll" style graphic editor (figure 6.6), where a note symbol's length and position on screen indicate its duration, its pitch, and its time placement in the sequence. Most graphic editors display and work with only note events, while some use different symbols to let you examine and edit non-note MIDI messages as well.

Just as with event editors, some graphic editors permit editing only one track or channel at a time, while others permit editing of all user-specified tracks or channels, with the same advantages and disadvantages to each approach as in event editors.

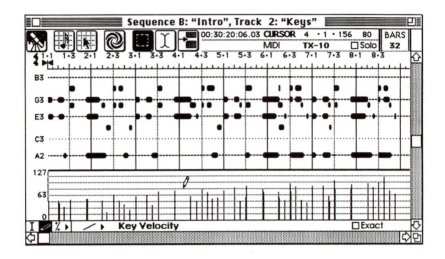

FIGURE 6.6   Vision sequencer "piano-roll" graphic editor (courtesy Opcode Systems, Inc.).

Unlike event editors, which display events as a continuous list of messages in a predetermined format, some graphic editors let you "zoom in" or "zoom out," showing a shorter or longer segment of your piece, so that you can work at the note or region level, as appropriate. (See the next section, "Region Editing," for more.)

Moving a cursor onto the MIDI message of interest should permit you to see or change its parameters. You should be able to specify the rhythmic increments by which the cursor moves so that it will jump smoothly from one note to the next. Generally, by setting the cursor to move in increments of the smallest rhythmic value in your piece, you would be able to edit any event and make homing in on the exact event you want as easy as possible.

Many graphic editor commands involve pointing at a note or segment of the sequence, so a well-designed mouse interface can make graphic editing faster and easier than equivalent cursor control commands. As mentioned above, "test drive" the mouse handling of the sequencers you evaluate if you plan to use a mouse with your computer.

Because each approach has its advantages, many sequencers include both event and graphic editors. Like event editors, though, some graphic editors have limited capabilities. Graphic editors can have all the capabilities of event editors described above, and vice versa. Before you choose your sequencer, try to determine in advance the capabilities you need for the type of music you make. Compare the features in each editor to the ones described here to find out what each sequencer's editor can do and, equally important, what it cannot. That way you will be more likely to choose an editor that meets your needs, without paying for features and capabilities you will not use.

Region Editing

Whether you use an event editor or graphic editor, you may want certain commands to act on more than one message at a time. Region editors let you mark a section within one or more tracks of your recorded sequence, either on the event list or on the graphics screen, then use commands that affect the entire marked region (figure 6.7). Some of the more useful region commands include:

Cut and paste—Mark a region of one or more tracks, then move or copy the marked region to a different location.

Splice—Like an audio tape recorder, some sequencers will let you completely remove the time period during which a marked section is recorded, shortening the overall length of the specified tracks by the length of the section "spliced out," or add the marked section into the middle of specified tracks, lengthening the total duration of those tracks by the duration of the segment "spliced in."

Transpose, invert, and retrograde—Rather than affecting the entire track (as described above under "Track Editing"), transposing, inverting, or retrograding a region affects only the notes in the marked region, leaving the remainder of the specified tracks as they were.

Quantize—By quantizing the notes in a specified region only, you can "clean up" passages with rhythmic inaccuracies without having to rerecord the passage or the entire specified tracks and without changing the rhythmic "feel" of the rest of the sequence.

Velocity change—Just as changing the velocity of a track affects the loudness of each note in the track, changing the MIDI velocity parameter in a marked region affects the loudness of the notes in that region. You may be limited to uniformly changing every note in the specified region by adding a specified amount to its velocity or multiplying each note's velocity by a specified percentage. As with track editing, the most powerful sequencers use region editing for crescendos and diminuendos, letting you specify the starting and ending velocity. The computer adjusts the velocity of each note within the region, progressing from the starting to the ending velocity you set. And as with track editing commands, you may be able to choose a linear or exponential curve for the specified region.

```
 File  Realtime  Mark  GoTo  Edit  Track  View  Settings  KeyMacro
                        ↓1    ┌──────────────────────────────────┐  ↓41
    1 Hat           P  ■···  │ Undo                     Alt-F1  │ ···········  ▲
    2 Kick/snare/tom P  ■■■■  ├──────────────────────────────────┤ ···········
    3 Ride/rim       P  ····  │ Copy...                  F2      │ ··■■···■■··■■
    4 Crash          P  ····  │ Cut...                   Ctrl-F2 │ ■■··········
    5 ─────────────  m  ····  │ Paste...                 Sh-F2   │ ···········
    6 Bass strings   a  ■·■■  │ Paste to One track...    Alt-F2  │ ··■·■■■·■■■·
    7 Bass           P  ■■■■  ├──────────────────────────────────┤ ···········■···■■■
    8 ─────────────  m  ····  │ Quantize...                      │ ···········
    9 Organ          a  ■■■■  │ Interpolate...                   │ ··■■■■■■■■■■
   10 Organ          a  ■■■■  │ Length...                        │ ··■■■■■■■■■■
   11 ─────────────  m  ····  │ Slide...                         │ ··■■■■■■■■■■
 → 12 ElecPiano/Vibes P ····  │ Retrograde...                    │ ··■■■■■■■■■■ ←
   13 ─────────────  m  ····  │ Pitch transpose...               │ ···········
   14 ─────────────  m  ····  │ Velocity scale...                │ ···········
   15 High strings   P  ····  │ Controller fill...               │ ■■■·■■·■·■··
   16 Bass strings   P  ····  │ Fit improvisation                │ ■■·········· ▼
 ┌───────────────────┐ ◄──── └──────────────────────────────────┘
 │Tempo►112 x1.00    │         CAL...                               Main►  5069
 │Meter►4/4   │Play │ Re                                            Scrap►     0
 │Key►C       └─────┘ └──┘    └────┘         IDEA7.WRK              Free►17424
 ┌────────────────────────────────────────────────────────────────────────┐
 │       33:01:000◄From       12:02:000◄Now        33:04:119◄Thru          │
 ◄────────────────────────────────────────────────────────────────────────►
Cakewalk Professional/MQX 3.0 Copyright (c) Greg Hendershott, 1988, 1989
```

FIGURE 6.7 Cakewalk sequencer region edit options (courtesy Twelve Tone Systems, Inc.).

Edit Filters

Whether you are using a track editor, event editor, measure editor, or graphic editor, you should be able to specify criteria for which of the selected events should be affected and which should be ignored. You might, for example, want to raise the velocity of only notes whose velocities fall below a certain threshold so that those notes would no longer be difficult to hear. Notes that were already sufficiently loud would not be affected.

A comprehensive edit filter (figure 6.8) lets you specify not only what type of event to edit—so that you could delete only numbered MIDI controller messages within a certain region—but also what range of values within that message type. With an event filter capable of selecting both event types and value ranges, you could delete Control Change 60 messages only or transpose notes in the highest octave only.

Meter and Tempo Changes

Many sequencers let you set only a single meter and a single tempo, which govern the entire sequence. While this is enough for many composers, you may require more sophisticated control over musical time. Some sequencers provide that control by offering programmable meter and tempo changes within a single sequence and, in some sequencers, within a single track of the sequence.

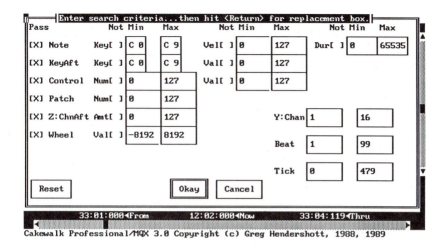

FIGURE 6.8 Cakewalk sequencer edit filters (courtesy Twelve Tone Systems, Inc.).

The most sophisticated sequencers in this respect provide enough flexibility and control over timing during recording that the composer can set up a metronome "click track" that begins, for example, with sixteen bars of $\frac{4}{4}$ meter at a tempo of sixty quarter notes per minute, then changes to a $\frac{3}{4}$ meter at ninety quarter notes per minute for twenty-four bars, then gradually slows over the next twelve bars to seventy-six quarter notes per minute. Once the click track is set up, the metronome will guide the player's performance during recording as usual.

Similarly, the most powerful editors let you change the meter and tempo as often as you like within a single sequence. Some sequencers that let you specify multiple different meters and tempos for different tracks within the sequence even warn you if the bars do not overlap in some regular ratio. Such capabilities might seem unnecessary when you are first learning to use sequencers, but rhythmic flexibility is characteristic of the best music in any genre, and many musicians quickly tire of sequences that are limited to a single meter and tempo throughout.

"Tap-Sync" Timing Control

Some sequencers will let you tap a key on the computer's typewriter keyboard—typically the space bar—and use the tap timing for the sequencer's beats-per-minute metronome control. Minimally implemented, this feature lets you enter metronome control by tapping it in rather than by typing in the number of beats per minute. In its most sophisticated implementation, such a facility will let you change the tempo of a recorded sequence as the sequence plays back, adjusting the recorded sequence's tempo to the taps. Periodic tempo adjustments can help overcome the "mechanical" rhythmic feel that too often characterizes sequencer music, and tap-sync metronome adjustment is one of the easiest ways to accomplish this.

MIDI Program Changes

For any but the simplest MIDI setups and sequences it is important to be able to add MIDI Program Change messages to an existing sequence so that the sequence will cause a specified synthesizer to change its internally stored configuration or "patch" while the sequence is playing back.

MIDI does not specify that any particular program number be assigned to any particular patch, so playing a sequence through different synthesizers usually selects a different patch from each one, sometimes with surprising results. Make sure that there is a way to add, delete, and change Program Change messages within the sequences you have recorded.

If your sequencer has enough tracks, it is often a good idea to record the notes and such non-note data as Program Change messages onto separate tracks. This simplifies editing and also makes it possible to record different Program Change message tracks for each synthesizer you will be using. Another advantage is the ability to record alternative program change tracks, deferring until later the choice of which one to use. If you start to run out of tracks, you can always merge the chosen program change track into the track containing the notes (assuming your sequencer supports track merging—see "Track and Channel Bounce and Merge" below).

System Exclusive Messages

System Exclusive messages are designed and implemented by each manufacturer specifically for its own hardware. For a detailed discussion of System Exclusive messages see chapter 8, "Understanding MIDI Messages." SysEx messages are often used to modify the "patch" information for a particular sound, since the MIDI specification does not address how manufacturers implement their sound generators. Your MIDI hardware has to be able to generate SysEx messages if your sequencer is to record them, so check each synthesizer's or keyboard's documentation.

If your hardware has that capability, being able to record, edit, and play back SysEx messages in your sequencer gives you more control over your MIDI gear. You may never change a patch once it has been selected by a program change, but if you do want to adjust the patch as the sequence plays, a sequencer that can handle SysEx messages can provide a way to manage it automatically.

You can also use your SysEx-recording sequencer as a bulk patch librarian for synthesizers capable of "SysEx dumps," even storing synthesizer patches in the same sequence that contains the notes!

Track and Channel Bounce and Merge

Bouncing data from one track or channel to another lets you make a copy of the data. You might want two different synthesizers to play the same passage in unison, for example. Or you might want to preserve a copy of a track before editing the original. Then, if you are dissatisfied with how the edited results sound, you can erase the track or channel you changed and use the copy with the original version.

Merging lets you combine two or more tracks or channels into one. If you have run out of available tracks or channels, merging will free one up. Or you might record each voice of a polyphonic passage on a separate track, edit each one, then merge them together for playback over a single channel of a polyphonic synthesizer.

Some editors let you bounce or merge specified regions of the tracks or channels, while others are restricted to bouncing or merging the entire tracks or channels. With bounce and merge control over regions, you could record several versions of the same solo, mark the best segments of each version, then bounce and merge them to a single track which would represent the best of all the solos.

PLAYBACK FEATURES

Fast Forward to Mark

By setting a mark—typically a single letter or short name—at a particular point in your sequence, you can subsequently instruct the sequencer to "fast forward" directly to that mark. Most sequencers set marks in the event editor or a separate window, while others also let you set marks on the fly, usually by pressing a key on the computer's typewriter keyboard during playback when you hear the start of the segment you want to mark.

Fast Forward Cuing

Some sequencers, like some tape recorders, let you listen to your recording at faster or slower than normal speed—typically, double or half speed. You should be able to cue from one mark to another, or from the beginning of the sequence onwards. This feature can be a great help when you are trying to locate a particular passage but are not sure where to look for it in the event editor or graphic editor. You can listen at faster than normal speed while you locate the general area you are looking for, switch to normal speed as you approach the precise segment, then to slow speed as you home in on the precise event. Even if fast forward cuing is not implemented as a convenient special feature, you can achieve the same effect by manually changing the tempo (see below).

Tempo Change

The ability to easily change the tempo of recorded passages is one of the great advantages sequencers have over tape recorders, for, unlike tape, changing the tempo of a recorded passage does not change the pitch or timbre of the recorded music. Some sequencers let you "preview" tempo changes while the recorded sequence plays, temporarily changing the tempo from the one built into the sequence. Changing tempo during playback can help you more quickly find the right tempo for a recorded sequence or judge the effects of tempo changes within the sequence.

Solo and Mute

As sequences become more complex, using multiple channels and multiple tracks, you may want to select which tracks you want to hear played back at different times. Setting one track of your multitrack sequence to solo lets you hear only that one track on playback. Some sequencers only allow a single track to be soloed, while other sequencers permit multiple solo tracks on playback.

Muting a track, on the other hand, causes the sequencer to suppress that track on playback. Most sequencers that incorporate muting will let you mute as many tracks at one time as you like, so you can simulate soloing on sequencers that provide only muting by muting all except the track you want to hear.

Channel Reassignment

You may often want to redirect the output of a track to a MIDI channel other than that over which it was recorded. Make sure your sequencer provides an easy way to do this—generally a playback "switch" that can be set to the desired channel or channels.

STANDARD MIDI FILES

Although all MIDI sequencer software records similar data, the original MIDI specification did not address the specific placement and arrangement of data, or format, in which MIDI message data is stored in disk files. As a result, each sequencer used its own unique file storage format. The result was incompatibility among sequencers and frustration for sequencer users who could not exchange sequence files among different sequencer programs. And becoming "locked in" to a particular file format made it harder to switch sequencers or upgrade to a better one without losing access to your previous work.

As so often happens, a de facto standard MIDI sequence file format arose. Several sequencer programmers followed the lead of MIDI software developer Opcode Systems, who early on campaigned for a common sequence file format. Eventually, their efforts were recognized by the MIDI Manufacturer's Association, which in 1988 formally adopted Standard MIDI Files (SMF) as an addendum to the MIDI specification. (The Appendix to this book contains only the overview and tables from the MIDI specification itself. To get a copy of the Standard MIDI Files specification or other addenda, contact the International MIDI Association, whose address is listed in chapter 11.)

Most sequencer programs still use proprietary formats as their primary means of storing MIDI data but provide the option of storing that data as a Standard MIDI File (often called exporting) or reading in a sequence stored in SMF format (importing) so that the user can take advantage of SMF compatibility among different sequencers as necessary (figure 6.9). Some sequencers always store data in their proprietary format but provide special programs that convert files from that format to SMF format, and vice versa.

The Standard MIDI Files specification defines those elements that are common to all sequencers, ignoring those elements such as looping and interpolation curves, which are implemented in a unique fashion by each sequencer.

Musicians can now exchange sequences almost as easily as composers can exchange scores, provided that all parties to the exchange use sequencers that support Standard MIDI Files. If so, they can exchange diskettes with sequences stored on them (provided both computers use the same diskette storage format) or communicate computer to computer over telephone lines, using telephone modems connected to the computers at each end.

At its most basic, SMF permits musicians to transfer sequence files between two different sequencer programs that adhere to the SMF

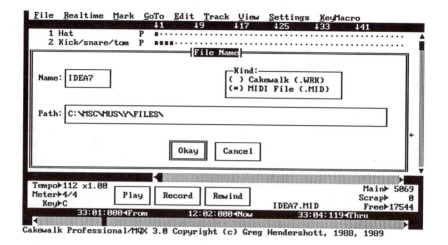

FIGURE 6.9   Cakewalk sequencer MIDI files option (courtesy Twelve Tone Systems, Inc.).

specification. This permits different musicians to collaborate on a single sequence or a single musician to work on a sequence using several different sequencer programs, taking advantage of the unique strengths of each.

By extension, a musician with a modem-equipped computer and appropriate telecommunications software can upload a Standard MIDI File to a computer bulletin board system, where other musicians can retrieve it, permitting collaboration by musicians who are separated by distance or time. (For more on modems, telecommunications, and computer bulletin board systems, see chapter 11, "Getting Help.")

SMF Structure

Standard MIDI Files consist of groups of data called chunks. Each chunk consists of a four-character chunk identifier, a 32-bit value specifying the length (in bytes) of the chunk, and the actual chunk data.

Two chunk types are currently in use: header chunks and track chunks. Other chunk types may be introduced in subsequent extensions of the SMF specification, so programs must be able to recognize unknown chunk identifiers and ignore them.

The header chunk is always at the very beginning of a Standard MIDI File, beginning with four bytes representing the ASCII symbols for the letters "MThd." (Those letters, like the letters "MTrk" that begin a MIDI track chunk, were chosen arbitrarily and have no particular significance.

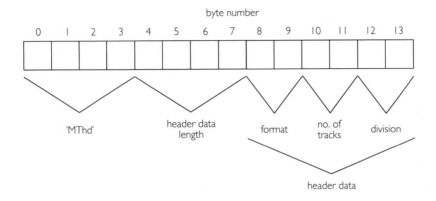

byte number

0 1 2 3 4 5 6 7 8 9 10 11 12 13

'MThd'   header data
           length   format   no. of   division
                                 tracks

header data

FIGURE 6.10   Standard MIDI Files header chunk format.

They simply identify a chunk as a header or track chunk, respectively.)
Header data includes the file format, number of tracks, and division (figure
6.10). The number of tracks simply indicates how many track chunks
follow in the file; format and division are discussed below.

Formats

The SMF specification defines three different formats,
called Format 0, 1, and 2. Each contains different numbers and types of
tracks, though the MIDI data in each is largely the same for all three
formats.

Format 0, the simplest of the three, consists of a single multichannel
track. Tempo maps are included within the single track, so sequencer
tempo map readers must ignore MIDI events included among the tempo
data.

Format 1 consists of several tracks, played back simultaneously, each of
which has meters and tempos that occur concurrently. The first track of a
Format 1 SMF contains the tempo map that is used for all subsequent
tracks of the file. Most sequencers that are organized as multiple tracks of
MIDI data are likely to use Format 1 for their implementation of Standard
MIDI Files.

Format 2 incorporates any number of independent tracks, each with its
own unique meters and tempos. It provides for tremendous versatility and
flexibility—more than any sequencer to date has chosen to implement!
For now, Format 2 is not much more than a curiosity, but it is an example
of the foresight shown by the developers of the MIDI specification and a
challenge to designers of the next generation of sequencer software.

Division

The division value can be interpreted in either of two ways, corresponding to quarter-note timing resolution or SMPTE synchronization protocol. Figure 6.11 shows the allocation of bits within each interpretation of the two-byte division value.

If the most significant bit of the two-byte division value is 0, the remaining fifteen bits specify the timing resolution of a quarter note. A 1 in the most significant bit of the two-byte division value specifies a SMPTE frame rate and frame division. The remaining seven bits of the most significant byte represent either 24, 25, 30, or 29, corresponding to the four most common SMPTE frame rates—twenty-four, twenty-five, or thirty frames per second, or thirty frames per second "drop-frame" format, respectively.

The least significant byte of that same two-byte division value specifies the division of each SMPTE frame—4 for quarter-frame MIDI Time Code, 80 for full SMPTE resolution. (For a discussion of MIDI Time Code and SMPTE synchronization, see chapter 9, "Synchronization.")

Track Chunks

(The following discussion will likely be confusing to those who are not already familiar with MIDI messages, which are discussed fully in chapter 8, "Understanding MIDI Messages." In that case, you may want to look ahead to that chapter now for an overview of MIDI messages or skip this section and come back to it after you have read chapter 8.)

A track chunk contains everything needed to describe one complete sequencer track. A track chunk begins with four bytes representing the ASCII symbols for the letters "MTrk", followed by four bytes specifying the length (in bytes) of the track data to follow, followed by the data itself (figure 6.12). Each track chunk data element is a MIDI message, differing from a normal MIDI message only in that each is preceded by a delta time, which specifies how much time has elapsed since the previous track event. Each MIDI message and its delta time is called a track event, representing a MIDI event, a system exclusive event, or a meta-event—special data such as timing, key signature, or track name.

The most common track events are MIDI channel messages such as the Note On or Note Off message, with or without Running Status. Only MIDI channel messages occur in Standard MIDI Files — most system messages, which govern real-time occurrences, do not make sense in a stored file.

Delta Times

As mentioned above, each track event begins with its delta time, the elapsed time since the preceding track event. Since delta

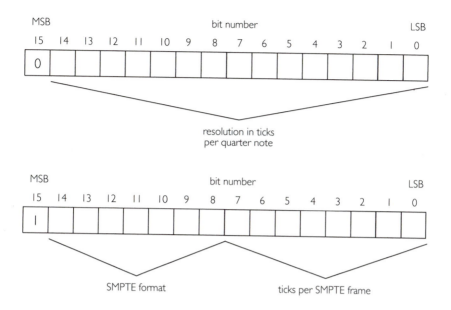

FIGURE 6.11 Standard MIDI Files division value format.

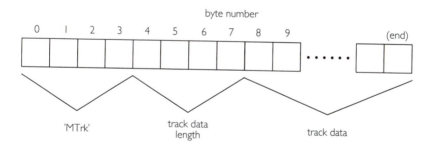

FIGURE 6.12 Standard MIDI Files track chunk format.

times may be values of indeterminate size, the number of bytes needed to represent a delta time depends on its size.

The most significant bit of each delta time byte is used as a signal—an MSB of 1 indicates that more delta time bytes follow; an MSB of 0 specifies the last delta time byte.

Since the MSB of the eight-bit value is used as a signal, the delta time data bytes must be regrouped from a series of eight-bit values to a similar series of seven-bit values, to which the appropriate MSB is attached.

For example, if 267 clock ticks (specified by a positive resolution value— see above) have passed since the preceding track event, the delta time would be represented as follows:

267 decimal	=	00000001 00001011 binary
regrouped by seven bits		00 0000010 0001011
add MSB: 0 for last (rightmost) byte, 1 for all others		10000010 00001011
delta time	=	820B hexadecimal

If only thirty-eight clock ticks had passed, the delta time would be represented as:

38 decimal	=	00100110 binary
regrouped by seven bits		0100110
add MSB: 0 for last (rightmost) byte, 1 for all others		00100110
delta time	=	26 hexadecimal

These two examples use small delta times for the sake of simplicity, but because each delta time byte except the last has 1 for its MSB, SMF software simply reads delta time bytes until a 0 MSB is encountered, then strips off the MSBs and reassembles the delta time from the remaining data. A delta time may theoretically be as large as necessary and use as many bytes as needed to represent it.

Although a variable-length delta time representation allows for unlimited delta times, the SMF specification currently limits delta times to values that can be represented by a maximum of four bytes. This should be plenty: At 240 beats per minute and a resolution of 1,128 clock ticks per quarter note, the maximum delta time would last almost a week.

SysEx Messages in Standard MIDI Files

System Exclusive messages can be included in an SMF track chunk. System Exclusive messages affect only specific equipment made by a specific manufacturer. Like channel messages, when SysEx messages are used as an SMF track event, they are preceded by a delta time.

In addition to the delta time, there is another difference between the format of a regular SysEx message and one stored as an SMF track event. According to the MIDI specification (as discussed in chapter 8), a SysEx message begins with a byte whose value is F0 and ends with one whose value is F7 (both values expressed in hexadecimal format), with the intervening bytes representing the actual SysEx data values. In an SMF SysEx

byte number

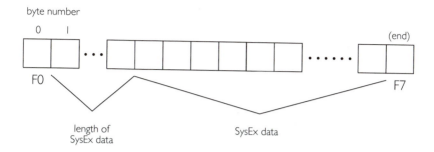

FIGURE 6.13   Standard MIDI Files SysEx track event format.

track event, a variable length value representing the length (in bytes) of the data to follow is inserted immediately after the F0 byte, which signals the start of the SysEx message. That length value includes the end-of-message F7 byte in its count of the bytes to follow. Figure 6.13 shows the structure of a system exclusive track event.

Since SysEx data lengths vary from one sequence to another and can range from a few to many thousands of bytes, Standard MIDI Files encode the SysEx data length value in the same fashion as variable-length delta times, discussed above.

Meta-Events

A Standard MIDI File containing only the data described so far would specify a workable sequence, but the SMF specification also includes meta-events, providing facilities for such things as track names, lyrics, key signatures, and instrument names. Following the delta time, a meta-event begins with a byte whose value is FF (hexadecimal), followed by a one-byte event type, followed by a variable length value representing the length (in bytes) of the meta-event data which follows, followed by the meta-event data itself.

More than a dozen meta-event types are already defined, and a total of 128 meta-event types may eventually become part of the SMF specification, so a program that uses Standard MIDI Files must be prepared for meta-event types it does not recognize. For a current list of all meta-event types and data formats in the SMF specification, contact the International MIDI Association.

Programming with Standard MIDI Files

One of the great advantages of SMF is the opportunities it affords MIDI programmers. With an understanding of SMF, a MIDI programmer can add features to extend the capabilities of existing sequencer software by manipulating the files the sequencer stores in SMF format, or create special SMF sequences for playback by any sequencer that supports the Standard MIDI Files specification.

Figure 6.14 shows a complete Format 0 file, including Header chunk and Track chunk, meta-events, and Note On/Note Off events.

OTHER CONSIDERATIONS

Synchronization

The subject of synchronization is important enough and complex enough that it is covered separately in chapter 9. Still, for the purposes of evaluating sequencers, certain features regarding synchronization are particularly important.

A sequencer can provide the clock pulse to which other events can be synchronized, in which case it functions as the master. Or, the sequencer can synchronize its events according to a clock pulse provided by another program or device, in which case it becomes the slave. In order to assume either role, the sequencer must be able to synchronize its events to its own internal clock or to a clock signal provided by the external source. Any sequencer capable of synchronization will provide both internal and external clock options.

The most common synchronization clock type is called MIDI Clock. To synchronize other MIDI equipment such as a drum machine to your sequencer, set the sequencer's clock to Internal and the other equipments clock to External. To synchronize your sequencer to external equipment, set the sequencer's clock to External and use the Internal setting on the other piece of gear, which then provides the master clock.

A more precise synchronization scheme was formulated by the Society of Motion Picture and Television Editors. SMPTE time code is divided into hours, minutes, seconds, and frames. If you plan to synchronize your music to film or videotape, you will need a sequencer that can calculate and display time in terms of SMPTE time code, as well as a device that can generate and read SMPTE time code and convert between it and MIDI.

For more information about synchronizing to tape, multitrack tape recording, and converting between clock types, see chapter 9, "Synchronization."

Extensibility

Recognizing that no sequencer is likely to meet all the needs of every composer, a few sequencers have provided a way by which

HEADER CHUNK DATA
(in hexadecimal)

data	interpretation
4D 54 68 64	MThd
00 00 00 06	chunk length—6 bytes
00 00	format—0
00 01	tracks—1
00 60	resolution—96 ppqn

TRACK CHUNK DATA
(in hexadecimal)

data	interpretation
4D 54 72 6B	MTrk
00 00 00 40	chunk length—64 bytes

delta	track event	interpretation	musical meaning
00	FF 59 02 00 00	Key Signature meta event	C major
00	FF 58 04 03 02 18 08	Time Signature meta event	3/4 meter
00	FF 51 03 16 E3 60	Tempo meta event—500,000 microseconds/quarter note	quarter note = 120
00	90 45 40	Note On, channel 1, note=69, vel=64	A, octave 4, medium loud
81 40	45 00	(Running Status) note=69, vel=0, delta=192	release A4 after half note
00	2B 40	(Running Status) note=43, vel=64	G, octave 2, medium loud
60	2B 00	(Running Status) note=43, vel=0, delta=96	release G2 after quarter note
00	24 40	(Running Status) note=36, vel=64	chord: C, octave 2, medium loud
00	3C 40	(Running Status) note=60, vel=64	C, octave 4, medium loud
00	3F 40	(Running Status) note=63, vel=64	D♯, octave 4, medium loud
00	43 40	(Running Status) note=67, vel=64	G, octave 4, medium loud
81 40	24 00	(Running Status) note=36, vel=0, delta=192	chord: release C2 after half note
00	3C 00	(Running Status) note=60, vel=0	release C4 after half note
00	3F 00	(Running Status) note=63, vel=0	release D♯4 after half note
00	43 00	(Running Status) note=67, vel=0	release G4 after half note
60	FF 2F 00	End of Track meta-event, delta=96	end after quarter note rest

FIGURE 6.14   A complete Format 0 Standard MIDI File.

users who are not afraid to tackle the task of writing computer programs can add the features they want. The most common programming languages supported are LISP and C, though a very few sequencers permit extensions in the more widely used BASIC programming language.

A word of warning, though. Most sequencer authors rightly fear the damage that a careless or unskilled programmer can inflict on their program code and do not allow users the chance to "improve" on their work. If your sequencer does provide "hooks" that you can use to program new features into it, make a backup copy of the original program disks before you start tinkering with the code. No matter how good a programmer you think you are, a backup copy can return your program to the state it was in before you introduced your "improvements," and that backup can save you from embarrassment or worse.

MIDI is a wide-open field for programmers, and chapter 10, "Programming in MIDI," will tell you what you need to get started.

GETTING IT ALL TO WORK TOGETHER

. . . .

In planning for any computer system, the rule is "Choose the software, then find hardware to run it on." Planning a MIDI system is no different, whether or not you plan to include a personal computer in your MIDI setup. Make a list of the features and capabilities that are important to you, ranked in order of importance. You may not be able to afford everything you want, but by developing priorities you should be able to choose equipment that will fit your budget and fulfill your most important needs.

A priority list might include:

eight-voice multitimbral polyphony

a velocity-sensitive keyboard controller

a large-capacity sequencer with the capabilities that are most important to you

particularly good piano sounds and brass sounds

an editor/librarian for the synthesizer, for creating new sounds and managing sound banks

Armed with your list of needs and wants, you can compare different options such as a MIDI workstation or integrated keyboard synthesizer with built-in sequencer; separate keyboard controller, synthesizer, and hardware sequencer; or keyboard synthesizer and personal computer with sequencer software. You will learn the costs, trade-offs, and limitations involved in your selection and be able to make an informed decision rather than selecting equipment first and finding out only later that the equipment you have chosen lacks the one feature you most needed or wanted.

If you are buying two MIDI devices that work together as a system, such as a controller and synthesizer, both must implement a particular feature if you want to be able to use that feature. If your controller transmits aftertouch data, for example, and your synthesizer does not respond to aftertouch, the resulting sounds will not be affected by aftertouch control.

MIDI IMPLEMENTATION CHARTS

Fortunately, there is an easy way to predict most such implementation incompatibilities—the MIDI implementation chart. Most manufacturers include an implementation chart with their MIDI equipment; the chart is one of the best ways to compare the features of MIDI devices. Keep the chart for each device in your MIDI network, and make them part of your system's principal reference materials. Figure 7.1 shows a MIDI implementation chart for a typical keyboard controller, while figure 7.2 shows a MIDI implementation chart chart for a typical synthesizer.

The leftmost column of each chart, labeled Function, lists the categories of MIDI messages that are generally used by MIDI devices of that type (and, sometimes, messages commonly used by MIDI equipment—even if those features are not appropriate to that particular device). The second column, Transmitted, indicates whether that particular type of MIDI data is transmitted by the device. All incoming signals are normally passed through the MIDI Thru jack of a device; the Transmitted column indicates whether such a signal originates within the device for transmission at the MIDI Out jack. The third column, Recognized, indicates whether the device will respond to a particular type of incoming MIDI data. Any MIDI device can receive any type of MIDI message, but a particular device can respond only to certain categories of messages. Finally, a fourth column lists remarks. The remarks might describe the way a particular message is handled or indicate how the device interprets the message.

For each message type, there will be an "o" in the Transmitted column if the device transmits that message type or an "x" if the device does not transmit that message type. An "o" or "x" in the Recognized column similarly indicates whether the device can or cannot act upon that message type.

In order for two devices to use a certain type of MIDI message, both devices must implement the message. For example, the controller's implementation chart in figure 7.1 shows an "o" in the Transmitted column

FUNCTION		TRANSMITTED	RECOGNIZED	REMARKS
Basic Channel	Default Changed	1–16 1–16	all ch x	
Mode	Default Messages Altered	3 or 4 OMNI OFF,M,P	x OMNI OFF,M,P	
Note Number	True Voice	22–108	0–127	‛
Velocity	Note ON Note OFF	o 9n v = 1–127 x 9n v = 0	o o	
After Touch	Keys Channels	o o	o o	
Pitch Bender			o	o
Control Change	1 64 67 1–121	o o o o	o	
Program Change	True #	o (0–127)	o 0–127	
System Exclusive		x	o	‛
System Common	Song Pos Song Sel Tune	x x x	o o o	
System Real Time	Clock Commands	o o	o o	
Aux Messages	Local ON OFF All Notes OFF Active Sense Reset	x o (123) o x	o o (123–127) o x	
Notes		Recognized messages are only merged into MIDI Out.		

FIGURE 7.1 A MIDI implementation chart for a typical keyboard controller.

for key aftertouch messages, but the synthesizer's implementation chart in figure 7.2 shows an "x" in the Recognized column for key aftertouch messages. Since both devices do not implement key aftertouch, the resulting sounds can be affected by channel aftertouch control only since both charts show an "o" for channel aftertouch. You will be able to hear sounds with key aftertouch response only if the controller (which generates MIDI messages) can transmit key aftertouch and the synthesizer (which acts on incoming MIDI messages) can recognize key aftertouch.

SETTING UP THE HARDWARE

The more planning you do before setting up a MIDI studio, the more efficient it will be to work in and the less you will need to move components around later. If you typically use a particular keyboard or other device as the primary controller, make sure it is readily accessible and located close to the first device its signal will be routed to.

If your MIDI setup involves a computer, it too should be easy to reach. The keyboard should be located at a convenient height and the monitor should be easily visible from any work station.

Connecting the Cables

The most important requirement for successful system setup is an understanding of signal flow, the transmission of streams of MIDI data from one device to another. A MIDI port either transmits or receives data, never both. MIDI data travels in one direction only over a particular MIDI cable.

A cable connected to a MIDI In port must carry data destined for that port. Data received at a MIDI In port is passed to the microprocessor of the device the MIDI In port is attached to. Any device that receives MIDI data must have one or more MIDI In ports.

A cable connected to a MIDI Out port carries data away from that port, for transmission to the MIDI In port of a second device. With such a data flow, the first device can control the second or send the second device data to store or process.

With an understanding of signal flow and the single purpose of any MIDI port, cabling two devices together is a simple matter. Every properly connected MIDI cable passes data from a MIDI port that transmits the data to a MIDI port that receives it.

If one device (the master) is to control another (the slave), like a keyboard controller and a synthesizer, a single cable connects the MIDI

FUNCTION		TRANSMITTED	RECOGNIZED	REMARKS
Basic	Default	1–16	1–16	memorized
Channel	Changed	1–16	1–16	
	Default	x	1,2,3,4	memorized
Mode	Messages		Poly, Mono	
	Altered		x	
Note		x	0–127	
Number	:True Voice	x	13–108	
Velocity	Note ON	x	o vel = 1–127	
	Note OFF	x	x	
After	Keys	x	x	
Touch	Channels	x	o	
Pitch Bender		x	o 0–12 semitones	
	1	x	o	modwheel
	2	x	o	breath control
	4	x	o	foot control
Control	5	x	o	portamento
				time
Change	7	x	o	volume
	10	x	o	pan
	64	x	o	sustain
	65	x	o	portamento
Program		o (0–127)	o 0–127	
Change	True #		0–183	
System Exclusive		o	o	voice
				parameter
System	Song Pos	x	x	
	Song Sel	x	x	
Common	Tune	x	x	
System	Clock	x	x	
Real Time	Commands	x	x	
Aux	Local ON OFF	x	o	
	All Notes OFF	x	o (123,126,127)	
Messages	Active Sense	x	o	
	Reset	x	x	
Notes				

FIGURE 7.2   A MIDI implementation chart for a typical synthesizer.

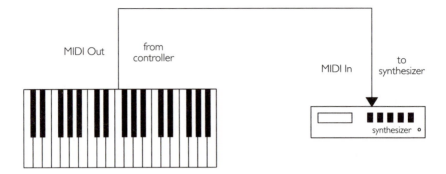

FIGURE 7.3   MIDI data flow between a keyboard controller and a rack-mount synthesizer.

Out port on the master to the MIDI In port of the slave. Figure 7.3 illustrates the signal flow between a keyboard controller (the master) and a rackmount synthesizer (the slave).

If two devices must exchange signals, like a keyboard synthesizer and sequencer during recording and playback, a second cable is necessary. One transmits data from the keyboard's MIDI Out to the sequencer's MIDI In during recording, and a second cable transmits data from the sequencer's MIDI Out to the synthesizer's MIDI In during playback. Figure 7.4 illustrates the signal flow between a hardware sequencer, which both records and transmits data, and a keyboard synthesizer, which both generates and receives data.

When two devices exchange signals in this manner, the possibility of MIDI feedback exists. If the keyboard synthesizer transmits a message, the message the sequencer receives may be retransmitted out the sequencer's MIDI Out port back to the synthesizer's MIDI In port. This can cause every note played by the keyboard to be sounded twice. To turn off retransmission by the sequencer, set the value of its Patch Thru or Keyboard Thru command to off. An alternative is to switch the synthesizer's Local Control to off so that only the echo note is heard, not the note the keyboard originally plays.

An even worse type of MIDI feedback can take place with a very few MIDI synthesizers and drum machines that implement a combined MIDI Out and Thru port. If such a synthesizer's Patch Thru is switched on and the sequencer is also retransmitting MIDI data, an infinite feedback loop can result.

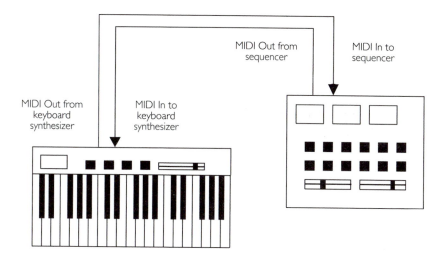

FIGURE 7.4   MIDI data flow between a hardware sequencer and a keyboard synthesizer.

Connecting Multiple Devices

You cannot connect one master device to two slaves with a Y-connector, as you would an audio signal. MIDI is a 5 milliamp current-loop circuit; splitting a MIDI cable would cause the current to drop by half in each cable after the split, rendering the signals unreadable. Instead, MIDI data can be transmitted sequentially from one slave to the next using MIDI Thru ports.

A MIDI Thru port copies signals received at the MIDI In port of the same device and retransmits them to the MIDI In of the next device. Since the signal is copied and retransmitted without being sent to the device's microprocessor, the device adds no data to the signal at its Thru port.

If each device in a MIDI system has a MIDI Thru port, they can be connected in a daisy chain network. Signals at the MIDI Out jack of the originating device—keyboard, sequencer, computer, or controller—are connected to the MIDI In jack of the first responding device. Signals at the MIDI Thru jack of that responding device are connected to the MIDI In jack of the next responding device, and so on for each successive responding device in the chain. Figure 7.5 shows the MIDI data signal flow from a hardware sequencer (or computer) controlling several rack-mount synthesizers in such a daisy chain network.

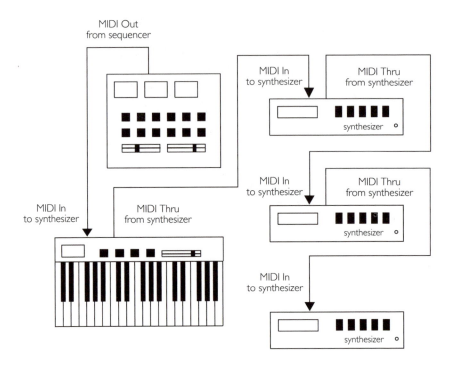

FIGURE 7.5 Signal flow diagram of a daisy chain network.

MIDI Thru Boxes and MIDI Patch Bays

Most MIDI devices have MIDI Thru connectors, even though the MIDI specification does not require it. If only one of your devices lacks a MIDI Thru port, it can be placed at the end of the daisy chain. If more than one device lacks a Thru port, or if you want the flexibility of being able to reconfigure your MIDI setup by pressing a few buttons or switches, you will need to buy a MIDI Thru box or MIDI patch bay.

A MIDI Thru box (figure 7.6) takes the incoming signal at its MIDI In port and replicates it, distributing first generation copies to its multiple MIDI Thru ports. Figure 7.7 shows the MIDI data signal flow in the same MIDI setup as in figure 7.5, but using a MIDI Thru box instead of daisy chaining.

MIDI patch bays (not to be confused with MIDI-controlled audio patch bays) have multiple MIDI In ports and multiple MIDI Thru ports. A MIDI patch bay acts like a "traffic controller," routing data from a set of specified MIDI devices to other devices according to a particular set of instructions, or program, that can be set using the unit's front panel. Most MIDI patch

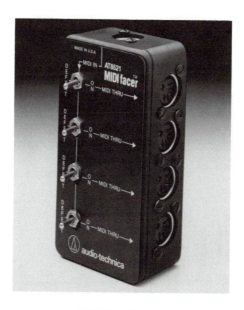

FIGURE 7.6 AT8521 MIDIfacer MIDI Thru box (courtesy Audio-Technica U.S., Inc.).

bays permit these setups to be called up via MIDI Program Change messages from another MIDI device.

A POTENTIAL PROBLEM—"MIDI LAG"

Daisy chaining MIDI devices will not normally cause appreciable delays in the transmission of MIDI signals down the chain. The time it takes for electrical signals to pass down MIDI cables is negligible. Furthermore, each device in the MIDI chain copies the MIDI signal electrically as it comes in through the device's MIDI In port, passing the copied signal directly to its MIDI Thru port. Thus, computation time by the devices' central processors is not a factor.

When devices in the chain act upon the MIDI signal in some way, however, a perceptible MIDI lag may develop as the computation time accumulates. Such devices may include MIDI mergers and MIDI message filters (discussed below), MIDI patch bays that include optional filtering, and computers running sequencer software with Patch Thru switched on. Unlike a piece of MIDI hardware, a computer must process incoming MIDI messages in order to retransmit them.

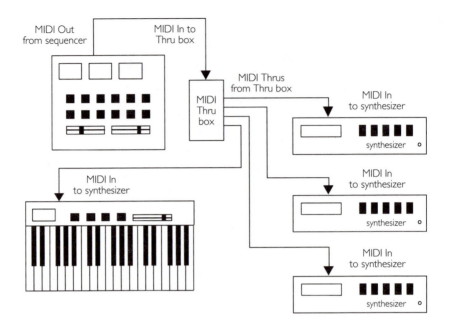

FIGURE 7.7   Signal flow diagram using a MIDI Thru box.

Occasionally the varying response times of synthesizers may create an illusion of MIDI lag. Synthesizers may take from 2 to 12 milliseconds (thousandths of a second) to produce a sound after receiving a Note On message. If the slowest synthesizers are positioned at the end of a MIDI daisy chain, the user may be fooled into thinking a MIDI lag problem has occurred. In addition, sounds with slow attacks become audible later than sounds with fast attacks.

If varying response or attack times are a problem, you may want to buy a MIDI delay device. These can be used to introduce a slight delay in the MIDI signals sent to the faster synthesizers so that they sound at the same time as the slower ones. An alternative if you are using a sequencer is to edit in a tiny offset delay at the beginning of the tracks being sent to the faster synthesizers.

ANOTHER POTENTIAL PROBLEM—"MIDI CHOKE"

The MIDI specification established 31,250 baud, a measure of transmission speed, as the rate at which messages must be transmitted over a MIDI cable. Each MIDI message can be made up of one or a great many MIDI words; it takes 320 microseconds for MIDI to transmit a word. Thus, there is a limit to the number of messages per second that the cable can effectively carry.

If the only messages are Note On and Note Off messages, with perhaps an occasional Program Change message, the message volume is low enough that MIDI choke does not usually occur unless you attempt to play back a thick sequenced passage at a superhumanly fast tempo.

But certain types of messages, such as continuous controller data, can occur hundreds of times each second. If each of several MIDI devices transmits several different types of continuous controller messages at the same time, the system can become overloaded with message traffic, as the volume of messages exceeds the capability of the cable to transmit them all. MIDI choke or MIDI clog describes that condition, and it can be solved only by cutting down the traffic of message flow.

In a daisy-chain MIDI network, continuous controller messages transmitted by any device in the network are transmitted to all devices farther along the chain. If the continuous controller messages from one device need to go only to the next device in the chain, the copies of those messages are still passed along and add to the message traffic, even if they are no longer needed.

A MIDI filter removes unwanted messages. Some MIDI patch bays and most sequencers include filtering capability, or the MIDI filter can be a separate device with a single MIDI In port and a single MIDI Out port. Whatever its form, the filter is programmable so that you can specify which message types to filter out and which to let pass through.

Once a MIDI filter is inserted into the chain, it gobbles up any messages it is programmed to filter out, passing along only what is left. MIDI devices farther along the chain than the MIDI filter, then, receive less data, and the likelihood of MIDI choke is lessened.

COMBINING TWO MIDI DATA STREAMS

Just as a cable carrying MIDI Out data cannot be split like audio Y-cables, two MIDI In message streams cannot be merged using Y-cables, either. Each message must be properly synchronized, and a cable alone cannot provide the synchronization. In addition, a single MIDI command may consist of anything from two bytes of data to thousands of bytes. Once a message starts it cannot be interrupted, and each cable in the Y has no way to judge when the other's messages are finished. Furthermore, using a Y-cable could result in electrical feedback and damage to the equipment.

Instead, a MIDI merger is used to merge incoming signals from two MIDI devices into a single MIDI data stream. If, for instance, a performer using a keyboard controller and a second performer using a woodwind controller want to share a single multitimbral synthesizer, each can connect a cable from their instrument's MIDI Out to the MIDI In of the merger. A cable from the merger's MIDI Out is connected to the MIDI In of the synthesizer. The MIDI data from the two performers will be merged into a single data stream. If each performer's controller is set to a different channel and the synthesizer is set to Mode 4, as described in the following section, the single data stream transmitted from the MIDI merger can control two synthesizer voices, one for each controller, at the same time.

SELECTING CHANNELS AND MODES

A single MIDI cable can carry data over as many as sixteen different channels at once, just as a single telephone cable can route each of many messages to its particular destination simultaneously. Many MIDI messages include a channel number as part of the message, and the channel number can be used to route the message to a particular device.

Do not confuse MIDI channels with sequencer tracks, which specify different data storage areas within the sequencer hardware or computer memory. A sequencer may use a few, a few dozen, or a few hundred tracks, but before transmitting its data the sequencer must assign each track (or, optionally, each message) to one of MIDI's sixteen channels.

Channels do not designate data storage areas but data communication paths. If several synthesizers are connected to a sequencer, for example, each synthesizer can be assigned a specific channel, and as the sequencer transmits messages over all the channels, a particular synthesizer will respond only to those incoming messages tagged with its own channel, ignoring all other incoming messages.

Similarly, if a sequencer is driving a multitimbral synthesizer, each of the timbres can be assigned to a specific channel within the synthesizer. As the sequencer sends data to the synthesizer, the data messages can specify which channel the message is intended for, and only that channel of the synthesizer will respond.

There may be many devices in a MIDI system, and we might want each one to respond to messages only on a specific channel. Alternatively, we might want some or all of the devices to respond to any message, regardless of its channel. The MIDI specification designates four different modes, each of which describes a different way that a MIDI device responds to messages that include a channel specification.

Each mode indicates how many channels the device will respond to and how many notes it can respond to over its specified channel(s). The four modes are determined by two messages: Omni On/Off and Poly/Mono. Omni On specifies that the device will respond to messages regardless of their channel, while Omni Off specifies that the device will respond to incoming messages only on specific channels. Poly or Mono specify whether the device can respond to multiple notes per channel or only one note per channel, respectively.

The combination of Omni On/Off and Poly/Mono yields four possible configurations, each of which is designated in the MIDI specification by a mode number. Mode 1, Omni On/Poly, is the simplest to use. If both a master and slave device are set to Mode 1, the slave will respond to any data transmitted by the master, regardless of the channel number. Furthermore, the slave will receive and respond to as many different notes at once as the master transmits, up to the limits of the polyphonic capability of the slave.

Mode 1 is most useful when setting up, testing, or trouble-shooting a MIDI setup because it eliminates any considerations of channel or polyphony. If two devices are cabled together properly and the slave is set to Omni On/Poly, the slave should respond to notes transmitted by the master over any channel.

In Mode 2, Omni On/Mono, the slave will still respond to notes transmitted by the master regardless of their channel assignment, but the slave will respond to only one note at a time, no matter how many notes the master sends at once and no matter how many notes the slave is capable of producing at once. This mode has little purpose and is rarely used. It limits the very capabilities we want from a polyphonic device, so many MIDI devices no longer implement Mode 2.

In Omni Off/Poly, Mode 3, the slave no longer responds to incoming messages irrespective of their channel. Instead, the slave responds only to messages transmitted over a specified channel. Within that channel, the slave will receive and respond to as many different notes at once as the master transmits, up to the limits of the polyphonic capability of the slave. The most important consideration in using Mode 3 is that the master and slave must communicate over the same channel if the slave is to respond.

Mode 4, Omni Off/Mono, is perhaps the most powerful of the four. A multitimbral synthesizer set to Mode 4 can assign a particular synthesizer voice to each of its MIDI channels. Most MIDI messages contain a channel "tag" within the message, so a single multitimbral synthesizer in Mode 4 can route each incoming message to its specific channel, which is assigned a particular voice. The number of different voice timbres that can sound at once are limited only by MIDI's sixteen channels and the synthesizer's polyphonic capacity.

Although Mode 4 originally meant that each channel would respond monophonically, synthesizer manufacturers have extended the meaning of Mode 4 to include polyphony within each channel voice. This extended version of Mode 4 is often called Multi Mode.

CONFIGURING THE SOFTWARE

If a computer is part of your MIDI setup, it too is a MIDI device and should be treated accordingly. Start by making sure that each cable is connected to the proper port on the computer's MIDI interface. In addition, each software program must be configured, just as a hardware device performing the same function would be.

Most often, that involves setting channel and mode assignments, volume, and MIDI Thru status. In addition, you may need to set the software's clock assignment (see chapter 9, "Synchronization"), timebase (in MIDI clock ticks per quarter note), master tuning, or other parameters.

TROUBLE-SHOOTING

Be prepared for trouble before it begins by periodically backing up the data from any device that permits backup. Some MIDI devices include floppy disks, some use RAM cards or data cartridges, some interface to a computer for backup, and some can back up only to data cassette.

Regardless of the backup medium, there is only one rule governing backups—do it. By making system backups a regular part of your routine, you will ensure that when the inevitable problems occur they will only slow you down, not wipe you out.

If a problem occurs and you cannot determine which device is causing the problem, the cables are the best place to begin. MIDI cables probably cause more problems than any other part of a MIDI system.

Start with the device where the MIDI data originates—often a keyboard controller or sequencer. Follow the cable from the MIDI Out port of that first device, and make sure it is connected to the MIDI In port of the device you want to receive the data. Follow each cable in a similar fashion—drawing a signal flow diagram showing each device and data path will be helpful—until you are sure that all the cables are connected properly. That step alone is likely to solve a great many problems.

Much of the trouble-shooting process is based on isolating the problem before trying to solve it. If a particular device is not responding at all, try using different MIDI cables. (Always turn off the devices at each end of a MIDI cable before plugging in or unplugging the cable.) Also check any volume controllers on both the slave device and its master, and slowly increase the setting of any volume controller that is off, muted, or at a very low setting.

If the physical connections, power switches, and volume controllers are not the cause of the problem, channel assignments may be. The master may be transmitting on a channel the slave is not set to receive on. Set the channel assignment on the slave to the same one as the transmitting device, referring to the owner's manual of each if you do not know how.

If setting both devices to the same channel does not solve channel communications, put the slave device into Omni On mode. If it responds at all, you can be sure that MIDI data is getting through over at least one channel. Then you must determine which one and set the channel assignment to it.

Sometimes the wrong device responds, or devices may respond improperly, making it difficult to isolate the problem within the context of a complex MIDI system. In that case, power down, unhook everything, and choose a single transmitting device and a single receiving one. Use a single cable to connect the transmitter's MIDI Out port to the receiver's MIDI In. If there is no response after powering on, try repeating the process with a different transmitter device, a different receiver, or different cables until a MIDI system of two devices works properly. Reconnect one device at a time, and continue the process until everything is working as it should or you have identified any devices in the system that are not working properly.

MIDI MONITORS

A MIDI monitor, as the name suggests, lets you follow the flow of MIDI messages that pass through the monitor. The monitor may be a software program, a special mode within a sequencer or synthesizer, or a special-purpose monitor box.

The monitor displays each MIDI message as it passes through—in real time. Typically, the monitor will display the actual MIDI data in binary, hexadecimal, or decimal format as well as the equivalent English description. If the monitor displays the MIDI message traffic from a controller to a synthesizer, for example, it will show whether the controller is transmitting aftertouch, breath control, or other controller data. If the synthesizer is not responding to the controller data shown on the monitor, the problem is with the synthesizer. It may be unable to respond to that particular type of message, or it may not be configured to respond correctly.

Using a MIDI monitor requires an understanding of MIDI messages, of course. While it is possible to use a MIDI system without any awareness of the specific messages passing through the cables, knowing what the messages mean enables a MIDI user to exercise the greatest degree of flexibility and control over each device in the system. The next chapter will describe each message type and provide examples of how each affects specific devices.

UNDERSTANDING MIDI MESSAGES

■ ■

MIDI messages are the means by which one MIDI device communicates information to another MIDI device. Each message specifies a musical event—in order to understand why a particular device acts in a particular manner, you must understand what messages it is receiving and transmitting. Most sequencers, and some other devices, can display MIDI messages (often in a variety of formats), allowing sequencer users to examine and alter MIDI messages one by one.

MIDI messages consist of one or more bytes of digital data. Since a MIDI cable carries voltages representing digital 1s and 0s—the binary digits, or bits that are the building blocks of computer data—rather than continuously varying voltages representing analog sound data, the output from a MIDI port should never be connected to an audio input, nor should an audio output be connected to a MIDI In port. Damage to both pieces of equipment could result.

Each MIDI message byte begins with a start bit (logical 0), followed by eight message bits sent with the least significant bit first, and terminated by a stop bit (logical 1), for a total of ten bits per serial byte (figure 8.1). Each eight-bit message byte specifies either a status or data value; the first byte of each message is the status byte, which specifies the type of message and how many additional data bytes follow to make up the complete message. Status bytes always have a most significant bit of 1, while data bytes always have a most significant bit of 0. Data bytes thus always range from a minimum value of 0 to a maximum value of 127 (decimal).

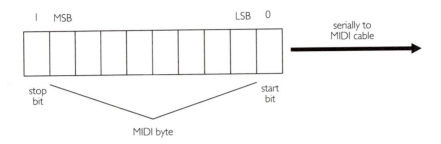

FIGURE 8.1   Transmission protocol of a MIDI byte.

CATEGORIES OF MIDI MESSAGES

MIDI messages may be grouped into two major categories, channel messages and system messages. Channel messages specify a particular MIDI channel within the message and generally control such aspects of performance as Note On/Off, Continuous Controller, and Program Change. System messages affect the MIDI system as a whole, without respect for a particular MIDI channel. These include such functions as System Exclusive (SysEx) messages, which provide a way to communicate manufacturer-specific data that is not part of the MIDI specification and timing clock messages used for synchronization (see chapter 9.)

Channel messages may themselves be grouped into channel mode messages and channel voice messages, while system messages may be grouped into system real time and system common messages and the single System Exclusive message, as shown in figure 8.2.

CHANNEL MODE MESSAGES

Channel mode messages affect the device that receives them only when they are sent over the channel to which the receiving device is assigned. That assignment of basic channel cannot be set or changed by any MIDI mode or voice message but may be set in one of three ways: permanently by the device's manufacturer; from the front-panel controls of the device; or by transmitting an appropriate System Exclusive message to the device.

Channel mode messages are used primarily to select one of the four MIDI modes described in the previous chapter. Each channel mode message is three bytes long. The four most significant bits of the channel mode

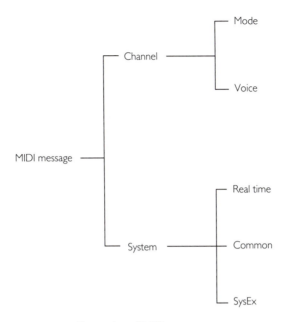

FIGURE 8.2 Categories of MIDI messages.

status byte are 1011, while the four least significant bits designate one of MIDI's sixteen channels, from 0000 for channel 1 to 1111 for channel 16.

The status byte of a channel mode message is identical to the status byte of a Control Change message, described below. It is the value of the second byte, from 01111001 (121 decimal) to 01111111 (127 decimal), that identifies the message as a channel mode message; a value of 01111100 (124 decimal) specifies Omni Off, a value of 01111101 (125 decimal) specifies Omni On, a value of 01111110 (126 decimal) specifies Mono On, and a value of 01111111 (127 decimal) specifies Poly On.

The third byte of a Mono On message specifies the number of channels over which monophonic channel voice messages are to be sent, using the values 1 to 16 (decimal). If the third byte of a Mono On message has a value of 0, the message directs the receiving device to assign its voices one per channel, from its basic channel through channel 16, until all available voices are used.

Three other channel mode messages are also worth noting, though not commonly used. All Notes Off turns off any voices turned on via MIDI messages. The MIDI specification does not require that receiving devices respond to All Notes Off, nor does All Notes Off turn off voices played by pressing the keys of a MIDI keyboard, but it can be useful for trouble-shooting and under certain unusual circumstances that leave notes sounding that cannot otherwise be turned off. The first data byte of All Notes Off is 01111011 (123 decimal), and the second data byte has a value of 0.

Sending a Reset All Controllers message causes the device receiving the message to reset the condition of all its controllers—continuous controllers, switches, pitch bend, and pressure—to what the device considers the optimum initial status. Generally, this will set the value of the Mod Wheel to 0 (no modulation), the pitch bend to center (no pitch bend), and so forth. The first data byte of Reset All Controllers is 01111001 (121 decimal), and the second data byte is 0.

The Local Control message is used to enable or disable the connection between the keyboard and the sound-generating circuitry of a MIDI synthesizer. The value of the first data byte of Local control is 01111010 (122 decimal); if the value of the second data byte is 0, Local Off disables the connection, and keyboard data goes only to the synthesizer's MIDI Out port—the synthesizer's sound-generating circuitry is controlled only by incoming MIDI data. On the other hand, if the second data byte is 01111111 (127 decimal), Local On restores normal operation where pressing a key causes a note to sound.

Most keyboard synthesizers provide local control from the front panel, but Local Control messages can also be useful when performing live along with a stored sequence. The sequence can turn the synthesizer's local control on and off at the appropriate times, while the keyboard alternates between specifying synthesizer notes and controlling other MIDI equipment in the performance setup.

For a summary of channel mode messages, see Table IV of the *MIDI 1.0 Detailed Specification,* included at the end of this book.

CHANNEL VOICE MESSAGES

Channel voice messages specify the nature of sounds produced by the synthesizer that receives the messages, using the channel number embedded in the status byte of the message. The events described by channel voice messages include Note On, Note Off, Channel Pressure, Polyphonic Key Pressure, Program Change, Control Change, and Pitch Bend.

Note On

A Note On message signals the device receiving it to begin playing a note. Note On messages are generated by a MIDI keyboard when a key is pressed or when some other MIDI device is similarly triggered.

Like all MIDI messages, the first byte of the Note On message is its status byte. The four most significant bits of the status byte, 1001, identify the message as a Note On and specify that two additional bytes of MIDI data will follow. The four least significant bits of the Note On status byte indicate which channel the message is intended for—from 0000 for channel 1 to 1111 for channel 16.

The second byte of the Note On message identifies which note is called for. Since it is a data byte, its most significant bit is 0. The MIDI specification designates 128 different notes, numbered from 0 to 127, indicated by the remaining seven bits of the second Note On byte. A MIDI note number does not designate a particular pitch; rather, the note generated depends on the note mapping and tuning determined by the synthesizer or sampler producing the note, though synthesizers most commonly assign MIDI note 60 to middle C and interpret each higher value as an additional half-step above middle C. Under this typical synthesizer's interpretation of Note On messages, MIDI note 66 would represent the F-sharp above middle C, MIDI note 54 would represent the F-sharp below middle C, and so forth.

The third byte of the Note On message indicates the velocity (usually interpreted as loudness), from 0 to 127, in the same manner as the second Note On byte specifies note number. Just as the note number does not specify a particular pitch, the velocity value does not specify a particular loudness, which is instead determined by the velocity map of the synthesizer or sampler.

Note Off

Each Note Off message signals the end of a note by signaling the device receiving it to turn off one of the notes it is playing. Like Note On, it is a three-byte message—status byte, note data byte, and velocity data byte. The only difference between the two is that the four most significant bits of a Note Off status byte are 1000, while a Note On has 1001 in the corresponding positions.

A higher velocity value usually is implemented as a note whose release occurs more quickly—a velocity value of 127 specifies the fastest possible release. Release data generally controls how a note dies away; a low velocity value would thus cause the note to die away slowly and a high velocity value would cause it to die away quickly. Not all MIDI devices implement Note On velocity; fewer still implement Note Off velocity. In such cases, the device transmits a velocity value of 64 for each Note On or Note Off message it transmits or ignores any note off velocity values it receives.

Channel Pressure

Channel Pressure messages are sent by those devices that can sense overall pressure on their keys but are not able to distinguish the pressure put on each individual key. That is, whichever key is pressed hardest determines the channel pressure value for the entire keyboard. In the same fashion, certain wind controllers transmit channel pressure information based on increasing breath pressure after the initial attack of a note. Depending upon the device, it may transmit one or, more commonly, a stream of Channel Pressure messages during the duration of a held note.

How a device receiving a Channel Pressure message responds depends on the particular device. Some devices use channel pressure for aftertouch volume; that is, pressing a key harder once the note has begun sounding causes the note to become louder. Other devices use channel pressure to control vibrato—harder pressure results in a faster or wider vibrato. Still other devices use channel pressure to control other parameters or allow you to assign the parameter yourself.

A Channel Pressure message contains two bytes. The status byte has 1101 as its four most significant bits; like all channel messages, the four least significant bits of the status byte specify the channel. The second byte of the Channel Pressure message specifies a data value from 0 to 127, with 0 indicating minimum pressure and 127 indicating maximum pressure.

The value of a Channel Pressure message affects all the notes currently sounding for that particular MIDI channel—provided that the device receiving the message has implemented a feature that causes it to respond to Channel Pressure messages. Otherwise, incoming Channel Pressure messages are simply ignored by the receiving device.

Polyphonic Key Pressure

Polyphonic key pressure acts in a manner similar to channel pressure, except that the Polyphonic Key Pressure message contains an additional data byte specifying a particular note and affects only that note rather than every note of the specified channel. In order for Polyphonic Key Pressure messages to have any effect, the device transmitting messages must be capable of detecting the different pressures put on each of its keys, and the device receiving messages must be able to act upon incoming Polyphonic Key Pressure messages.

The most significant bits of a Polyphonic Key Pressure message status byte are 1010; the least significant bits specify the channel. Unlike the Channel Pressure message, the second byte of a Polyphonic Key Pressure message specifies a particular note, using the values from 0 to 127 in the same manner as a Note On message, within the channel specified by the status byte. The third byte of the Polyphonic Key Pressure message represents the pressure value, from 0 to 127.

Program Change

The terms *program, patch,* and *voice* are used to refer to a particular setting of a synthesizer's controls when the setting produces a specific instrumental timbre or other musical sound. The terms may also refer to the settings on some other MIDI device such as a digital reverberator that, for example, produce a particular reverberation pattern. ("Program," used in this context, should not be confused with a computer program, a set of instructions that directs a computer to perform a particular task.)

A Program Change message does not specify the synthesizer settings themselves; rather, the settings are associated with a patch number by the synthesizer, and the Program Change message simply calls up whatever settings the synthesizer associates with that number. Since the settings that produce a sound vary widely from one synthesizer to another, it is much simpler for MIDI just to specify a program number and leave the particulars of what that program number represents to the synthesizer. (By contrast, System Exclusive messages, described below, can be used to change a synthesizer's parameters governing sound production—but such messages are often hundreds, or even thousands, of bytes long.)

A Program Change message has only a status byte and a single data byte. The status byte of a Program Change message has 1100 as its four most significant bits; like all channel messages, the four least significant bits of the status byte specify the channel.

The data byte of the Program Change message selects a patch on the device receiving the message, from patch 0 to 127. Upon receipt of a Program Change message, the device receiving the message calls up the patch corresponding to the patch value in the message.

But because patch numbers are likely to produce very different results on different synthesizers, selecting the same patch number on two different synthesizers offers no assurance that the resulting two sounds will be similar. In other words, patch number 47 might be associated with a flute sound on one synthesizer and a trombone sound on a different synthesizer. General MIDI, described in chapter 4, provides a minimum level of patch compatibility among synthesizers that implement the General MIDI specification. Even then, patches beyond the 128 specified by General MIDI are likely to differ from one synthesizer to another.

Some synthesizers store fewer than the 128 patches the Program Change message can select. If a synthesizer receives a value higher than the number of stored patches, it may ignore the message, select a default patch, or "wrap" the high value around the number of patches to find a value that is the remainder.

Other synthesizers and MIDI devices can store many more than 128 patches. In such a case, the user can assign 128 of the device's patches to MIDI's 128 patch numbers at any given time; only those 128 patches (sometimes referred to as the MIDI program table) are accessible using Program Change messages.

Even some synthesizers that cannot store more than 128 patches have a user-definable MIDI Program Table. In that way, the user can associate patches on a synthesizer receiving Program Change messages with the same program change numbers used by a transmitting synthesizer or sequencer for similar sounds, but which the receiving synthesizer had previously associated with a different patch number.

Control Change

A Control Change message affects a sound that has already been initiated by a Note On message, altering such parameters as volume or modulation of the note in progress. The message can specify any of 121 specific MIDI controllers—though most transmitting devices generally implement only a few. These include continuous controllers, On/Off switch controllers, data controllers, and undefined controllers.

Continuous controllers can transmit control data over a range of values—normally 0 to 127 (or 0 to 16,383 in the case of high-resolution controllers, discussed below). On/Off switch controllers transmit only one of two possible values—0 to represent off or 127 to represent on. Data controllers transmit specific data values directly or increment or decrement the value previously sent. Finally, undefined controllers may operate in the same fashion as continuous controllers, switches, or data controllers, but they use controller numbers that have not been assigned within the MIDI specification.

Control Change messages consist of three bytes. The four most significant bits of the first (status) byte, 1011, identify the message as a control change, and the four least significant bits indicate which channel the message is intended for—from 0000 for channel 1 to 1111 for channel 16.

The second byte specifies a controller number, from 0 through 120 (decimal). As described in the section on channel mode messages above, a second-byte data value of 121 through 127 does not specify a Control Change message at all but rather a channel mode message.

The third byte specifies the setting value for the particular controller specified by the previous byte. Setting values range from 0 to 127, but as we will see, Control Change messages for a particular continuous controller can be linked together to yield an effective range of 0 to 16,383.

Controller numbers 0 through 31, as specified by the second byte of a Control Change message, are for continuous controllers—those that generate data over a range of values, such as pedals, levers, wheels, and so forth. Some continuous controllers, called bidirectional continuous controllers, are at a centered position while at rest. Using such a controller involves moving it above or below its centered position. Upon release, a bidirectional continuous controller returns once again to its at-rest, centered position.

The data byte for each continuous controller uses 0 to represent the minimum position of the controller and 127 to represent the maximum position. In the case of bidirectional continuous controllers, a value of 64 is used to represent the centered position, while lower or higher values represent a change from the at-rest position.

If more than 128 steps of resolution is needed, controller numbers 32 through 63 can be used to represent the least significant byte of a two byte value whose most significant byte is represented by the corresponding controller number 0 to 31. For example, if an instrument sends volume control to adjust a note's volume from its initial setting (as specified by the velocity value of the note's Note On message), controller number 7 (volume) may be used. A single Control Change message using controller number 7 can represent any of the 128 settings for that controller. If finer resolution is required, controller number 39, the corresponding controller number to controller number 7, is also sent. The seven-bit data value from the controller 7 message represents the most significant byte, while the seven-bit data value from the controller 39 message represents the least significant byte. Together, the two messages specify a fourteen-bit data value for the volume setting, providing a resolution of 16,384 steps instead of 128 steps.

Once the most significant byte and corresponding least significant byte of a single Control Change pair have been sent, subsequent fine adjustments to the controller can be made by sending only the three-byte Control Change message for the least significant byte—the message for the most significant byte does not have to be transmitted again.

By agreement between the MIDI Manufacturers Association and the Japan MIDI Standards Committee, certain controller numbers are designated for certain standard musical applications. Some of the most important of these include: controller number 1, modulation wheel or lever; controller number 2, breath controller; controller number 4, foot controller; controller number 7, main volume; controller number 65, portamento; controller number 66, sostenuto; and controller number 67, soft pedal. For a summary of controller number assignments, see Table III of the *MIDI 1.0 Detailed Specification,* included at the end of this book.

Controllers produce a particular effect, and the third byte of the Control Change message specifies how much effect is produced. In most cases, a value of 0 specifies no effect, while a value of 127 specifies maximum effect.

Three defined MIDI controllers work in a different fashion, however. These are controller number 8, balance; controller number 10, pan; and controller number 11, expression.

The balance controller determines the volume balance between two different sound sources. A controller 8 value of 0 specifies full volume for the left or lower half, while a value of 64 specifies equal balance, and a value of 127 specifies full volume for the right or upper half.

The pan controller determines where a single sound source will be located within a stereo sound field. A controller 10 value of 0 specifies hard left, while a value of 64 specifies center, and a value of 127 specifies hard right.

Expression is an accented volume above the main volume of a note. Controller 11 values are thus added to the programmed or main volume value.

Although the MIDI specification defines 121 controllers, an instrument manufacturer may choose to implement a controller in a manner different from what the specification might lead you to expect. For example, controller numbers 64 through 69 are assigned functions normally associated with on/off switches, such as sustain and soft pedals. However, manufacturers may choose instead to implement these controller numbers as continuous controllers, simply by using the third byte of the Control Change message to specify a range of values from 0 to 127 rather than just 0 (off) and 127 (on).

In the same fashion, a controller number that is normally used for continuous controller data such as controller number 1 (mod wheel) may be implemented as an on/off modulation switch by sending only third-byte values of 0 and 127, respectively. The only certainty of Control Change messages is that a second-byte value represents the most significant byte of a high-resolution controller number 0–31, while a second-byte value represents the least significant byte of the corresponding controller number 32–63.

Pitch Bend

A Pitch Bend Change message transmits a new setting for a pitch bend controller. It is a special case of Control Change message, with a unique status byte value, whose four most significant bits are 1110.

Unlike other Control Change messages, Pitch Bend messages are always sent with 14-bit resolution. Following the first (status) byte, the second byte of a Pitch Bend message specifies the least significant byte value, and the third byte of the message specifies the most significant byte value. Maximum downward pitch bend corresponds to data byte values of 0, followed by 0. The center (no bend) position corresponds to data byte values of 0, followed by 64. Maximum upward pitch bend corresponds to data byte values of 127, followed by 127.

Sensitivity to Pitch Bend Change messages is a function of the receiving device. That is, the actual amount of pitch bend that results from a message specifying maximum downward pitch bend may vary from one device to another, depending on the settings of the receiving devices.

For a summary of channel voice messages, see Table II of the *MIDI 1.0 Detailed Specification,* included at the end of this book.

Bank Select

Most recent synthesizers incorporate many more than 128 patches. MIDI program tables, which map specific patches to each of the patches accessible through Program Change messages, are not only cumbersome to set up but do nothing to make more than 128 patches available at once. Bank Select, an extension of the MIDI Program Change message, addresses this problem by making it possible to quickly and easily access any of 16,384 different banks of 128 patches each without setting up MIDI program tables.

Bank select uses continuous controllers 0 and 32 (decimal) to communicate the most and least significant bytes, respectively, of a single bank number. Using two data bytes to specify a single bank number provides for 16,384 individual banks, each containing up to 128 different patches—more than any current synthesizer might need, but enough that the Bank Select message should serve for the foreseeable future, when tens of thousands of patches might be immediately accessible from optical storage or other high-speed storage devices.

Three separate MIDI messages make up a single Bank Select command. Two three-byte Control Change messages are followed by a single two-byte Program Change message; each is structured like the Control Change and Program Change messages described above.

The four most significant bits of each Bank Select Control Change message status byte, 1011, identify the message as a control change, and the four least significant bits indicate which channel the message is intended for—from 0000 for channel 1 to 1111 for channel 16. The second byte of the first Control Change message, 00000000, specifies that the Bank Select message's most significant data byte follows, while the second byte of the second Control Change message, 00100000, specifies that the Bank Select message's least significant data byte follows. Together, the seven data bits of each Control Change message's third-byte data value specify one of the 16,384 possible banks. Finally, the two-byte Program Change message, just as above, specifies a particular patch in the specified bank.

The two Bank Select Control Change messages must be transmitted as a pair before the Program Change message is transmitted. Fourteen-bit Bank Select message values correspond to bank numbers in table 8.1. A complete Bank Select message on MIDI channel 3 calling up bank 2, program number 7, would appear as:

10110010	00000000	00000000	Control Change, channel 3, MSB = 0
10110010	00100000	00000001	Control Change, channel 3, LSB = 1
11000010	00000110		Program Change, channel 3, data value = 6

SYSTEM MESSAGES

Some MIDI messages affect an entire device in a MIDI system or affect every device in the system, without regard for any specific MIDI channel. Such system messages are of three types: system common messages, system real-time messages, and a single System Exclusive (SysEx) message.

System common messages are one or two bytes long; system real-time messages are each one byte long; and System Exclusive messages may be of any length, with a minimum length of three bytes.

The most significant bits of every system message status byte are 1111. Because system messages affect an entire MIDI device rather than just a single channel of that device, system messages contain no channel identifier data. Instead, the four least significant bits of a system message status byte are used to identify the particular type of system message.

MOST SIGNIFICANT BYTE	LEAST SIGNIFICANT BYTE	BANK NUMBER
0000000	0000000	1
0000000	1111111	128
0000001	0000000	129
1111111	1111111	16,384

TABLE 8.1   Bank Select message data and corresponding bank numbers.

System Common Messages

System common messages perform such functions as establishing a common tuning for all devices in a MIDI system or coordinating the selection of a song whose individual parts may be distributed among several MIDI devices. The MIDI specification includes seven system common messages, though only five of these are currently defined. They are: Tune Request, Song Select, Song Position Pointer, End of Exclusive (EOX), and MIDI Time Code Quarter Frame.

Tune Request

Tune Request is a one-byte (status only) message whose value is 11110110 (246 decimal). The message directs all devices receiving it to tune themselves. A MIDI system that includes only digital synthesizers would probably never need to issue a Tune Request since one advantage of digital synthesizers is that they do not drift out of tune if they are working properly.

Some MIDI setups may include older, analog synthesizers with MIDI retrofits, along with digital synthesizers. Also, certain MIDI manufacturers have continued to make analog synthesizers because some musicians prefer the types of sounds analog synthesizers produce. But such analog synthesizers use electronic oscillators, which are more likely to have tuning problems during routine use than all-digital synthesizers.

If your MIDI setup includes such analog synthesizers, you may want to issue a Tune Request message between songs. If the master device in a MIDI network is an analog keyboard synthesizer, the keyboard may have a Tune Request switch; pushing the switch would transmit a Tune Request message down the cable to all subsequent devices in the network, including other analog synthesizers. Alternatively, the message could be stored at the beginning of each recorded sequence and transmitted by the sequencer to all the devices in the setup.

Song Select

The term *song* is used to describe a completed sequence that is ready for playback, whether the song consists of a series of drum machine patterns grouped together, a sequence in chorus-and-verse structure stored within a single synthesizer, or a complex, through-composed sequence involving multiple MIDI devices and stored in a personal computer.

Many sequencers and drum machines have the capability to associate particular songs with numbers that identify them, just as synthesizers associate patch settings with program numbers. And just as a synthesizer patch can be called up by its identifying number using a MIDI Program Change message, a stored song can be called up using the Song Select message.

Song Select is a two-byte message. The first byte, status, has a value of 11110011 (243 decimal), and the value of the second byte, data, can range from 0 to 127, selecting the song associated with that number.

Some receiving devices do not respond to Song Select, in which case the device ignores incoming Song Select messages. And just as patches on two different synthesizers are unlikely to correspond, there is no requirement that songs be numbered consistently from one device to another. It is the responsibility of the user to ensure that the correct song has been mapped to the appropriate song number within each device that will respond to incoming Song Select messages.

Song Position Pointer

The MIDI specification states that each musical duration represented by a quarter note be divided into twenty-four "ticks" of the MIDI clock (also called timing clock). Other musical durations can similarly be expressed in terms of their MIDI clock lengths—one half note equals forty-eight ticks and one sixteenth note equals six ticks, for example.

A MIDI clock tick does not represent a specific elapsed time since the length of a musical duration such as a quarter note is a function of tempo — at a faster tempo, a quarter note represents a shorter elapsed time than the same quarter note at a slower tempo. Rather, MIDI clock ticks form the basis for establishing musical durations and synchronization.

Most MIDI sequencers and drum machines can count MIDI beats from the beginning of a song, with six ticks considered a single MIDI beat. Since six ticks of the MIDI clock correspond to one sixteenth note, a MIDI beat is equivalent to a sixteenth note. A sequencer's song position, then, is the number of elapsed MIDI beats since the start of the song, ranging from 0 to a maximum of 16,383 MIDI beats. (Bear in mind that a MIDI beat is not equivalent to a musical beat, which varies with the time signature of each piece of music.)

To further complicate matters, a particular sequencer may implement greater precision than MIDI's twenty-four ticks per quarter note. Typically, the sequencer's timebase would be a multiple of the MIDI clock—that is, forty-eight ticks per quarter note, ninety-six ticks per quarter note, or some similar multiple.

The Song Position Pointer message consists of a status byte followed by two data bytes that specify song position. The status byte has a value of 11110010 (242 decimal). It is followed first by the least significant byte of song position data, then the most significant data byte. Since each data byte is a seven-bit value, the two bytes combined have 14-bit precision, representing the 16,384 possible song position values.

Song position is normally set to 0 when a master sequencer's start control is activated. All other sequencers that derive their timing clock from the master would then also begin playing their sequences from the beginning. As the combined sequences play, song position is automatically incremented every sixth MIDI clock tick until the master sequencer's stop control is activated. If the master sequencer's continue control is activated, song position is again incremented from its current value.

Song Position Pointer messages are effective only if they are sent before a sequencer begins to play a song; they cannot be used to synchronize devices to a song that is already playing. Upon receipt of a Song Position Pointer message, every device set to MIDI sync (external) clock mode sets its own song position pointer to that of the incoming Song Position Pointer message.

For example, if the value of song position is 20 at the time a Song Position Pointer message is transmitted, and a device receiving the Song Position Pointer message uses a resolution of 96 internal clock ticks per quarter note, that device would set its internal clock as follows:

1. Song Position (20) × 6 MIDI clock ticks per MIDI beat = 120 MIDI clock ticks.

2. 120 MIDI clock ticks × (96 internal clock ticks per quarter note / MIDI's timebase of 24 clock ticks per quarter note) = 480 internal clock ticks.

The device receiving the Song Position Pointer message would therefore set its internal clock to begin playback 480 ticks into the sequence.

Song Position Pointer messages provide only the most basic of synchronization capabilities—the capability to start two clock-sensitive devices at some point other than the beginning of a sequence. Furthermore, the MIDI specification does not require MIDI devices to implement Song Position Pointer, and it seems to be implemented by only a few manufacturers. Other MIDI messages related to Song Position Pointer are grouped under system real-time messages and will be discussed below. For more on synchronization, see chapter 9.

End of Exclusive (EOX)

A System Exclusive message may contain any number of bytes, so the End Of Exclusive message alerts devices receiving the SysEx message that it is the last byte of that SysEx message. End of Exclusive is a single-byte message whose value is 11110111 (247 decimal). Although the MIDI specification classifies EOX as a system common message, it functions only in connection with a System Exclusive message, so it will be discussed further in the section below covering SysEx messages.

MIDI Time Code Quarter Frame

MIDI Time Code (MTC) is a synchronization system and will be covered in chapter 9. MTC Quarter Frame is a two-byte message whose status byte value is 11110001 (241 decimal). It specifies a high-resolution timing value for other devices to synchronize to.

For a summary of system common messages, see Table V of the *MIDI 1.0 Detailed Specification,* included at the end of this book.

System Real-Time Messages

As the name implies, system real-time messages coordinate and synchronize the timing of clock-based MIDI devices such as sequencers, drum machines, and synthesizers during performance or playback. Consequently, such messages must be sent at regular, precise intervals to ensure that every device in a MIDI system marches to the same beat—so much so that they are sometimes inserted between bytes of other multi-byte messages.

Many MIDI devices have no clock or synchronization capabilities, and such devices simply ignore incoming system real-time messages.

All system real-time messages consist of only a single status byte, without any subsequent data bytes. Since system real-time messages affect an entire MIDI device rather than just a single channel of that device, they—like all system messages—contain no channel identifier data.

Timing Clock

The one-byte value of a Timing Clock message is 11111000 (248 decimal). When a master sequencer plays a song, it transmits Timing Clock messages at a rate of twenty-four per quarter note, interspersed among the other MIDI messages it transmits. The master (transmitting) sequencer is thus able to transmit tempo and duration information by adjusting the rate at which it sends Timing Clock messages according to the tempo and rhythmic values. Any clock-based MIDI systems set to MIDI (external) clock mode synchronize to the incoming Timing Clock messages, providing a means to synchronize the entire system using MIDI messages. To avoid confusion, only one device in a MIDI system should serve as the master clock at any given time; all other clock-based devices in the system should be set to receive timing information from the external clock.

Start

Start—a one-byte, status-only message whose value is 11111010 (250 decimal)—is sent when the Play control on a master timing device is activated. It directs any receiving devices that respond to incoming system real-time messages to start play from the beginning of their stored song or sequence. Timing Clock messages then serve to initiate and maintain synchronization from that point.

Those devices that implement Song Position Pointer also return their song position value to 0 upon receipt of a Start message.

Stop

The one-byte, status-only Stop message is sent when playback is stopped on the device that supplies master timing clock information to the rest of the system. Its value is 11111100 (252 decimal). Any receiving devices that respond to incoming system real-time messages will cease playback immediately upon receiving a Stop message. Song position within each of the devices does not change from its current value as of when the Stop message was transmitted or received.

Continue

Continue—a one-byte, status-only message whose value is 11111011 (251 decimal)—initiates playback on any receiving devices that respond to incoming system real-time messages, in the same manner as the Start command. The difference is that a Start message initiates playback from the beginning of the song or sequence and resets song position to 0, while Continue initiates playback starting with whatever the current value of song position is at the time the message is received.

Some transmitting devices have a separate Continue control, while others send a Start message if the Song Position value of the transmitting device is 0, and a Continue message if the value is greater than 0. If receiving devices have not been set to external synchronization until after the playback has begun and been stopped on such a transmitting device, their Song Position values might not correspond to the master's, so they might not play back in proper synchronization to the master upon receipt of a Continue message generated by activating the master device's Play control.

The above example is one illustration of the limitations of MIDI sync. It cannot provide true chase-lock synchronization, in which receiving devices automatically synchronize correctly to the transmitting device, regardless of the point at which the transmitting device begins playback.

Despite their limitations, Stop, Start, and Continue messages provide a way to stop playback, then resume without having to begin once again from the beginning.

Active Sensing

Active sensing, like system reset (below), solves an infrequently encountered problem; as a result, few MIDI devices implement it. The single-byte, status-only Active Sensing message has a value of 11111110 (254 decimal). It is sent at least as often as every 300 milliseconds by transmitting devices that implement it, whenever there is no other MIDI data being transmitted.

Once an Active Sensing message has been received by a device that also implements active sensing, that device will continue to look for Active Sensing messages at regular intervals and at those times when there are no other incoming MIDI messages. If it fails to receive the expected Active Sensing messages and no other MIDI messages appear along the incoming MIDI cable, it would likely be because the cable connecting the two devices had become unplugged.

An unexpected cable disconnection can cause a variety of problems. At best, the receiving device will simply fail to respond to subsequent messages from the transmitting device. At worst, if the MIDI cable became unplugged after the transmitting device sent a Note On message, but before the transmitter sent its companion Note Off message, the receiving device will continue to sustain its note indefinitely—the dreaded "stuck" or "hung" note.

Although implementing active sensing can avoid the problems described above, it creates problems of its own. Sending repeated messages at frequent intervals contributes to MIDI choke, the overloading of the MIDI data stream described in chapter 7. Since MIDI choke is more likely to become a problem under normal circumstances than disconnected cables, implementing active sensing carries a high price.

Choosing not to implement active sensing causes no compatibility problems, so most manufacturers omit it. A receiving device that does implement active sensing must first receive an Active Sensing message from the transmitter before it starts looking for subsequent Active Sensing messages—if the transmitting device does not implement active sensing, active sensing will not be initiated in the receiving device. In the same manner, if a receiving device does not implement active sensing, it ignores any Active Sensing messages it receives.

System Reset

The one-byte, status-only System Reset message has a value of 11111111 (255 decimal). Upon receiving a System Reset message, the device receiving the message should return all its controls to their default settings—that is, the initial values of the controls at power-up.

Those default settings may vary from one device to another, so a system reset can have different effects on different devices. But as a general guideline, the MIDI specification lists the following as its system reset conditions:

1. MIDI Mode 1—Omni On/Poly;

2. Local On;

3. all voices off (no notes playing);

4. reset all controllers to minimum or centered position;

5. stop playback of any sequencer or song currently playing;

6. clear Running Status (see below for an explanation of Running Status);

7. reset other parameters to their values at power-on.

The MIDI specification further suggests that system reset be used sparingly and be transmitted under manual control rather than as a stored sequencer message. It should generally only be used as a last resort to return all devices to a known condition, not as part of an initialization routine. Many MIDI devices retain their most recent settings upon power down so that the same settings are maintained upon the following power up. This capability can be a time saver when a session must be interrupted and continued later, but those settings might be lost if a system reset is performed.

For a summary of system real-time messages, see Table VI of the *MIDI 1.0 Detailed Specification,* included at the end of this book.

System Exclusive Messages

The designers of the MIDI specification recognized that they could not include messages to address the unique needs of each MIDI device and that it would be unwise to try. Instead, they provided System Exclusive messages, which communicate device-specific data that falls outside the scope of standard MIDI messages.

MIDI devices made by a single manufacturer can use SysEx messages to transmit and receive data that is unique to that manufacturer's devices. Indeed, any manufacturer may use the system exclusive codes of any existing product without the permission of the original manufacturer; one manufacturer, then, could use SysEx messages to transmit data to a different manufacturer's device. Whether between devices from the same or different manufacturers, such data might include synthesizer patch parameters or sampler data values.

If SysEx messages are to be useful, they must represent data that is compatible with the transmitting and receiving device. For example, a SysEx message containing parameter data for an FM synthesizer will have no corresponding meaning to an additive synthesizer, even if the two are made by the same manufacturer.

Each System Exclusive message begins with a status byte whose value is 11110000 (240 decimal). The first data byte following a SysEx status byte is used to identify a specific manufacturer, using an ID number that must be obtained from the MIDI Manufacturers Association or Japan MIDI Standards Committee. Such ID values range from 0 to 127—for example, ID number 1 specifies devices manufactured by Sequential, while ID number 67 specifies devices manufactured by Yamaha. An ID whose value is 0 specifies that the following two bytes are used as extensions to the manufacturer's ID: for example, the three-byte ID 0, 0, 7 specifies Digital Music Corp., while the three-byte ID 0, 0, 16 specifies DOD Electronics. (All the above IDs are given in decimal notation.)

Three ID numbers are reserved for specific purposes: 01111101 (125 decimal) is reserved for noncommercial use and may not be used by any product released to the public; 01111110 (126 decimal) identifies a non-real-time System Exclusive message; and 01111111 (127 decimal) identifies a real-time System Exclusive message.

Both real-time and non-real-time System Exclusive messages use the same format. The status byte 11110000 is followed by the ID code data byte, followed by a channel number byte, a sub-ID #1 byte, a sub-ID #2 byte, any number of data bytes, and the EOX message byte 11110111 to conclude the real-time or non-real-time SysEx message.

For a list of currently defined system exclusive ID numbers, see Table VIII of the *MIDI 1.0 Detailed Specification,* included at the end of this book.

Once a receiving device determines that the manufacturer's ID in the incoming message is the same as its own, it attempts to act on the incoming SysEx message. If the incoming SysEx message specifies a manufacturer other than the maker of the receiving device, the device ignores the rest of the incoming SysEx message.

Any number of data bytes may follow the manufacturer ID, provided that each is a true MIDI data byte—that is, the most significant bit of each data byte must be 0.

The SysEx message ends with an End of Exclusive (EOX) message, the one-byte, status-only system common message whose value is 11110111 (247 decimal).

Once a SysEx message has begun, no other MIDI status or data bytes should be sent until after an EOX has terminated the SysEx message. The only exception is system real-time messages, which may be inserted between bytes of any other MIDI message and which are received even by devices that are ignoring the SysEx message bytes the system real-time messages are interleaved between. However, if a status byte other than real time or EOX is received during a SysEx message transmission, receipt of the System Exclusive message is terminated, and any SysEx data bytes that follow are ignored.

For a summary of System Exclusive messages, see Table VII of the *MIDI 1.0 Detailed Specification,* included at the end of this book.

RUNNING STATUS

Running status is not a type of MIDI message but a short-cut technique of transmission that is used to minimize message traffic volume and help avoid the problems that arise from an overloaded MIDI data stream. Under running status, once a message of a particular type has been sent, subsequent messages of the same type that follow immediately after the first are sent without repeating the status byte for each subsequent message.

For example, a series of notes would normally be transmitted as follows: Note On status, Note Number data value, Velocity data value; Note On status, Note Number data value, Velocity data value; Note On status, Note Number data value, Velocity data value; and so on for each note in the group. Under running status, the same series of notes would be transmitted as follows: Note On status, Note Number data value, Velocity data value; Note Number data value, Velocity data value; Note Number data value, Velocity data value; and so on. As long as the subsequent data consists of Note On messages using the same MIDI channel as the first complete Note On message, the status bytes of the subsequent messages need not be transmitted. Once a device receives a status byte, it must interpret subsequent data bytes as the same status until it receives a new status byte; in other words, it must maintain the most recent, or "running," status.

Running status is most appropriate for transmitting Note On messages and continuous controller data. In the case of Note On messages, running status can take advantage of the fact that notes can be turned off by transmitting a Note On message with a velocity value of 0 rather than by transmitting a Note Off message for the same note.

Figure 8.3 shows the savings achieved using running status for a series of three Note On messages as compared to normal Note On transmission, and for three Note On messages (the second of which has a velocity value of 0) instead of Note On/Note Off/Note On messages.

A FINAL WARNING

Even if you know and understand all the messages that pass back and forth between MIDI devices, it is easy to overlook this basic principle of MIDI message transmission: Few MIDI devices implement every variety of MIDI message. The MIDI specification does not require

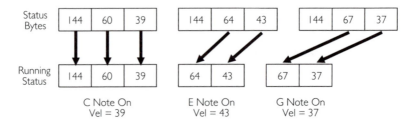

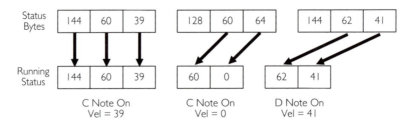

FIGURE 8.3   Status bytes versus running status.

that MIDI devices implement any but a very few core features. Unless a device implements a particular feature, it will not respond to incoming messages that call upon that feature. Even if the device does implement a feature, how it implements the feature may be different from how another device implements it. The only way to be sure is to understand the messages entering a device and observe how the device responds.

SYNCHRONIZATION

• •

Human beings in live ensemble performance hear what is being played and adjust their own playing to what they hear, maintaining a sense of ensemble through constant, near-instantaneous reactions and adjustments. MIDI instruments and tape recorders rely instead on synchronization to ensure that each device plays back stored material at the same rate, from the same starting point, as all the other devices that contribute to ensemble playback. Each device is locked together in time, or synchronized, so that the entire ensemble of devices functions as a single system.

The most widespread use of synchronization in the MIDI studio is to interlock sequencers, drum machines, and multitrack tape recorders. One device functions as a master, and the slave machines automatically and continuously match the timing of their recording or playback to the master's, establishing synchronism between devices.

Applications of synchronization include matching a drum machine's prerecorded pattern to a recorded sequence; mixing down individual sequencer tracks, each with its own signal processing, in multiple passes on a single multitrack tape recorder; and command of multiple audio/video machines and MIDI devices in an advanced multimedia production.

Synchronization systems fall into one of two general categories. The first type uses what might be called a click track. One device generates a steady stream of clicks—alternating voltage changes or electronic pulses. Other devices sense the click rate generated by the first device, comparing it to and adjusting their own click track so that each machine runs at the same speed. As long as each device starts at the same time, all the devices should remain "in sync." But because each click is like every other, there is no way for any device to know which click is which—the devices must start from the very beginning of a piece each time it is played, or each device might begin playback from a different point.

SYNCHRONIZATION SIGNAL	INTERPRETATION
Clock Sync	advance 1 unit
MIDI Clock	advance 1/24 quarter note
FSK	advance 1 unit
Song Position Pointer	MIDI beats since start
SMPTE	hours, minutes, seconds, frames
MIDI Time Code	hours, minutes, seconds, frames

FIGURE 9.1   Synchronization methods.

The second type of synchronization uses addresses, in which each click has a unique label. The label may represent elapsed time from some starting point or a count of musical durations. Address codes require that more timing-related data be transmitted among devices but provide more flexibility in synchronizing from any starting point.

Figure 9.1 shows each of the synchronization methods that will be discussed in this chapter, as well as MIDI Song Position Pointer, covered in chapter 8. The first grouping includes click track methods, while the second group includes address methods.

CLOCK SYNCHRONIZATION

One of the simplest synchronization techniques, found in some pre-MIDI electronic instruments, many drum machines, and in certain MIDI equipment, is clock sync. A clock emits a steady stream of voltage changes, alternating between a minimum and maximum voltage value. The clock is simply turned on at the beginning of the piece of music and continues churning out its alternating voltages until it is turned off at the end of the piece. A device receiving clock voltages places events at the appropriate number of clock pulses from the beginning by counting the number of voltage changes it receives.

Clock rates are usually specified in parts per quarter note (ppqn), so that a clock tick represents a musical time rather than an absolute time. That is, the elapsed time between ticks depends on the tempo of the music—at a slower tempo, more time will elapse between ticks than at a faster tempo, since the number of quarter notes per unit of elapsed time (and therefore the number of ticks) will be lower at a slower tempo.

The greater the number of parts per quarter note, the higher the resolution—the capability to place complex rhythmic units exactly. Two ppqn provides resolution to within an eighth note—that is, every event would have to occur on an eighth-note boundary. With 24 ppqn, resolution as precise as sixty-fourth note triplets is possible, as shown in figure 9.2. Figure 9.3 shows musical rhythmic units and the equivalent number of clock ticks for each, at 24 ppqn resolution.

While many manufacturers use a 24 ppqn clock rate, other clock rates are also commonly used. If two devices use different clock rates, they will not operate in sync—unless one or both devices is connected to a clock-rate converter, which synchronizes devices with different clock rates by converting the disparate clocks to a common rate.

In order for a clock-based synchronization system to work, one device must serve as the master clock, providing the timing reference to all other devices in the system. Each of the slave devices must have an external clock input jack, just as the master must have a clock output jack. Once connected, the master device must be set to internal clock, while each slave must be set to external clock. When the master clock begins "ticking," each of the slave devices begins counting, so that each slave can make its contribution to the music at the correct count of clock ticks. Of course, the system depends on a common clock rate reference so that all the devices count the same number of clock ticks per quarter note.

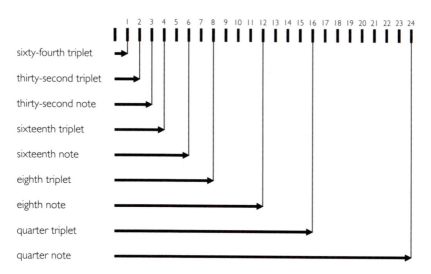

FIGURE 9.2   MIDI clock rate at 24 ppqn resolution.

whote note	=	96 ticks
half note	=	48 ticks
half note triplet	=	32 ticks
quarter note	=	24 ticks
quarter note triplet	=	16 ticks
eighth note	=	12 ticks
eighth note triplet	=	8 ticks
sixteenth note	=	6 ticks
sixteenth note triplet	=	4 ticks
thirty-second note	=	3 ticks
thirty-second note triplet	=	2 ticks
sixty-fourth note triplet	=	1 tick

FIGURE 9.3 Musical rhythms and equivalent clock representations, at 24 ppqn resolution.

MIDI CLOCK

As we saw in chapter 8, the MIDI specification established twenty-four parts per quarter note as a universal standard. Any MIDI device that is capable of synchronizing to MIDI Clock is compatible with the 24 ppqn clock rate. Such MIDI messages as Start, Stop, and Continue provide basic synchronization from the beginning of a piece of music, while Song Position Pointer provides the capability for synchronized playback beginning from anywhere within the piece.

The essence of MIDI Clock synchronization is the real-time clock messages that are transmitted at a rate of twenty-four parts per quarter note. Those messages provide the only timing reference for a MIDI device set to external MIDI Clock. If twenty-four ticks per quarter note were the maximum possible resolution for such externally clocked devices, as was the case among the earliest MIDI hardware, music involving more precise synchronization than the MIDI standard permits would be impossible.

Instead, newer sequencers and externally clocked MIDI devices often incorporate interpolation, using incoming timing pulses as a reference for the device's own higher internal resolution. In that way, the device can time its events as precisely as its own internal resolution permits, placing each event in the correct location relative to the incoming twenty-four tick per quarter note MIDI Clock.

If a high-resolution device is unable to synchronize complex rhythmic events to an external MIDI Clock without forcing each event to the nearest MIDI Clock tick, its user-selectable resolution may be on too low a setting. Setting the device to its highest resolution should solve the problem in high resolution MIDI devices that implement MIDI Clock interpolation.

TAPE SYNCHRONIZATION USING FSK

Recording brief, intermittent clock pulses directly to audio tape provides an unreliable synchronization reference signal. Recordings of intermittent signals are prone to dropouts, which occur when metal oxide particles become detached from the tape backing, taking with them whatever signals are recorded on those particles. Discontinuous signals, like clock pulses, are also prone to tape stretching, which occurs when tape is repeatedly stopped and started, especially at high speeds during rewind and fast forward. As the tape stretches, the recorded clock pulses move farther apart, degrading the regularity of the master clock signal.

A more reliable recorded clock signal can be achieved by alternating between two frequencies to represent successive clock voltage changes. This representation of the clock signal, called frequency shift key, or FSK, produces a signal that tape machines can more easily record and is less likely to be affected by dropout.

Unfortunately, just as devices can use different clock rates, different manufacturers may use different (and incompatible) FSK standards. Like different clock resolutions, the problem can be overcome with converters, but that solution adds additional expense and complication to what is already a complicated process.

A clock-based device that synchronizes to FSK uses an FSK Out jack, which is connected to one audio input of a multitrack tape recorder, and an FSK input jack, which is connected to the output of the tape recorder's track on which the FSK sync signal is recorded, as shown in figure 9.4.

Many MIDI devices convert the MIDI Clock signal to FSK for recording the tape synchronization clock signal. Some have FSK Out and FSK In jacks, which can be connected directly to tape input and output jacks, respectively. Other devices, particularly older ones, may have only MIDI Clock Out and In jacks. Those, too, can be converted to FSK by connecting them to a MIDI Clock/FSK converter. Route clock signals through the converter as they pass between the device and tape recorder.

Synchronizing to tape using FSK works similarly to synchronizing two clock-based devices. The taped FSK clock serves as the master; its signal is fed to all other devices, whose own clocks must be set to External (FSK) Clock.

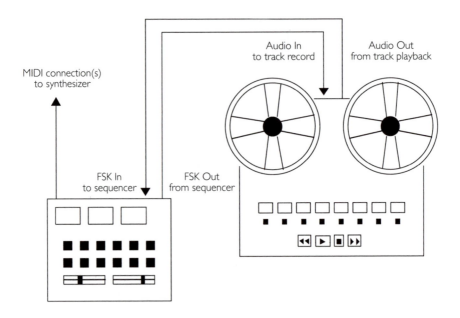

FIGURE 9.4 Connections between an FSK device and a multitrack tape recorder.

As an example, consider the problem of taping a sequence on an eight-track tape recorder. Six sequencer tracks, each using its own MIDI channel, play a multitimbral polyphonic synthesizer with only monaural or stereo outputs. Even with six signal processors (such as reverberators), you could not add different signal processing to each track and record the whole sequence at once since at least three tracks would have to share an output.

Instead, by synchronizing to tape using FSK, you could record each sequencer track separately, adding unique signal processing to each. First, record the synchronization signal by itself—usually you would record it onto track 8 of the tape recorder. Connect the FSK Out from the sequencer, MIDI interface, or MIDI/FSK convertor to the audio input jack of tape recorder track 8. Set the sequencer to Internal clock. Enable tape recorder track 8 and begin recording, then start the sequencer playback from the beginning. Let the sequence play to its completion before stopping the tape.

Then connect the tape recorder's track 8 audio Out to the FSK In connector of the sequencer, computer's MIDI interface or MIDI/FSK convertor. Rewind the tape. Disable tape recorder track 8 for recording.

To record one sequencer track in synchronization with the others:

1. Connect the synthesizer's audio Out to the signal processor's audio In. Select the signal processing settings, then route the signal processor's audio Out to the first available tape recorder track audio In—we will use the tape recorder's track 1. (Route signals through a mixing console if necessary.)

   Figure 9.5 shows the audio and MIDI connections at the end of this step for a setup involving a sequencer program running on a personal computer; the computer's MIDI interface with FSK; the synthesizer and eight-track tape recorder described above; and a single digital signal processor.

2. Set the sequencer to External clock. Mute all the sequencer tracks except the one you want to record.

3. Enable the tape recorder track that the synthesizer's audio Out is connected to.

4. Start the sequencer playback from the beginning, then begin recording. The sequencer will wait to receive its clock signal from the tape recorder and begin playback when it receives it.

5. Let the sequence play to its completion before stopping the tape and rewinding.

Repeat the above five steps for each sequencer track, rewinding the tape recording to the beginning before each time through. As long as the sequencer's clock is set to External, it will wait for the tape recording to start up before beginning playback at the correct time. Set the sequencer clock to Internal if you need to hear the sequence without recording it to tape, then back to External when you are ready to record.

TIME CODE

Time code is a signal that uniquely identifies each location on a tape recording or in a recorded sequence. It provides a built-in timing reference so that other devices can synchronize their recording or playback to the recorded time code. Time code performs two functions: it establishes the common pulse or clock for all devices and provides address information to the entire system of synchronized devices.

The development of time code allows true programmable synchronization. Using time code, two or more devices can be operated in near perfect synchrony. Complex timing functions such as predetermined

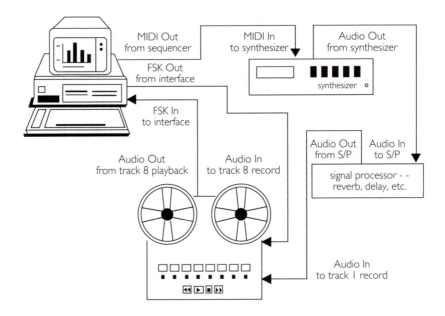

FIGURE 9.5   Audio and MIDI connections for multitrack tape recording.

switching between machine outputs can be performed, permitting electronic editing within timing accuracies as precise as 1/30 of a second.

Time code has also made it possible for automated mix information to be stored in a personal computer or sequencer rather than on tape itself, reducing the number of tape tracks required for mix information to one — the time code track itself. Automated mix information with its identifying time code can then be synchronized to the time code recorded on the single tape track.

One example that demonstrates the use of time code is punch-in/punch-out. A certain portion of a recorded sequence might need to be replaced, without having to rerecord the remainder as well. First, the user would set the precise time code locations where the new material to be recorded over the old should begin and end. Since the sequencer would be synchronized to the recorded time code, it would begin playback a specified interval before recording should begin (called pre-roll), then shift into record mode at precisely the right location, then back to playback again, allowing the user to "punch in" the new material.

SMPTE TIME CODE

Synchronization is not a problem for the film medium; sprocket-driven, discrete-frame film can be synchronized by lining up picture, dialogue, music, and effects—each recorded on separate pieces of film stock—on an editing table's sprocket drives, making adjustments to the placement and position of an individual piece of stock as necessary.

Video tape, like audio tape, has no discrete divisions similar to film frames, so another synchronization method is required. In 1971, the Society of Motion Picture and Television Engineers, the professional organization that sets and maintains standards for the video, film, and television industries, adopted as a standard an address code system originally developed by NASA to accurately and precisely time-stamp incoming data transmitted from space. It has become known as SMPTE (pronounced "simp-tee") time code and is the most widely used synchronization technique.

SMPTE time code is the closest thing to a universal synchronization standard, used in the audio world as well as in film and television. Its universality enables projects begun in a MIDI studio to move to a professional production or postproduction studio for completion. Audio recordings can be developed separately from their video or film counterparts, then synchronized together when each is complete.

Originally, SMPTE time code was used only to synchronize tape machines, but it has proved so versatile and effective that it can now be found in sequencers and other MIDI devices as well. The adoption of MIDI Time Code (discussed below) as part of the MIDI specification means that SMPTE has become the most widely implemented synchronization system among better-quality MIDI devices.

SMPTE time code provides frame-accurate timing information, updated thirty times each second, to uniquely identify every video frame in a twenty-four hour period, normally by recording the time of day (which may, but need not, correspond to actual local time) along with the frame number of each of the multiple video frames within each second. An event marked by SMPTE time code is identified by a unique address measured in hours, minutes, seconds, and frames.

There are two varieties of SMPTE time code; both consist of an analog signal describing digital data. The signal is created by a SMPTE code generator and recorded on tape. Vertical interval time code (VITC) is stored as video information in discrete segments stored vertically on video tape, interspersed with the video recording itself. Longitudinal time code (LTC) is stored as an audio signal along the length of an audio track used only for recording time code. LTC is used almost exclusively for audio applications, even audio-for-video production. Unless otherwise specified, audio SMPTE time code is LTC time code.

SMPTE Time Code Frame Rates

Four slightly different SMPTE time code systems are used throughout the audio and video world, each with a different frame rate. The different versions of SMPTE can cause problems in multistudio audiovisual productions, though audio-only productions in a particular studio usually involve only a single frame rate.

Film runs at twenty-four frames per second; SMPTE code for film applications generally runs at that rate. The frame rate used by European television is called EBU time code (named for the European Broadcasters Union, which is responsible for the standard); it uses twenty-five frames per second. The American black-and-white television standard (called NTSC monochrome, or just NTSC, named for the National Television Systems Committee) uses thirty frames per second, while the American color television standard (also called NTSC color) is 29.97 frames per second.

In the NTSC color system, the frames are still nominally counted at thirty per second, but over a period of one hour the difference between the actual number of elapsed NTSC color frames and the number of frames counted at thirty frames per second would result in a discrepancy of 108 frames (approximately 3.5 seconds' worth) between the time shown on a tape counter and actual elapsed clock time. To correct this discrepancy, two frames are skipped on the tape counter at the end of each minute, except for every tenth minute. The tape runs normally—only the frame counter is affected, by incrementing the counter by three frames instead of one, resulting in the necessary adjustment of 108 frames per hour (2 frames × 9 minutes × 6 ten-minute groups). The NTSC color time code format is also widely known as drop-frame time code, since the frame counter "drops" 108 frames per hour.

The thirty-frame-per-second rate is used almost exclusively in audio-only production and is the only frame rate implemented by many MIDI manufacturers. But if you must synchronize to tapes made by outside video or film studios, find out what frame rate is recorded on the tapes. If your MIDI gear or software operates only at thirty frames per second, you may need a SMPTE code converter. As the name implies, a SMPTE code converter accepts incoming SMPTE time code at one frame rate and converts it to another, preserving the correct timing relationships between devices running on different time code standards.

SMPTE Time Code Structure

Longitudinal SMPTE Time Code (LTC) consists of a stream of 80-bit digital words that identify each frame; at 30 frames/second the bit rate is 2,400/second. Each word is incremented with each passing frame, second, minute, and hour. Figure 9.6 shows the bit structure of longitudinal SMPTE Time Code.

Only twenty-six of the eighty bits represent the timing address information itself. The 80-bit code includes thirty-two undefined bits that can be assigned by the user for purposes other than time code data. Sixteen specific bits define the end of each word. Two bits are used as flags to signify the presence or absence of particular video conditions; another bit specifies one of two video fields; all are of little use in audio applications. Three bits are undefined and are reserved for future implementation.

The thirty-two user bits, organized into eight groups of four bits each called Binary Group 1 through Binary Group 8, may be assigned any value or function the user desires. Some SMPTE-oriented computer programs and SMPTE reader/generators enable the user to access and use those bits to label sequences or display time remaining in a particular recorded selection, for example.

The first four bits of LTC specify units of frames: 1, 2, 4, and 8 respectively. The next four bits are called Binary Group 1—the first four of thirty-two user bits. The next two bits specify tens of frames: ten and twenty frames, respectively. The two bits that follow are flags: a value of 1 in each bit represents drop frame time code and color frame flags, respectively. The next four bits are Binary Group 2—the second four of thirty-two user bits. The next four bits specify units of seconds: 1, 2, 4, and 8 respectively, followed by the four bits of Binary Group 3. The next three bits specify tens of seconds: 10, 20, and 40 seconds respectively. The twenty-eighth bit of LTC is used to specify one of two video fields (each video frame is made up of two interlacing fields, usually labeled "odd" and "even"). The next four bits are Binary Group 4.

The next four bits specify units of minutes: 1, 2, 4, and 8 respectively, followed by the four bits of Binary Group 5. The next three bits specify tens of minutes: 10, 20, and 40 minutes respectively. The bit that follows is undefined; it is followed by the four bits of Binary Group 6. The next four bits specify units of hours: 1, 2, 4, and 8 respectively, followed by the four bits of Binary Group 7. The next two bits specify tens of hours: 10 and 20 hours respectively. Those are followed by two more unassigned bits, then by Binary Group 8.

The final sixteen bits of the 80-bit SMPTE code are called the "sync word," whose value is 0011 1111 1111 1101. This unique bit pattern is

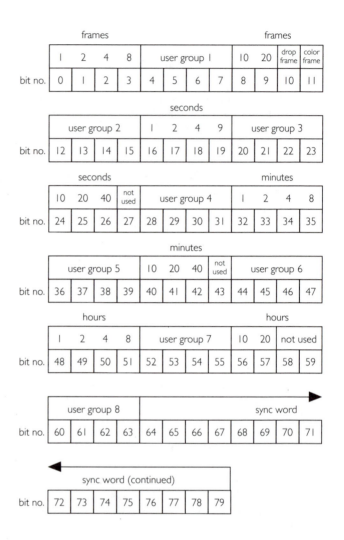

FIGURE 9.6   Longitudinal 80-bit SMPTE Time Code bit map.

found nowhere else in an 80-bit SMPTE code, so it is used to signal the end of a complete LTC address. The sync word is recognizable whether the tape it is recorded on is played forwards or backwards, so that a time code reader will always have a reference point from which to calculate the beginning and end of an LTC address.

SMPTE Tape Control Automation

Some better-quality multitrack tape recorders incorporate SMPTE control of tape transport functions. An autolocator permits the tape operator to program in a specific SMPTE time code address; the autolocator then rewinds or fast forwards the tape, stopping when it reaches the preprogrammed address (though some stop prior to the address, generally within thirty frames).

In the same fashion, autolocators typically permit the operator to program punch-in/punch-out addresses. The autolocator rewinds or fast forwards the tape, stopping prior to the punch-in address. Playback begins, then shifts into record at the specified punch-in address and back to play at the specified punch-out address.

Using SMPTE Time Code

Although video production facilities use a video sync generator (as the SMPTE standard specifies) to ensure that all SMPTE clocks agree on when each frame begins, it is not necessary for most audio studios to own one. If you are preparing audio for video postproduction and synchronizing to SMPTE, make sure that you receive a tape that already contains SMPTE time code generated at the postproduction facility; their video sync generator will ensure that the time code on tape matches the standard used throughout their studio.

An audio facility needs only a SMPTE generator, a synchronizer, and any necessary cables. The generator and synchronizer may be separate devices or they may be built into multitrack tape recorders, MIDI sequencers, or other devices. There are also software programs for personal computers that turn the computer into a SMPTE code generator, as well as compact discs containing recorded SMPTE time code which turn any compact disc player into a SMPTE time code generator.

The synchronizer analyzes the SMPTE time code previously recorded on one or more inputs (which may include tape machines, sequencers, or other devices), compares the time code to a master reference standard, and adjusts the tape location and speed of the slaves to match the reference standard. In the simplest case, the synchronizer continuously adjusts the position and speed of the slave devices so that their time code addresses always match that of the master.

Many synchronizers allow the user to select an offset, which is added to or subtracted from the master addresses before locking the slaves to that address. The case described above, where the slave addresses always match the master address, represents zero offset, a condition called frame lock.

But if, for example, a particular sound effect must be synchronized to a video picture, it may be necessary to program the synchronizer with a nonzero offset for the audio portion if the sound effect would otherwise occur slightly ahead of the video image it belongs with. Offsets can also be useful in audio-only situations. An effect similar to chorusing (in which a signal is split in two, then recombined after one of the two has been slightly delayed) can sometimes be achieved by adding a small offset to one of two identical inputs that would otherwise be perfectly locked together.

When SMPTE is used to synchronize two MIDI devices, no tape recording need be involved. Instead, one device (the master) generates SMPTE time code, while other devices (the slaves) synchronize to it. Some devices have a user-selectable choice of clock types—SMPTE, MIDI Time Code, or Song Position Pointer—so the correct clock type must be selected. In order for a system of several devices to synchronize using SMPTE, all the devices must implement SMPTE time code, the master device must be set to Internal (SMPTE) clock, and the slave devices must all be set to External (SMPTE) clock.

Synchronizing SMPTE-compatible MIDI devices to multitrack tape is somewhat more complicated since it involves recording the SMPTE time code to tape. The first step is to record time code over the full length of the tape, called striping the tape with time code. The time code source can be any SMPTE generator—sequencer, computer program, or time code compact disc. Rewind the tape to the beginning, start the time code generator, and record the time code until the end of the tape.

Experiment with different recording levels to find the one that works best for your equipment. Try recording at slightly less than the normal maximum level (a setting of -3 on a standard VU meter is a good level to try first). If you can switch off noise reduction for the track on which you are recording the time code, do so.

The outside (highest-numbered) track of a multitrack recorder is most often used for recording time code. If possible, do not record any material on the track next to the time code track. The empty track is called a guard band, and it can help isolate the time code signal from audio tracks. SMPTE time code sounds terrible to human ears, and normal audio can confuse a SMPTE reader; track-to-track bleed-through in either direction can cause problems.

If you are unable to leave a guard band because of the number of tracks you must record, try to record as little low-level audio material as possible on the track you would have used for the guard band.

Some engineers take the added precaution of recording SMPTE on the next-to-highest track, and using the track below as a guard band—for example, track 15 of a sixteen-track recorder for SMPTE, track 14 for guard band—since the outside tracks are most likely to be affected by improper handling and poor tape alignment. If your tape must travel from one studio to another for postproduction or mixdown and you have enough unused tracks, you may consider taking this extra precaution. If the entire production takes place in your studio, it probably is not necessary.

Make sure to record plenty of time code on tape before the location where the audio recording is to begin—at least 20–30 seconds' worth. Many synchronizers require a "resolve interval" before they begin their synchronization, so it is important to provide them a reference point before the recorded material begins. The best solution is to stripe the entire tape with time code from beginning to end before doing any audio recording. Record the first selection on tape well after the time code has begun, and leave a sufficient resolve interval without recorded program material between selections.

Multitrack Tape Synchronization Using SMPTE

One valuable synchronization technique can help overcome MIDI's sixteen-channel limitation by using a multitrack tape recorder to record multiple "passes" of sixteen-channel sequence playback. We will use a six-track tape recorder for our example, though the technique would work equally well with eight, sixteen, or twenty-four tracks. The example's MIDI studio includes two eight-voice multitimbral synthesizers, driven by a computer running sequencer software that implements SMPTE (though a SMPTE-capable hardware sequencer could be substituted for the computer in this example, just as an FSK-capable hardware sequencer could be substituted for the computer in figure 9.5).

First record a SMPTE time code reference signal from a SMPTE generator or SMPTE compact disc onto the outside track of the tape recorder, track 6. We will need to record only four tracks of synthesizer audio, so we will leave tape recorder track 5 for a guard band. Rewind the tape to a suitable starting point, remembering to leave an adequate resolving interval at the beginning of the tape.

Create a multipart, multivoice sequence, using thirty-two sequencer tracks. Set sequencer tracks 1–16 to play eight voices on each of the two synthesizers, with each track and corresponding synthesizer voice assigned a unique MIDI channel. Mute tracks 17–32 so that no sound is produced by those tracks on playback.

Connect the output of one synthesizer to tape recorder track 1 input and the other synthesizer to tape recorder track 2 input. Connect the output of tape recorder track 6 to the SMPTE input of the computer or sequencer. Make sure that the computer or sequencer is set to SMPTE clock. If you are not going to start recording from the beginning of the recorded SMPTE code, program the necessary offset into the sequencer.

Start the sequence's playback; the computer or sequencer should tell you that it is waiting for SMPTE. Start the tape recording. When it reaches the beginning of the recorded SMPTE code, the sequence should begin playback. Record the sixteen sequencer tracks, then rewind the tape to a location prior to where the first recording began. Figure 9.7 shows the connections between the synthesizers and multitrack recorder at the end of the first recording pass.

Now mute sequencer tracks 1–16 and unmute tracks 17–32. Set the sixteen unmuted tracks to play eight voices on each of the two synthesizers (using different synthesizer voices than before, if you prefer), with each track and corresponding synthesizer voice again assigned a unique MIDI channel.

Connect the output of one synthesizer to tape recorder track 3 input and the other synthesizer to tape recorder track 4 input. Leave the output of tape recorder track 6 connected to the SMPTE input of the sequencer. Start sequencer playback, then start recording as above. Record the sixteen new sequencer tracks, then rewind the tape to the beginning. On tape playback, you should hear thrity-two voices performing in perfect synchronization.

Trouble-shooting Time Code

If your system has been synchronizing effortlessly but suddenly intermittently fails to sync correctly or stops synchronizing altogether, the first device to suspect is the tape recorder. Check the connections to and from each tape machine. See that they are cabled correctly and that the cable connections are firm and tight. If you have some contact cleaner, apply it to each connector before reconnecting.

Consider cleaning the tape recorder heads if you have not cleaned them for a while. A small amount of dirt on the tape heads can interfere with time code recording or playback, even if there is no noticeable degradation in the audio program.

Sometimes, though, stretches of time code itself may be erased or lost due to accident or signal degradation. In that case, you will need a SMPTE time code reader/generator. A reader/generator analyzes existing SMPTE time code recorded on tape that appears at the reader/generator's input and generates a fresh version of the same time code at its output—even if the incoming time code has degraded or contains gaps. The generation of fresh time code in this manner is called jam sync and is used whenever existing time code must be copied. Copying the time code track like any other audio track subjects the time code to the same generation loss of fidelity as other audio copies, but time code is much more sensitive to such a drop in quality. Jam sync is the only proper way to copy time code.

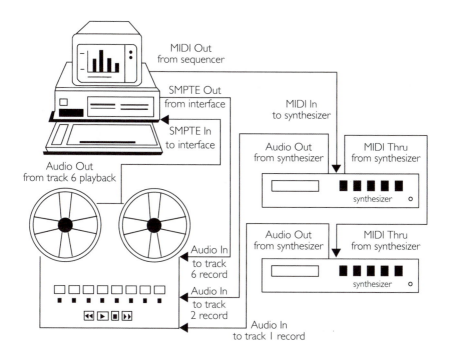

FIGURE 9.7   Audio and SMPTE connections for sequencing to multitrack tape.

To repair damaged or degraded time code, connect the output for the existing time code track to the input of the reader/generator and the output from the reader/generator to an unused recording track. Set the reader/generator to Continuous Jam and start recording. The reader/generator will output fresh time code for recording onto the previously unused track, maintaining the flow of fresh time code even when the source time code is damaged or missing.

SMPTE/MIDI Conversion

SMPTE to MIDI converters are available for MIDI devices that implement Song Position Pointer but lack SMPTE capabilities. Such converters translate each SMPTE address into the number of MIDI beats that have elapsed since the beginning of the tape, sending an appropriate Song Position Pointer message over a MIDI cable. To do so, the converter uses a tempo map to correlate SMPTE clock time to MIDI musical rhythmic values, converting one into the other.

If, for example, you start playback of a SMPTE-striped tape at a location corresponding to the first beat of measure 25, the converter will translate the incoming SMPTE address to the corresponding song position value and pass that value along to a MIDI device. If the MIDI device is set to External (MIDI) clock, it too will begin playback at the first beat of measure 25.

The expense and complication of SMPTE/MIDI conversion may be avoided by using a second tape track for time code. If one tape track is striped with SMPTE time code while the adjacent track is striped with FSK representing MIDI clock, the two tracks will always be synchronized to each other. Those devices that use SMPTE can get their timing reference from the SMPTE track, while MIDI clock devices can get theirs from the FSK track.

MIDI TIME CODE

Though both MIDI Clock and SMPTE time code provide ways to synchronize multiple devices and tape, the two are different in several important respects. MIDI is primarily a set of digital messages plus a means of communicating those messages from one device to another. The real-time messages described in chapter 8 are transmitted twenty-four times for each elapsed quarter note of musical time—the duration of a quarter note depends on tempo and is not a specific interval of time. SMPTE, by contrast, converts digital timing information into an audio signal that can be recorded on tape. That audio signal represents elapsed clock time, which is not directly related to musical note values.

As described above, one way to reconcile the two involves a SMPTE/MIDI converter, which translates SMPTE timing data into MIDI Song Position Pointer messages. That works well for synchronizing musical material, but as MIDI is increasingly used for video and film scoring, it has become important to synchronize MIDI events to clock time directly rather than having to determine which measure, beat, and tick a sampled car horn should occur on, for example.

The adoption of MIDI Time Code (MTC) as part of the MIDI specification created a standard interface between SMPTE time code and MIDI. The primary function of MTC is to transmit SMPTE time code data as MIDI messages over MIDI cables so that MIDI devices can synchronize directly to SMPTE clock time.

With MTC, the sampled car horn in the above example could be programmed to sound at the same SMPTE time code address that appeared on video tape at the time a driver pressed the car horn button. With Song

Position Pointer, the composer would have to calculate the corresponding number of MIDI beats and ticks—or more likely, find the right setting by trial and error. MTC has thus helped MIDI become a popular choice among film and video composers and sound effects specialists, who can simply make a list of SMPTE addresses where the music or effect is needed, then program a sequencer to generate a MIDI Note On message or play a sequence at the appropriate time.

Since MTC (like SMPTE) is a time code address, not a representation of musical rhythmic durations, the composer who uses MTC while scoring both music and effects gives up musical synchronization for time-accurate synchronization. As described above in "SMPTE/MIDI Conversion," one solution is to record tracks of both synchronization signals simultaneously and drive each device from the appropriate taped synchronization track.

Alternatively, a sequencer that implements both MIDI Clock and MTC and automatically converts internally from one to the other allows the composer to select MIDI Clock while planning musical passages, then switch to MTC for sound effects. Both music and effects can coexist within the same sequence, and the composer can choose either clock as the master while driving other instruments or generating the synchronization signal for tape, or select either form of external clock when the sequencer acts as a slave.

MTC Quarter Frame Messages

Two message types—Quarter Frame and Full—form the basis of MIDI Time Code. A third optional message can be used to encode SMPTE user bits.

Quarter Frame messages, like MIDI Timing Clock messages, provide the timing pulse for synchronization. Each message also includes four bits that are used to encode part of a SMPTE time code address.

As the name implies, Quarter Frame messages are transmitted at a rate of four messages per frame—120 messages per second for the thirty-frame-per-second SMPTE format normally used for audio-only synchronization. It takes eight messages to transmit one SMPTE address, so MTC updates addresses at a rate equivalent to every second SMPTE frame. That resolution is far better than MIDI Clock's twenty-four parts per quarter note; devices capable of SMPTE interpolation (similar to MIDI Clock interpolation described above) can provide even higher resolution.

When time code is running in the forward direction, as during recording and playback, a device transmitting MIDI Time Code sends Quarter Frame messages in a repeating sequence of eight, each consisting of a two-byte pair. The first (status) byte has a value of 11110001 (241 decimal). The second byte, like all data bytes, has a most significant bit of 0. The remaining three bits of most significant nibble specify the message type—which part of the SMPTE address the data represents. The least significant nibble in the data byte of the Quarter Frame message pair communicates the actual address data.

Message type values range from 0 to 7 (decimal), as follows:

000   frame count least significant nibble

001   frame count most significant nibble

010   seconds count least significant nibble

011   seconds count most significant nibble

100   minutes count least significant nibble

101   minutes count most significant nibble

110   hours count least significant nibble

111   hours count most significant nibble (and time code type)

The four Quarter Frame message data bits representing a least significant SMPTE count nibble match the least significant nibble of the data byte of the next Quarter Frame Message. The least significant nibble of the second Quarter Frame message data byte represents the most significant SMPTE count nibble. Together, the two Quarter Frame message data bytes' least significant nibbles compose a single SMPTE count data byte. Thus, it takes four Quarter Frame message bytes—status, data, status, data—to make up a SMPTE count data byte, since each Quarter Frame data byte yields a nibble of the SMPTE count data byte.

Once the two nibbles of the SMPTE count data byte are combined, they are interpreted according to whether the message type is frame, seconds, minutes, or hours:

The five least significant bits of a Frame Count message encompass values ranging from 0 to 29 (decimal).

The six least significant bits of a Seconds Count message encompass values ranging from 0 to 59 (decimal).

The six least significant bits of a Minutes Count message encompass values ranging from 0 to 59 (decimal).

The five least significant bits of an Hours Count message encompass values ranging from 0 to 23 (decimal).

Other than the 0 bit that begins every data byte and the bits described above, bits in Quarter Frame message data bytes are not defined—transmitting devices send 0s for those bits and receiving devices ignore them—with one exception. If the message type bits specify an Hours Count message, the two bits that follow the most significant (0) bit of the hours count (assembled from the least significant nibbles of two separate Quarter Frame message data bytes) specify the time code type, as follows:

00   24 frames per second

01   25 frames per second

10   30 frames per second (drop-frame)

11   30 frames per second (NTSC monochrome)

Figure 9.8 shows a complete eight-part series of Quarter Frame messages specifying the complete SMPTE address 19:42:37:18 (hours: minutes:seconds:frames) in NTSC monochrome.

Note that the hours/most significant nibble will always represent hours as 0 or 1, since hours cannot exceed 24 (16 + 8). The two middle bits of the hours/most significant nibble (in this case, 11) specify the SMPTE code type—thirty frames per second, nondrop in this example.

For all SMPTE frame rates except twenty-five frames per second, the MTC frame number will always specify an even-numbered frame. At twenty-five frames per second, the frame number may be even or odd and will alternate between the two for each twenty-five-frame group. Starting with frame 1, for example, the next 3 seconds of frames would be counted [1, 3, 5 ... 21, 23, 25] [2, 4, 6 ... 20, 22, 24] [1, 3, 5 ... 21, 23, 25].

STATUS	MESSAGE TYPE	DATA BITS
11110001	0 000	**0010**
11110001	0 001	**0001**
		Data Byte: 0001 0010 → 16 + 2 = frame: 18
11110001	0 010	**0101**
11110001	0 011	**0010**
		Data Byte: 0010 0101 → 32 + 5 = seconds: 37
11110001	0 100	**1010**
11110001	0 101	**0010**
		Data Byte: 0010 1010 → 32 + 10 = minutes: 42
11110001	0 110	**0011**
11110001	0 111	**0111**
		Data Byte: 0111 0011 → 16 + 3 = hours: 19
		SMPTE Type: 11 = 30 frames/second, non-drop

SMPTE Address: 19 hours, 42 minutes, 37 seconds, frame 18

FIGURE 9.8   A complete SMPTE address (NTSC monochrome.)

MTC Full Messages

Quarter Frame messages establish the ongoing "pulse" for MIDI Time Code. But when a device transmitting MTC messages is rewound or fast-forwarded, the address at which the device stops is important rather than the number of addresses it passed to reach its destination. Rather than transmitting numerous Quarter Frame messages at high speed and expecting receiving devices to keep up, a Full message transmits a complete SMPTE address in a single 10-byte message. Devices receiving an MTC Full message can then auto-locate to that address and await the next Quarter Frame message to signal that SMPTE time is "running" once again.

The first (status) byte of a Full message, whose value is 11110000 (240 decimal), identifies the message as a System Exclusive message. The next byte, 01111111 (127 decimal), specifies a real-time System Exclusive message. The third (channel) byte has a value of 01111111 (127 decimal) to specify that the message is intended for the entire system. The fourth and fifth bytes (sub-ID #1 and sub-ID #2) each have a value of 1, specifying MIDI Time Code and Full, respectively. The next four bytes specify the SMPTE counts for hours and type, minutes, seconds, and frames, using the same conventions as described above. The tenth and last byte, EOX, has a value of 11110111 (247 decimal) and signifies the end of the System Exclusive MTC Full message.

User Bits

As described above in "SMPTE Time Code Structure," the SMPTE specification provides thirty-two user bits whose purpose varies with the application—for example, to date-stamp a recording or add a reel number onto a SMPTE-striped tape. The user bits can accommodate up to four characters or eight digits.

A MIDI User Bits message, fifteen bytes long, sets the value of the SMPTE User Bits. The first four bytes of a MIDI User Bits message are the same as the Full message described above. The fifth byte, sub-ID #2, has a value of 2 to specify a User Bits message.

The next eight bytes provide the data corresponding to SMPTE Binary Groups 1 through 8. The eight bytes are broken into four pairs. The most significant nibble of each byte has a value of 0, while the least significant nibble of each byte provides one nibble of a SMPTE Binary Group byte. Thus, the least significant nibbles of the first pair form the most and least significant nibbles, respectively, of SMPTE Binary Group 1.

Each bit of the fourteenth (next to last) byte of the MIDI User Bits message has a value of 0, except for the two least significant bits. The values of those two bits represent the two Binary Group Flag Bits (also described above), as defined by the SMPTE specification.

A User Bits message may be sent whenever the specified User Bits values need to be changed within the devices that receive and respond to MIDI Time Code messages.

Other MTC Messages

MIDI Time Code uses another series of System Exclusive messages to transmit specialized MTC synchronization information. These Set Up messages permit such MIDI cuing functions as Time Code Offset, Punch In or Punch Out, and Cue Points. Such messages are typically used by devices that use Edit Decision Lists (EDLs). EDLs are often used in sound-effects and dialogue-replacement applications, in which a list specifies a particular effect or dialogue block stored on a particular device and a time at which that effect or dialogue should be played back for final mix-down. SMPTE-based devices that read EDLs can "fire off" the correct audio portion from the correct device at the correct time, automatically.

A few MIDI devices implementing MTC-based Edit Decision Lists have appeared, and more are likely as MIDI is increasingly used for film and video scoring. Readers interested in the specific implementation of Set Up messages should refer to the complete *MIDI 1.0 Detailed Specification.*

PROGRAMMING IN MIDI

MIDI is well-enough established that it supports a wide variety of software as well as hardware. Many musicians can meet all their software needs using commercially available programs. Such MIDI users may never need to develop their own programs and may wish to skip this chapter or read it only to get a better understanding of the programming principles underlying MIDI software.

But like any mass-market item, commercial software aims at the most common needs of the largest possible user base—your own needs may be considerably different. Developing custom programs lets you tailor the capabilities and features of your MIDI system to more exactly meet your specific needs. There are other advantages as well: writing a voice editor or librarian program for a new synthesizer may be faster than waiting for an acceptable one to appear; as the MIDI specification develops and the MIDI marketplace grows, there should be opportunities to market innovative original programs; and many people enjoy the challenge of designing and crafting quality software.

Writing computer programs for MIDI applications can be thought of more specifically as writing programs to control the passage of data through the computer's MIDI interface. If the correct MIDI messages are sent by the computer to the MIDI interface at the proper time and in the proper order, any MIDI device connected to the interface should receive the messages correctly.

Different types of MIDI interfaces implement the passage of messages differently from one another, however, so there is no single set of MIDI programming commands that works on all MIDI interfaces. For that reason, this chapter provides an overview of MIDI programming—the subject is complex enough to merit its own book, and several such books are available. In addition, refer to the technical documentation of your MIDI interface to determine the specific requirements for implementing a program on the particular MIDI interface you use.

CHOOSING A PROGRAMMING LANGUAGE

There are two primary factors that distinguish MIDI programming from most other software development. Unlike accounting programs for example, MIDI programs must deal with data that is timing-sensitive, often handling data as it is generated by MIDI devices in real time—as it occurs—rather than accumulating the data for subsequent processing. Similarly, MIDI programs must deal with MIDI devices that are external to the computer system itself, gathering input from those devices or sending them output in the form of MIDI messages.

MIDI software can be developed in any computer programming language, but the best choice is one that facilitates fast queuing (lining up) of serial (one-after-another) data streams and one that is designed to handle input and output quickly and efficiently. Many MIDI software developers use the C programming language because it excels at handling data queues quickly and because many C compilers can call assembly-language modules to perform input/output (I/O) or tasks where speed is particularly important. (Assembly language consists of commands that manipulate the computer's central processing unit and memory directly rather than being broken down from a high-level language such as C into the computer's native command set.) The C language also has a rich variety of commands that provide control over the computer hardware itself, particularly over how computer memory is allocated and used.

Memory management is an especially important consideration for MIDI programmers, even though memory capacity has grown significantly compared to earlier generations of personal computers. The simplest Note On message, for example, occupies three bytes, so an eight-voice chord would require a minimum of twenty-four bytes, and a single measure of four eight-voice chords would require a minimum of ninety-six bytes. It is easy to see how a large composition can require a similarly large amount of computer memory. Continuous Controller messages can occupy hundreds of bytes each; so can System Exclusive messages. Without some attention to memory management, even a relatively simple MIDI data storage program can quickly run out of memory space.

Well-designed C programs use memory conservatively and run quickly. However, the language has such a rich collection of data structures, operators, and machine control functions that some programmers find it more difficult to learn and use than other programming languages.

The LISP programming language, while very different from C, is likewise popular among MIDI software developers. "LISP" is a contraction of List Processor, and LISP's strength is its handling of data in the form of lists. This is particularly appropriate for MIDI processing since many MIDI programs deal with lists of MIDI events. Note lists, for example, are easy to control using LISP to implement transposition, retrograde, and inversion, making LISP well suited for music composition, printing, and other applications that manipulate note list data.

A further advantage of LISP is its extensibility. LISP programmers can add new capabilities to the programming language; subsequent programs can use the extensions as if they were part of LISP itself.

LISP is the language of choice among developers of expert systems, which can make decisions based on "best guesses" as well as clear rules. Music composition can be considered the flexible application of certain rules or guidelines; music composition programs called algorithmic composers are sometimes written in LISP.

FORTRAN, one of the earliest computer programming languages, was used to develop one of the first computer music synthesis programs, which ran on mainframe computers twenty years before the development of MIDI. Many variants of that original program, including Music 5 and a C language version, Csound, are still in use today by colleges and researchers with access to large computers. Music 5 and Csound have even been adapted to the MIDI studio on an experimental basis, and commercial versions of software incorporating concepts first used in Music 5 have also appeared.

Indeed, virtually any programming language can be used for MIDI software development. Though the Pascal programming language was originally conceived as a language for teaching programming skills and techniques, it is powerful enough that it, too, can be used by MIDI programmers.

Even the BASIC programming language—sometimes criticized as poorly structured and cumbersome to use—has been used successfully by MIDI software authors. In fact, special extensions of BASIC such as MIDI BASIC have been created specifically for developing MIDI programs. BASIC is often the first language many programmers learn, so MIDI BASIC may be the best choice for such programmers to use while learning to write MIDI programs. A version of BASIC with extensions for MIDI programming can be the fastest way to develop more complex MIDI programs as well, since much of the program code needed for the specialized requirements of

MIDI programming is already part of the language. For that reason, MIDI BASIC is popular among more experienced MIDI programmers as well as beginners.

MIDI PROGRAM MODULE LIBRARIES

The most common MIDI programming tasks include such operations as getting or sending a byte of data from or to the MIDI interface and sending a command to the interface. Other commonly used MIDI programming routines change the status or configuration of the MIDI interface; store incoming MIDI data in a buffer (a block of memory in the MIDI interface or computer used for temporary data storage); retrieve the stored messages, one by one, from the buffer; and clear any MIDI data from the buffer—as well as more complicated routines required for interrupt servicing (discussed below). Programs involving sequencing generally also contain routines to group, store, and manipulate MIDI data by sequencer track.

Inexpensive or public domain MIDI input/output program code modules to perform these common MIDI programming tasks are available for programming languages such as BASIC, Pascal, and C. They are often posted on computer bulletin board systems, where they are accessible to anyone whose computer is equipped with a modem, a device that allows computers to communicate over telephone lines. Program developers can implement these "off-the-shelf" modules into their own programs. (For more on computer bulletin board systems for MIDI users, see chapter 11, "Getting Help.")

Using a well-designed and well-documented function library can speed program development, implementation, and testing. The program developer can simply call upon the prewritten module when it is required, concentrating on the goal, organization and logic of the program and leaving most of the details of how the particular functions work to the library modules. The developer designs and implements the program in the usual manner, calling upon the library function, procedure, or module when needed. The program library can be considered a collection of "black boxes"—the program developer need not be concerned with how the library modules work, only that they produce the result described in the documentation for those modules.

The most important concerns in choosing a particular program library include the following: The library must be designed to work with the same programming language that the software developer uses; it may require that the program developer use a particular dialect or brand of the chosen programming language; it must implement most of the important functions that the program developer needs; and each module's documentation must be complete and clear.

PROGRAMMING TOOLS FOR NONPROGRAMMERS

Recently, a new generation of MIDI programming tools has taken the modular approach to MIDI programming a step farther. Often called object-oriented or iconic programming environments, these tools view the programming process as one of stringing together a series of modular tasks rather than developing a linear process from beginning to end. Such tasks might include getting or sending a byte of MIDI data, pressing a key to generate a MIDI Note message, or changing the position of a numbered controller.

Each task module is represented by an object, which can be a named process or a picture (icon) representing that process. The user connects the objects or icons in such a way as to accomplish the desired task, and the programming tool generates the necessary program code (figure 10.1). This approach frees the user from the need to learn the syntax of a programming language, minimizes the possibility that the resulting program will contain logic errors, speeds the program development process, and represents programming functions in a manner familiar to MIDI users.

As the principles and techniques of object-oriented programming become better understood, we are likely to see increasingly powerful MIDI development environments that free MIDI users from the need to learn traditional computer programming languages and skills.

PORTS

The computer and the MIDI interface exchange data through a port, a special-purpose computer memory location that transmits and receives data rather than storing it. Like memory, a port is referred to by its address—a program transmits data to a numbered port address rather than to the destination device, while the destination device looks for data at the same port address.

A typical arrangement uses one port for sending and receiving data and another port for sending and receiving commands. A third port may be used for reporting the status of the interface, though on some interfaces the command port is used to transmit status information as well as commands.

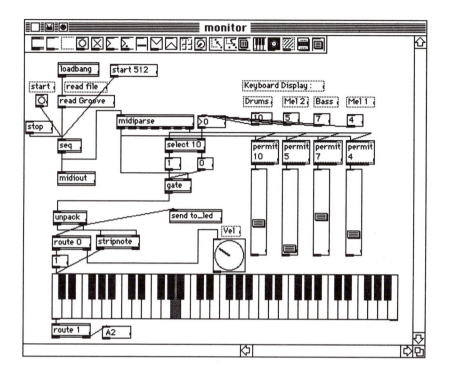

FIGURE 10.1   Max iconic MIDI programming environment
(courtesy Opcode Systems, Inc.).

Sending and receiving data to and from the interface is typically a
two-step process. The interface uses a port address to report its status, so
the program first has to check the status port to see if any data is waiting
or if the interface is ready to receive data. If the status indicates the correct
condition, data is then received or sent at another port address.

Commands are sent to the required port address. The interface may
send back an acknowledgement—a special byte pattern reserved for that
purpose—indicating that the interface received the command correctly.

SMART AND DUMB MODES

Most MIDI interfaces have two operating modes. In "smart"
mode, the interface keeps track of MIDI timing while the computer performs other tasks. Smart mode is generally used for complex multipurpose
MIDI programs such as sequencers. In "dumb" mode, the MIDI interface

simply receives and transmits data without changing it in any way, and the computer handles all timing and sequencing of data. Programmers familiar with serial interfaces can apply many of the same programming concepts to MIDI interface programming. (The serial interface protocol called RS-232, widely used for computer data communications, acts like a MIDI interface in dumb mode, simply passing along any data sent to it.)

In dumb mode, the primary function of receiving and transmitting data in most MIDI interfaces is performed by a logic chip known as a UART, for Universal Asynchronous Receive/Transmit. It too, is widely used for data communications applications. The UART sends incoming MIDI data along to the computer and passes data coming from the computer along to MIDI devices.

The default (ordinary) state of many MIDI interfaces is smart mode, which while more powerful requires more programming. Most simple programs require that the MIDI interface act as a "dumb" interface, so a user's program would need to set it to dumb mode before proceeding.

POLLING THE INTERFACE

One approach to MIDI interface programming, called polling, directs the computer to repeatedly check the status port waiting for the status message that reports a data byte in the interface waiting to be read.

Most computers can send and receive data faster than the MIDI interface, so the program might need to introduce delays between sending or receiving successive bytes. Otherwise it might poll the interface and read the same byte more than once before the interface has had time to change its status back to "no byte waiting."

INTERRUPTS

An alternative approach uses the capability of most MIDI interfaces to transmit interrupts—special signals a device sends to the computer when an unscheduled event occurs. By sending an interrupt, the interface can signal the computer to stop what it was doing, get a data byte from the interface and store it, then return to what it was doing before receiving the interrupt. Programming using polling is simpler than using interrupts, but polling wastes the computer's time repeatedly looking at an unchanged status port. Polling may also miss a data byte that arrived when the computer was not looking for it. Interrupts tell the computer when each data byte arrives, so the computer only needs to look at the interface when data is waiting.

One reason that interrupt programming is usually more complicated than polling is that many computers use a special logic chip to receive interrupts from external hardware. That chip, in turn, passes the interrupt to the computer's central processing unit. Techniques for programming the interrupt controller chip differ from one computer to another; if the computer you work with uses such a chip, you will need to determine exactly how it is programmed if you want to use interrupts in your MIDI programs.

Each MIDI program must have its own specially written interrupt handler since the desired response to an interrupt depends on the nature of the interrupt and the particular program. Programming interrupts for a complex program like a sequencer is similarly complex because of the different requirements of interrupts under different circumstances.

An interrupt service routine can quickly become complicated when it must assign priorities to several simultaneous interrupts, as in a multiport MIDI system. Failure to service an incoming interrupt quickly enough can result in the loss of a byte. Since MIDI contains no error detection or correction protocol, even a single lost byte can cause problems. Fortunately, most programming languages (including any that can call assembly-language routines) can assign appropriate priority levels to interrupts from different sources so that the most important source of interrupts is always serviced first.

GETTING STARTED

There are only two ways to learn computer programming: analyzing programs that others have written and writing your own. The guidelines in this chapter are only the beginning—you will need to gather the technical reference documentation for your MIDI interface and MIDI equipment, select an appropriate programming language, and choose a MIDI program module library or object-oriented MIDI programming environment if one that you like is available.

If you are already an experienced programmer, your computer and MIDI system documentation, together with an understanding of the specifics of each MIDI message (covered in chapter 8) should give you enough information to begin designing, coding, and testing some simple MIDI programs.

But if you are new to programming, you might want to study other MIDI programmers' work before undertaking a programming project of your own. Unfortunately for students of programming, most commercially available MIDI software is distributed as object code (machine-level instructions represented by ones and zeros) rather than source code, the human readable computer language that must be converted into machine-executable object code before a computer can run it.

Many examples of source code MIDI programs are readily available, however. Sources of such examples, and sources of other kinds of help as well, are covered in the next chapter.

GETTING HELP

This book is intended to provide an overview of the major aspects of MIDI—but much more information is available to the interested MIDI user. The information sources described here offer advice, free or low-cost instrument patches and computer software, opportunities to exchange information and views with other MIDI users, a marketplace for new or used equipment, and many other services.

MAGAZINES

Magazines are one of the best ways to keep up with the rapidly developing MIDI specification and MIDI equipment marketplace. A wide range of MIDI-oriented magazines is available, some suitable for beginners and others intended for more advanced MIDI users.

Electronic Musician is one of the most widely read magazines among MIDI users. Each issue contains several MIDI-related articles, including tutorials, reviews of MIDI equipment, and do-it-yourself projects. It is particularly appropriate for MIDI beginners and those who are unfamiliar with the terminology and theory of computers and electronics.

Keyboard has changed its emphasis during recent years. Though it still covers every aspect of keyboard technology, practice, and performance, *Keyboard* is now of particular interest to players of electronic keyboard instruments—particularly MIDI keyboards. Other MIDI users are likely to find information and reviews of interest as well since *Keyboard* also covers and reviews modular synthesizers and accessories that may be equally at home in a keyboardless studio.

R-E-P: Recording-Engineering-Production bills itself as "The Pro Audio Applications Magazine," and that is a fair description of its focus and content. Each issue contains a photo tour and technical discussion of a leading professional recording studio, as well as technical articles on such topics as multitrack tape recorders, automated mixing consoles, and the design of recording studio facilities. As MIDI has become commonplace in professional recording studios, articles about MIDI have become a regular feature of *R-E-P* as well. While perhaps too technical for the beginning MIDI user, the articles and regular columns covering MIDI-related topics are likely to interest more experienced MIDI users and music professionals.

Studio Sound, like *R-E-P,* is directed at audio and recording professionals, with an editorial content to match. Unlike *R-E-P* and *Mix* (described below), *Studio Sound* is published in Europe, not America, so it has a different perspective on audio issues, including MIDI. *Studio Sound* sometimes covers European MIDI developments before the stories reach American shores.

Mix calls itself "The Recording Industry Magazine," and as such its focus is more on developments of interest to recording studio owners and operators than to MIDI musicians. Yet as MIDI finds its way into a growing array of recording studio equipment, a growing number of MIDI-related articles have appeared in *Mix* as well. Recent articles have covered such subjects as digital audio tape (DAT) recorders, the design of mixing consoles, and MIDI-controllable equalizers. Each issue includes a tour of a professional recording studio, interviews with prominent musicians or studio engineers, and users' reviews of recording equipment and musical instruments—MIDI equipment among them.

Computer Music Journal was the first journal devoted to computer music and digital audio topics. It began publication in 1978 and has appeared quarterly ever since. Many concepts and technologies that are now commonplace in the computer music world first appeared in print in *CMJ,* and the journal continues to stay at the leading edge of computer music and digital audio research. Though many of its articles are too advanced for beginning MIDI users, more experienced MIDI users—especially those with some knowledge of computer architecture and programming, electrical engineering, or higher mathematics—may enjoy its focus, which is more technical than other magazines described here.

Music Technology delivers what its title suggests—articles and reviews of equipment, computers, and software designed for music applications. Rather than focusing on a particular type of instrument such as keyboards or guitars, it looks at MIDI from the system perspective. It sometimes includes articles of a somewhat technical nature, but it more often includes a wide range of information of interest even to beginning MIDI users. Despite its technology focus, a knowledge of computers and engineering is not required.

Several manufacturers also sponsor magazines, and those, too, can be worth a look—particularly since most are free for the asking. While primarily a vehicle for advertising the manufacturer's products and disseminating tips and techniques specific to those products, they often include tutorials and articles of more general interest. The best include the *Roland Users Group Magazine* and *The First Reflection,* published by MIDI and audio equipment manufacturer Alesis Studio Electronics.

New magazines start up all the time, and existing magazines often refocus their editorial content, change their name, or cease publication altogether. The *Reader's Guide to Periodicals* at your local library is a good reference for finding out what MIDI magazines are available—and many of the magazines may be available at your local library as well.

The list above is a representative but by no means exhaustive survey. If a title that is unfamiliar to you seems interesting, try to read a library copy or buy one from a newsstand or music store, then decide if you think it is worth subscribing to. Every MIDI user I know subscribes to at least one MIDI magazine, if only to keep current on new products of interest. It is a practice I strongly recommend.

MUSIC STORES

Many music stores have been unable to keep up with rapidly changing music technology, and a customer with detailed questions may have difficulty finding knowledgeable music store personnel who do not change jobs after a few months. Some stores, though, do invest in training their salespeople and work hard at retaining their personnel. Such stores deserve the support of their customers.

Better music stores have good-quality equipment and knowledgeable salespeople; some of the best stores offer other services as well, including on-site repairs, special rush repair service, computer bulletin boards (described below), or MIDI classes.

Unfortunately, too many prospective customers view music stores as a free information resource, depending on their local full-service store to answer questions and provide technical support, but spending their money at discount stores and mail-order houses. Recognize that music stores, like any commercial enterprise, are in business to make a profit. If you are lucky enough to find a full-service music store that does more than simply sell equipment, patronize it with your purchases as well as your information-gathering. Otherwise, full-service music stores may become reluctant to help anyone who is not already a customer or may start charging fees for information and assistance that is now offered free of charge.

BOOKS

The best single-volume introduction and overview of computer music principles and practice may be *Foundations of Computer Music,* edited by Curtis Roads and John Strawn. Roads and Strawn provide a perspective of the field based on their years of experience as composers, authors, and computer music professionals. The volume covers all aspects of computer music, so much of the material may be too technical or otherwise of limited interest to the MIDI musician, but it can provide a thorough grounding in the history, technology, and theory that underlies all computer music—of which MIDI is a small but significant part.

If you are finding this book too technical or otherwise difficult to understand, you might want to look at *MIDI for Musicians,* by Craig Anderton. A breezy, nontechnical introduction to MIDI, with interviews, product descriptions, and an overview of some subjects covered more deeply in this book, *MIDI for Musicians* can provide an introduction to the MIDI neophyte. Experienced MIDI users and those interested in moving beyond the introductory level are likely to find it inadequate for their needs, however.

Musical Applications of Microprocessors, by Hal Chamberlin, was one of the first books dealing with implementing computer music on personal computers. It predated MIDI, and many of the computers and programming techniques it describes are obsolete, but it can help the reader gain a broader perspective of the development of computer music and help provide a deeper understanding of some of the techniques used by computer music programmers.

Other books in the Computer Music and Digital Audio Series (of which this book is a part) bring together information resources covering topics on all aspects of computer music, including theoretical research and practical technology such as compact discs and digital audio engineering, as well as synthesizers and MIDI.

THE INTERNATIONAL MIDI ASSOCIATION

The International MIDI Association (IMA) is the single most important MIDI user's group. It serves as the official information network for the MIDI industry, disseminating information on behalf of the

MIDI Manufacturers Association. Any addenda or extensions to the MIDI specification are immediately published by the IMA, either in the IMA bulletin, which is mailed periodically to all IMA members, or in addenda to the *MIDI 1.0 Detailed Specification.*

The detailed specification is available directly from the IMA, at a discounted rate for IMA members. Other documents available from IMA include an extensive collection of system exclusive codes and standard MIDI implementation charts covering MIDI instruments from all MIDI manufacturers, several MIDI-related books, and a complete collection of IMA bulletin back issues.

MIDI User Group services offered by IMA include a telephone hotline for inquiries pertaining to MIDI and requests for technical support, a discount on the enrollment fee for PAN, the Performing Artists' Network (discussed below), and an industry referral service, through which members' resumes are entered into a database that is made available to interested companies. Every serious MIDI user should consider joining IMA—if only to take advantage of the member's discount on the detailed specification, the single most important MIDI reference text. That alone justifies the cost of membership, and with its other services, the IMA is a true bargain.

For more information, contact: International MIDI Association, 5316 West 57th Street, Los Angeles, California 90056, telephone 213-649-6434, facsimile machine 213-215-3380.

USERS' GROUPS

Many communities support their own MIDI users' groups, which offer a variety of services to local MIDI users. Users' groups provide their members with a forum for asking questions, airing complaints, and exchanging information. Some groups maintain MIDI reference libraries, offer collections of public domain MIDI programs, host presentations by local musicians or MIDI experts, publish newsletters, or sponsor equipment swap meets. Each users' group is likely to be unique in some respect— and that is what makes them worth finding out about.

Your local music stores may know if there is a MIDI users' group in your area. Other leads might come from your local library, music school, or college music department. Talk to other MIDI users you know; if no one knows of a MIDI users' group nearby, consider starting one. All it takes is a meeting place (school cafeterias, library conference rooms, and music stores often provide meeting space at no charge), some publicity, and a few hours devoted to making the necessary arrangements. The potential rewards are great.

COMPUTER BULLETIN BOARD SYSTEMS

Personal computers can be equipped with a modem, which converts digital information into audio signals for transmission over telephone lines and converts incoming modulated telephone audio signals back into digital information—a process called modulation/demodulation. Modem software is also required, in addition to the modem hardware. The software typically includes capabilities to transmit (upload) data files prepared off line—prior to establishing the modem connection—to a remote computer, and to capture (download) information from the remote computer, storing it on the user's system.

A computer bulletin board system (CBBS) allows modem-equipped personal computers to leave messages for others and retrieve messages that have been posted on the bulletin board. Some CBBSs permit person-to-person messages, but messages are more commonly posted on a public basis—that is, anyone with access to the CBBS can read them.

Some CBBSs are operated at no charge to users by system operators (sysops) who enjoy providing such a forum. Others charge a nominal fee to offset expenses, while still others operate on a for-profit basis and typically provide other on-line information services as well. If the bulletin board's access telephone number is a long-distance call, users generally must pay any long-distance telephone charges involved.

Most CBBSs are structured into conferences or special interest groups (SIGs), organized by topic so that callers need only browse through those messages covering topics of interest to them. MIDI SIGs are among the most popular, and CBBSs can be a good source of low-cost MIDI information.

If there is a computer club in your area, it may operate a CBBS or be able to tell you who does and how to gain access to it. Other leads might come from local computer stores, public libraries, schools, or colleges.

ON-LINE DATABASE SERVICES

While some computer bulletin board systems are operated as a public service, others charge a fee for the services they provide. Most often, such subscription computer networks also provide access to specialized databases, organized collections of information with certain rules for accessing them. Some database services focus exclusively on MIDI, while others have a more general orientation.

As a general rule, the more specialized a service is, the more it is likely to cost. Generic services of interest to a large market—such as access to news organizations' wire services—are typically less expensive than those that specialize in a particular professional specialty or area of interest. Many specialized database services charge a one-time membership fee, with a required monthly minimum charge that is offset by charges for actually using the system, based on how many minutes the customer is on line. Some database services further segment their charges into charges for connect time, the number of minutes your computer is connected to the host system that provides the database, and computer charges, the number of seconds or minutes that the host computer actually spends processing your information requests. Many services also charge different rates at different times of day, with higher rates during prime time daylight hours and lower charges at night.

Modem transmission speed is measured in baud, with baud rates ranging from 300 to 9,600 baud. Higher baud rates minimize time-related connect charges, though not all database services and CBBSs support all baud rates. The most commonly supported baud rates are 300, 1,200, and 2,400 baud—though as high-speed modems become competitively priced, more database services and CBBSs are likely to support the higher speeds.

Most users of database services are located in cities far from the host computer. Rather than charging differential costs based on long-distance fees, most major database providers use telecommunications services such as Tymnet and Telenet, which provide a local phone number that users located in major metropolitan areas can call. The local number serves as a gateway to the distant host computer, so the end user pays only for the database service itself, not the added long-distance charges as well.

Some on-line information services are operated by large corporations. They generally serve mass-market customers, offering airline schedules, sports information, stock market and investment data, and so forth. While such mass-market commercial database services may be worth investigating, they are likely to provide little of particular interest to musicians, though they sometimes offer CBBS capabilities and SIGs similar to the CBBSs described above.

THE PERFORMING ARTISTS' NETWORK

One on-line computer network and database oriented specifically toward musicians is PAN, the Performing Artists' Network. PAN offers a variety of SIGs covering audio topics, particular synthesizers, and aspects of MIDI, along with sample and patch databases. It is available twenty-four hours a day and accessible by modem from almost every city in the Western world. Most of the programs and utilities available on PAN are machine-specific; that is, intended for a particular brand and model of synthesizer or computer.

While PAN is musician-oriented, not all of PAN's services are music-specific. Like many such on-line services, PAN offers electronic mail, or E-mail. This allows individuals to send and receive messages to and from other specified individuals, regardless of the time of day. Transmission is instantaneous, and users can "check their mail" any time, at their convenience. Some musicians use PAN's private mail facilities to send song or sequence files to colleagues, permitting collaborative efforts by musicians in far-flung locations.

PAN also provides CBBS facilities, but these are intended to serve musicians' needs—instruments for sale, music production services offered, and requests for information about discontinued synthesizers, for example.

Another on-line service PAN has adapted for musicians is the teleconference, a "real time" communication between two or more individuals using PAN at the same time. It can be particularly powerful when many people log on to the teleconference at a prearranged time to discuss a predetermined subject such as a new-product announcement or for a group "interview" with a leading industry figure or manufacturer's representative.

PAN also features a manufacturer-specific hotline system that allows customer service functions on a twenty-four-hour basis. The PAN user can select a company (whose product they have a question or comment about) from a menu—an extensive list of companies that are part of the PAN user support network. The system then helps the user complete an electronic questionnaire and routes it to the electronic mailbox of the company's on-line customer service representative.

PAN's databases are what distinguish it from other computer networks providing services like those described above. Any PAN user can download sound patches from PAN's patch library database or contribute original patches to the database by uploading their patch files to PAN.

Patch files in the PAN library are stored on line and indexed so that users can browse through the catalog of patches or do a specific search, downloading just those sounds that are appropriate for the user's synthesizer or computer equipment, soundfile format, and personal preference.

All these capabilities come at a cost. In addition to a one-time membership fee, PAN levies charges for each minute of user connect time, along with applicable administrative charges for such services as mailbox maintenance and user data storage. For additional information, contact:

The PAN Network, PO Box 162, Skippack, Pennsylvania 19474, USA, telephone (215) 584-0300.

OTHER DATABASE SERVICES

While PAN offers perhaps the most extensive database services of interest to MIDI musicians, other MIDI databases are also worth investigating and often cost considerably less than PAN. Some are sponsored by manufacturers and provide manufacturer-specific synthesizer patches, software updates, and utilities. Generally, manufacturer-sponsored boards do not charge users for access to the system. For only the cost of applicable long-distance charges, synthesizer and MIDI-controlled audio equipment owners can download patch files, post questions for customer service representatives, and learn about the manufacturer's new products, often before they are publicly announced.

As MIDI has become a part of school and college music curricula, some schools and other institutions have begun offering on-line MIDI database services. While usually less comprehensive than PAN, such systems generally offer some of the same services, without many of the charges levied for using PAN. In most cases, downloadable files include patch libraries and collections of useful MIDI utility programs. Some school-sponsored CBBSs charge a nominal registration fee to cover administrative costs, while others are available free of charge (except for long-distance telephone charges).

MIDI computer bulletin boards and database services appear (and disappear) frequently. Check with other MIDI users, music stores, and school music departments for information on services in your area or new systems that might be of interest. Many CBBSs contain listings of other systems along with access information or contacts, so one call to a CBBS can provide a gateway to many more.

While on-line services can be expensive, they often provide the fastest, most comprehensive information available, and judicious use of the services' information sources and databases can save time and money, compared to available alternatives.

CONCLUSIONS

Finally, remember that one information source can often provide leads to others. Many of the sources described in this chapter contain such "pointers." For example, the Classifieds sections of MIDI magazines are an excellent source of leads to new MIDI bulletin boards and database services, as well as numerous other MIDI products and services.

Manufacturer advertising has information value, too. Most MIDI magazine ads include "bingo card" numbers, corresponding to numbers on information request cards bound into the magazine. Circle the numbers of products of interest, return the bingo card, and your mailbox will be filled with information. Its primary purpose is to sell new products, of course, but by studying specifications, comparing features, and learning to separate fact from fluff, you will get a better understanding of products before purchasing them and learn more about MIDI in general.

MIDI has evolved from a simple interconnect scheme to a complex, extensible protocol that provides a wealth of capabilities to musicians. Yet its history has barely begun, and even more dramatic developments are sure to occur. This is an exciting time to be a musician, and the ongoing evolution of the MIDI specification makes it likely that the excitement will continue for a long time to come.

MIDI 1.0 DETAILED SPECIFICATION: OVERVIEW AND TABLES

CONTENTS

SECTION ONE — OVERVIEW

Introduction

MIDI, the Musical Instrument Digital Interface, was established as a hardware and software specification which would make it possible to exchange information (musical notes, program changes, expression control, etc.) between different musical instruments or other devices such as sequencers, computers, lighting controllers, mixers, etc. This ability to transmit and receive data was originally conceived for live performances, although subsequent developments have had enormous impact in recording studios, audio and video production, and composition environments.

This document has been prepared as a joint effort between the MIDI Manufacturers Association (MMA) and the Japan MIDI Standards Committee (JMSC) to explain the MIDI 1.0 specification. This document is subject to change by agreement between the JMSC and MMA. Additional MIDI protocol may be included in supplements to this publication.

Hardware

The hardware MIDI interface operates at 31.25 (+/− 1%) Kbaud, asynchronous, with a start bit, 8 data bits (D0 to D7), and a stop bit. This makes a total of 10 bits for a period of 320 microseconds per serial byte. The start bit is a logical 0 (current on) and the stop bit is a logical 1 (current off).

Circuit: (*See Schematic*—figure A.1). 5 mA current loop type. Logical 0 is current ON. One output shall drive one and only one input. To avoid ground loops, and subsequent data errors, the transmitter circuitry and receiver circuitry are internally separated by an optoisolator (a light emitting diode and a photo sensor which share a single, sealed package). Sharp PC-900 and HP 6N138 optoisolators have been found acceptable. Other high-speed optoisolators may be satisfactory. The receiver must require less than 5 mA to turn on. Rise and fall times should be less than 2 microseconds.

Connectors: DIN 5 pin (180 degree) female panel mount receptacle. An example is the SWITCHCRAFT 57 GB5F. The connectors shall be labelled "MIDI IN" and "MIDI OUT." Note that pins 1 and 3 are not used, and should be left unconnected in the receiver and transmitter. Pin 2 of the MIDI In connector should also be left unconnected.

The grounding shield connector on the MIDI jacks should not be connected to any circuit or chassis ground.

When MIDI Thru information is obtained from a MIDI In signal, transmission may occasionally be performed incorrectly due to signal degradation (caused by the response time of the optoisolator) between the rising and falling edges of the square wave. These timing errors will tend to add up in the "wrong direction" as more devices are chained between MIDI Thru and MIDI In jacks. The result is that, regardless of circuit quality, there is a limit to the number of devices which can be chained (series-connected) in this fashion.

Notes:

1. Optoisolator currently shown is Sharp PC-900 (HP 6N138 or other optoisolator can be used with appropriate changes).

2. Gates "A" are IC or transistor.

3. Resistors are 5%.

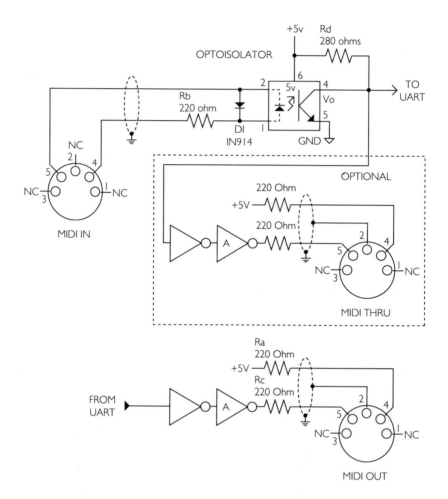

FIGURE A.1   MIDI Standard Hardware

Cables shall have a maximum length of fifty feet (15 meters), and shall be terminated on each end by a corresponding 5-pin DIN male plug, such as the SWITCHCRAFT 05GM5M. The cable shall be shielded twisted pair, with the shield connected to pin 2 at both ends.

A MIDI Thru output may be provided if needed, which provides a direct copy of data coming in MIDI In. For long chain lengths (more than three instruments), higher-speed optoisolators should help to avoid additive rise/fall time errors which affect pulse width duty cycle.

Data Format

MIDI communication is achieved through multi-byte "messages" consisting of one Status byte followed by one or two Data bytes. Real-Time and Exclusive messages are exceptions.

A MIDI-equipped instrument typically contains a receiver and a transmitter. Some instruments may contain only a receiver or only a transmitter. A receiver accepts messages in MIDI format and executes MIDI commands. It consists of an optoisolator, Universal Asynchronous Receiver/Transmitter (UART), and any other hardware needed to perform the intended functions. A transmitter originates messages in MIDI format, and transmits them by way of a UART and line driver.

MIDI makes it possible for a user of MIDI-compatible equipment to expand the number of instruments in a music system and to change system configurations to meet changing requirements.

MIDI messages are sent over any of 16 channels which are used for a variety of performance information. There are five major types of MIDI messages: Channel Voice, Channel Mode, System Common, System Real-Time and System Exclusive.

A MIDI event is transmitted as a "message" and consists of one or more bytes. The diagrams in figures A.2 and A.3 below show the structure and classification of MIDI data.

Message Types

Messages are divided into two main categories: *Channel* and *System.*

Channel Messages

A Channel Message uses four bits in the Status byte to address the message to one of sixteen MIDI channels and four bits to define the message (see Table II). Channel messages are thereby intended for the receivers in a system whose channel number matches the channel number encoded into the Status byte.

An instrument can receive MIDI messages on more than one channel. The channel in which it receives its main instructions, such as which program number to be on and what mode to be in, is referred to as its "Basic Channel." An instrument may be set up to receive performance data on multiple channels (including the Basic Channel). These are referred to as "Voice Channels." These multiple-channel situations will be discussed in more detail later.

There are two types of Channel messages: *Voice* and *Mode.*

Voice: To control an instrument's voices, Voice messages are sent over the Voice Channels.

TYPES OF MIDI BYTES:

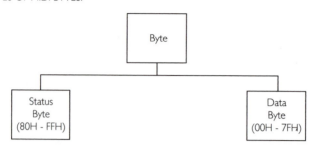

TYPES OF MIDI MESSAGES:

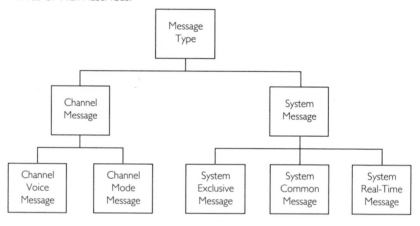

FIGURE A.2

Mode: To define the instrument's response to Voice messages, Mode messages are sent over an instrument's Basic Channel.

System Messages

System messages are not encoded with channel numbers. There are three types of System messages: *Common, Real-Time,* and *Exclusive.*

Common: Common messages are intended for all receivers in a system regardless of channel.

Real-Time: Real-Time messages are used for synchronization and are intended for all clock-based units in a system. They contain

STRUCTURE OF A SINGLE MESSAGE:

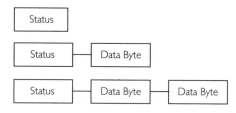

STRUCTURE OF SYSTEM EXCLUSIVE MESSAGES:

FIGURE A.3

Status bytes only—no Data bytes. Real-Time messages may be sent at any time—even between bytes of a message which has a different status. In such cases the Real-TIme message is either acted upon or ignored, after which the receiving process resumes under the previous status.

Exclusive: Exclusive messages can contain any number of Data bytes, and can be terminated either by an End of Exclusive (EOX) or any other Status byte (except Real-Time messages). An EOX should always be sent at the end of a System Exclusive message. These messages include a Manufacturer's Identification (ID) code. If a receiver does not recognize the ID code, it should ignore the following data.

So that other users and third party developers can fully access their instruments, manufacturers must publish the format of the System Exclusive data following their ID code. Only the manufacturer can define or update the format following their ID.

Data Types

There are two types of bytes sent over MIDI: *Status bytes* and *Data bytes.*

Status Bytes

Status bytes are eight-bit binary numbers in which the Most Significant Bit (MSB) is set (binary 1). Status bytes serve to identify the message type, that is, the purpose of the Data bytes which follow it. Except for Real-Time messages, new Status bytes will always command a receiver to adopt a new status, even if the last message was not completed.

Running Status

For Voice and Mode messages only. When a Status byte is received and processed, the receiver will remain in that status until a different Status byte is received. Therefore, if the same Status byte would be repeated, it can optionally be omitted so that only the Data bytes need to be sent. Thus, with Running Status, a complete message can consist of only Data bytes.

Running Status is especially helpful when sending long strings of Note On/Off messages, where "Note On with Velocity of 0" is used for Note Off.

Running Status will be stopped when any other Status byte intervenes. Real-Time messages should not affect Running status.

Unimplemented Status

Any Status bytes, and subsequent Data bytes, received for functions not implemented in a receiver should be ignored.

Undefined Status

All MIDI devices should be careful to never send any undefined Status bytes. If a device receives any such code, it should be ignored without causing any problems to the system. Care should also be taken during power-up and power-down that no messages be sent out the MIDI Out port. Such noise, if it appears on a MIDI line, could cause a data or framing error if the number of bits in the byte are incorrect.

Data Bytes

Following a Status byte (except for Real-Time messages) there are either one or two Data bytes which carry the content of the message. Data bytes are eight-bit binary numbers in which the Most Significant Bit (MSB) is always set to binary 0. The number and range of Data bytes which must follow each Status byte are specified in the tables in section 2. For each Status byte the correct number of Data bytes must always be sent. Inside a receiver, action on the message should wait until all Data bytes required under the current status are received. Receivers should ignore Data bytes which have not been properly preceded by a valid Status byte (with the exception of "Running Status," explained above).

Channel Modes

Synthesizers and other instruments contain sound generation elements called voices. Voice assignment is the algorithmic process of routing Note On/Off data from incoming MIDI messages to the voices so that notes are correctly sounded.

Note: When we refer to an "instrument" please note that one physical instrument may act as several virtual instruments (i.e. a synthesizer set to a 'split' mode operates like two individual instruments). Here, "instrument" refers to a virtual instrument and not necessarily one physical instrument.

Four Mode messages are available for defining the relationship between the sixteen MIDI channels and the instrument's voice assignment. The four modes are determined by the properties Omni (On/Off), Poly, and Mono. Poly and Mono are mutually exclusive, i.e., Poly disables Mono, and vice versa. Omni, when on, enables the receiver to receive Voice messages on all voice Channels. When Omni is off, the receiver will accept Voice messages from only selected Voice Channel(s). Mono, when on, restricts the assignment of Voices to just one voice per Voice Channel (Monophonic). When Mono is off (Poly On), a number of voices may be allocated by the Receiver's normal voice assignment (Polyphonic) algorithm.

For a receiver assigned to Basic Channel "N" (1–16), the four possible modes arising from the two Mode messages are:

Mode Omni

1	On	Poly	Voice messages are received from all Voice Channels, and assigned to voices polyphonically.
2	On	Mono	Voice messages are received from all Voice Channels, and control only one voice, monophonically.
3	Off	Poly	Voice messages are received in Voice Channel N only, and are assigned to voices polyphonically.
4	Off	Mono	Voice messages are received in Voice Channels N thru $N+M-1$, and assigned monophonically to voices 1 thru M, respectively. The number of voices "M" is specified by the third byte of the Mono Mode Message.

Four modes are applied to transmitters (also assigned to Basic Channel N). Transmitters with no channel selection capability should transmit on Basic Channel 1 (N = 1).

Mode Omni

1	On	Poly	All voice messages are transmitted in Channel N.
2	On	Mono	Voice messages for one voice are sent in Channel N.
3	Off	Poly	Voice messages for all voices are sent in Channel N.
4	Off	Mono	Voice messages for voices 1 thru M are transmitted in Voice Channels N thru $N+M-1$, respectively. (Single voice per channel.)

A MIDI receiver or transmitter operates under only one Channel Mode at a time. If a mode is not implemented on the receiver, it should ignore the message (and any subsequent Data bytes), or switch to an alternate mode, usually Mode 1 (Omni On/Poly).

Mode messages will be recognized by a receiver only when received in the instrument's Basic Channel—regardless of which mode the receiver is currently assigned to. Voice messages may be received in the Basic Channel and in other Voice Channels, according to the above specifications.

Since a single instrument may function as multiple "virtual" instruments, it can thus have more than one Basic Channel. Such an instrument behaves as though it is more than one receiver, and each receiver can be set to a different Basic Channel. Each of these receivers may also be set to a different mode, either by front panel controls or by Mode messages received over MIDI on each basic channel. Although not a true MIDI mode, instruments operating in this fashion are described as functioning in "Multi Mode."

An instrument's transmitter and receiver may be set to different modes. For example, an instrument may receive in Mono mode and transmit in Poly mode. It is also possible to transmit and receive on different channels. For example, an instrument may receive on Channel 1 and transmit on Channel 3.

Power-up Default Conditions

It is recommended that at power-up, the Basic Channel should be set to 1, and the mode set to Omni On/Poly (Mode 1). This, and any other default conditions for the particular instrument, should be maintained indefinitely (even when powered down) until instrument panel controls are operated or MIDI data is received. However, the decision to implement the above, is left totally up to the designer.

SECTION TWO — TABLES

Hex	STATUS Binary D7–D0	NUMBER OF DATA BYTES	DESCRIPTION
Channel Voice Messages			
8nH	1000nnnn	2	Note Off
9nH	1001nnnn	2	Note On (a velocity of 0 = Note Off)
AnH	1010nnnn	2	Polyphonic Key Pressure/Aftertouch
BnH	1011nnnn	2	Control Change
CnH	1100nnnn	1	Program Change
DnH	1101nnnn	1	Channel Pressure/Aftertouch
EnH	1110nnnn	2	Pitch Bend Change
Channel Mode Messages			
BnH	1011nnnn (01111xxx)	2	Selects Channel Mode
System Messages			
F0H	11110000	*****	System Exclusive
	11110sss	0 to 2	System Common
	11111ttt	0	System Real-Time

Notes

nnnn: N−, where N = Channel #, i.e. 0000 is Channel 1, 0001 is Channel 2, and 1111 is Channel 16.

*****: iiiiiii, data, ..., EOX
iiiiiii: Identification
sss: 1 to 7
ttt: 0 to 7
xxx: Channel Mode messages are sent under the same Status byte as the Control Change messages (BnH). They are differentiated by the first Data byte which will have a value from 121 to 127 for Channel Mode messages.

TABLE I Summary of Status Bytes

STATUS		DATA BYTES	DESCRIPTION
Hex	Binary		
8nH	100nnnn	0kkkkkkk	Note Off
		0vvvvvvv	vvvvvv: note off velocity
9nH	1001nnnn	0kkkkkkk	Note On
		0vvvvvvv	vvvvvv ≠ 0: velocity
			vvvvvv = 0: note off
AnH	1010nnnn	0kkkkkkk	Polyphonic Key Pressure (Aftertouch)
		0vvvvvvv	vvvvvv: pressure value
BnH	1011nnnn	0ccccccc	Control Change (See Table III)
		0vvvvvvv	ccccccc: control # (0–120)
			vvvvvv: control value
			ccccccc = 121 thru 127: Reserved. (See Table IV)
CnH	1100nnnn	0ppppppp	Program Change
			ppppppp: program number (0–127)
DnH	1101nnnn	0vvvvvvv	Channel Pressure (Aftertouch)
			vvvvvv: pressure value
EnH	1110nnnn	0vvvvvvv	Pitch Bend Change LSB
		0vvvvvvv	Pitch Bend Change MSB

Notes:

1. nnnn: Voice Channel number (1–16, coded as defined in Table I notes)

2. kkkkkkk: note number (0–127)

3. vvvvvv: key velocity
   A logarithmic scale is recommended.

4. Continuous controllers are divided into Most Significant and Least Significant Bytes. If only seven bits of resolution are needed for any particular controllers, only the MSB is sent. It is not necessary to send the LSB. If more resolution is needed, then both are sent, first the MSB, then the LSB. If only the LSB has changed in value, the LSB may be sent without re-sending the MSB.

TABLE II   Channel Voice Messages

CONTROL NUMBER (2nd Byte value)		CONTROL FUNCTION
Decimal	Hex	
0	00H	Undefined
1	01H	Modulation wheel or lever
2	02H	Breath Controller
3	03H	Undefined
4	04H	Foot controller
5	05H	Portamento time
6	06H	Data entry MSB
7	07H	Main volume
8	08H	Balance
9	09H	Undefined
10	0AH	Pan
11	0BH	Expression Controller
12–15	0C–0FH	Undefined
16–19	10–13H	General Purpose Controllers (#'s 1–4)
20–31	14–1FH	Undefined
32–63	20–3FH	LSB for values 0–31
64	40H	Damper pedal (sustain)
65	41H	Portamento
66	42H	Sostenuto
67	43H	Soft pedal
68	44H	Undefined
69	45H	Hold 2
70–79	46–4FH	Undefined
80–83	50–53H	General Purpose Controllers (#'s 5–8)
84–90	54–5AH	Undefined
91	5BH	External Effects Depth
92	5CH	Tremolo Depth
93	5DH	Chorus Depth
94	5EH	Celeste (Detune) Depth
95	5FH	Phaser Depth
96	60H	Data increment
97	61H	Data decrement
98	62H	Non-Registered Parameter Number LSB
99	63H	Non-Registered Parameter Number MSB
100	64H	Registered Parameter Number LSB
101	65H	Registered Parameter Number MSB
102–120	66–78H	Undefined
121–127	79–7FH	Reserved for Channel Mode Messages

TABLE III Controller Numbers

Parameter LSB	Number MSB	Function
00H	00H	Pitch Bend Sensitivity
01H	00H	Fine Tuning
02H	00H	Coarse Tuning

TABLE IIIa Registered Parameter Numbers

STATUS		DATA BYTES	DESCRIPTION
Hex	Binary		
Bn	1011nnnn	0ccccccc 0vvvvvvv	Mode Messages

ccccccc = 121:Reset All Controllers
vvvvvvv = 0

ccccccc = 122:Local Control
vvvvvvv = 0, Local Control Off
vvvvvvv = 127, Local Control On

ccccccc = 123: All Notes Off
vvvvvvv = 0

ccccccc = 124: Omni Mode Off (All Notes Off)
vvvvvvv = 0

ccccccc = 125:Omni Mode On (All Notes Off)
vvvvvvv = 0

ccccccc = 126: Mono Mode On (Poly Mode Off) (All Notes Off)
vvvvvvv = M, where M is the number of channels.
vvvvvvv = 0, the number of channels equals the number of voices in the receiver.

ccccccc = 127: Poly Mode On (Mono Mode Off) (All Notes Off)
vvvvvvv = 0

Notes:

1. nnnn: Basic Channel number (1–16)

2. ccccccc: Controller number (121–127)

3. vvvvvvv: Controller value

TABLE IV Channel Mode Messages

STATUS		DATA BYTES	DESCRIPTION
Hex	Binary		
F1H	11110001	0nnndddd	MIDI Time Code Quarter Frame
			nnn: Message Type
			dddd: Values
F2H	11110010		Song Position Pointer
		01111111	1111111: (Least significant)
		0hhhhhhh	hhhhhhh: (Most significant)
F3H	11110011	0sssssss	Song Select
			sssssss: Song #
F4H	11110100		Undefined
F5H	11110101		Undefined
F6H	11110110	none	Tune Request
F7H	11110111	none	EOX: "End of System Exclusive" flag

TABLE V   System Common Messages

STATUS		DATA BYTES	DESCRIPTION
Hex	Binary		
F8H	11111000		Timing Clock
F9H	11111001		Undefined
FAH	11111010		Start
FBH	11111011		Continue
FCH	11111100		Stop
FDH	11111101		Undefined
FEH	11111110		Active Sensing
FFH	11111111		System Reset

TABLE VI   System Real-Time Messages

STATUS		DATA BYTES	DESCRIPTION
Hex	Binary		
F0H	11110000		Bulk dump, etc.
		0iiiiiii	iiiiiii: identification (See note 1)
		(0ddddddd)	
		.	Any number of data bytes may be sent here,
		.	for any purpose, as long as they all have a
		.	zero in the most significant bit.
		(0ddddddd)	
F7H	11110111		EOX: "End of System Exclusive"

Notes:

1. iiiiiii: identification ID (0–127). If the ID is 0 the following two bytes are used as extensions to the manufacturer ID.

2. All bytes between the System Exclusive Status byte and EOX must have zeroes in the MSB.

3. All manufacturer's ID number can be obtained from the MMA or JMSC.

4. Status or Data bytes (except Real-Time) should not be interleaved with System Exclusive.

5. No Status Bytes (other than Real-Time) should be sent until after an EOX has terminated the System Exclusive message. If however, a Status byte other than EOX is received during a System Exclusive message, the message is terminated.

6. Three System Exclusive ID numbers have been set aside for special purposes: 7DH is reserved for non-commercial use (e.g. schools, research, etc.) and is not to be used on any product released to the public; 7EH (Non-Real Time) and 7FH (Real Time) are used for extensions to the MIDI specification.

TABLE VII   System Exclusive Messages

SUB-ID #1	SUB-ID #2	DESCRIPTION

Non-Real Time (7EH)

00	--	Unused
01	(not used)	Sample Dump Header
02	(not used)	Sample Data Packet
03	(not used)	Sample Dump Request
04	nn	MIDI Time Code
	00	Special
	01	Punch In Points
	02	Punch Out Points
	03	Delete Punch In Point
	04	Delete Punch Out Point
	05	Event Start Point
	06	Event Stop Point
	07	Event Start Points with additional info.
	08	Event Stop Points with additional info.
	09	Delete Event Start Point
	0A	Delete Event Stop Point
	0B	Cue Points
	0C	Cue Points with additional info.
	0D	Delete Cue Point
	0E	Event Name in additional info.
05	nn	Sample Dump Extensions
	01	Multiple Loop Points
	02	Loop Points Request
06	nn	General Information
	01	Identity Request
	02	Identity Reply
7C	(not used)	Wait
7D	(not used)	Cancel
7E	(not used)	NAK
7F	(not used)	ACK

Real Time (7FH)

00	--	Unused
01	nn	MIDI Time Code
	01	Full Message
	02	User Bits

Notes:

1. The standardized format for both Real-Time and Non-Real Time messages is as follows: F0H <id number> <channel number> <sub-ID#1> <sub-ID#2> F7H

TABLE VIII Currently Defined Universal System Exclusive ID Numbers

NUMBER	MANUFACTURER	NUMBER	MANUFACTURER
	American Group		European Group
01H	Sequential	20H	Passac
02H	IDP	21H	SIEL
03H	Octave-Plateau	22H	Synthaxe
04H	Moog	24H	Hohner
05H	Passport Designs	25H	Twister
06H	Lexicon	26H	Solton
07H	Kurzweil	27H	Jellinghaus MS
08H	Fender	28H	Southworth
0AH	AKG Acoustics	29H	PPG
0BH	Voyce Music	2AH	JEN
0CH	Waveframe Corp	2BH	SSL Limited
0DH	ADA	2CH	Audio Veritrieb
0EH	Garfield Elec.	2FH	Elka
0FH	Ensoniq	30H	Dynacord
10H	Oberheim		
			Japanese Group
11H	Apple Computer		
12H	Grey Matter Response	40H	Kawai
14H	Palm Tree Inst.	41H	Roland
15H	JL Cooper	42H	Korg
16H	Lowrey	43H	Yamaha
17H	Adams-Smith	44H	Casio
18H	Emu Systems	46H	Kamiya Studio
19H	Harmony Systems	47H	Akai
1AH	ART	48H	Japan Victor
1BH	Baldwin	49H	Meisosha
1CH	Eventide	4AH	Hoshino Gakki
1DH	Inventronics	4BH	Fujitsu Elect
1FH	Clarity	4CH	Sony
		4DH	Nisshin Onpa
00H 00H 07H	Digital Music Corp.	4EH	TEAC Corp.
00H 00H 0BH	IVL Technologies	4FH	System Product
00H 00H 0CH	Southern Music Sytems	50H	Matsushita Electric
00H 00H 0DH	Lake Butler Sound	51H	Fostex
00H 00H 10H	DOD Electronics		
00H 00H 14H	Perfect Fretworks		
00H 00H 16H	Opcode		
00H 00H 18H	Spatial Sound		
00H 00H 19H	KMX		
00H 00H 20H	Axxes		

TABLE IX System Exclusive Manufacturer's ID Numbers, Current as of June 1988

INDEX